# UNDER
# THE
# OSAKAN
# SUN

# UNDER
# THE
# OSAKAN
# SUN

## A FUNNY
## INTIMATE
## WONDERFUL
## ACCOUNT OF
## THREE YEARS
## IN JAPAN

## HAMISH
## BEATON

AWA PRESS

First edition published in 2008
by Awa Press, 16 Walter Street, Wellington,
New Zealand.

National Library of New Zealand Cataloguing-in-
Publication Data
Beaton, Hamish, 1978-
Under the Osakan sun : a funny, intimate, wonderful
account of three years in Japan / Hamish Beaton.
ISBN 978-0-9582750-2-6
1. Beaton, Hamish, 1978-
2. Japan—Social life and customs.
3. Japan—Description and travel. I. Title.
952.05—dc 22

Cover design by Athena Sommerfeld, Auckland
Typeset by Jill Livestre, Archetype, Wellington
Printed by McPherson's Printing Group, Australia
This book is typeset in Fournier.

To Mum and Dad, who inspired me to get out
and experience the world

# About the author

Hamish Beaton was born in Christchurch, New Zealand. He graduated in Japanese and French at Canterbury University, and after travelling in Europe, spent three years living and teaching in Japan under the JET programme. He now lives and works in London.

# Contents

# Prologue

''*Wax on, wax off*'—*it was perhaps not the most enlightened teaching available to mankind, but at age ten I had been enchanted. The elderly Japanese karate teacher Mr Miyagi and his protégé, Daniel-san, had entered my life via* The Karate Kid *movies. I stared up at the television screen and was awestruck by Daniel-san's oversized bandana and heroic super-crane flying kick. I marvelled at Mr Miyagi's ability to catch flies with chopsticks, and dispatch villains with a tweak of the nose.*

*I bought a copy of the book and decorated my bedroom with a poster of Daniel-san performing a flying kick. I dreamed of wearing my own oversized bandana, and karate-kicking an arch-enemy off a rickety bamboo bridge to rescue a princess.*

*My devotion to these superheroes would soon be submerged by an embarrassing period in my life when I obsessed on* Beverly Hills, 90210 *and sported a tragic '90s haircut that my mother had helped choose—but my interest in things Japanese had begun.*

*At age thirteen, I was thrust into three months of Japanese language lessons. A bespectacled Japanese woman with the unlikely name of Mrs Lutnaant—her husband was German—encouraged me to practise formal greetings, and patiently tolerated my attempts at writing basic characters on the blackboard. I was a poor student, completely unable to keep up with the bright girls, and my interest in long, ridiculous-sounding words started to wane. But Mrs Lutnaant had seemingly detected a small glimmer of potential. 'Beaton-san, you must try harder,' she would exhort. 'You can speak very good Japanese, but you must try harder.'*

*I was baffled when at the end of the term I received an A minus. The following term I decided to continue: Mrs Lutnaant's absurdly generous grade had not only given me a new level of self-esteem, but had rekindled my interest. I now approached my studies with enthusiasm, spending weekends memorising vocabulary and perfecting my handwriting.*

*I continued to receive good grades, but Mrs Lutnaant was never satisfied. 'Beaton-san,' she would lecture, 'you should know this word. Beaton-san, you should study harder.'*

*During my third year, when I was sixteen, Mrs Lutnaant made a comment that profoundly affected me. 'Beaton-san,' she said in her usual sharp tone, 'one day you will live in Japan.'*

*I was electrified. Suddenly, I had a goal. I was no longer ingesting copious vocabulary lists just to get an A on a report card; I was gaining skills for an adventure.*

*Sadly, once I got to university, Japanese lectures proved to be less than inspirational, consisting of monotonous expositions of Japanese characters and grammar. I could see no point memorising academic vocabulary and translating dense university texts. There was no personal interaction, no fun, and no hint of practical relevance. Several times I came close to chucking in the towel, but Mrs Lutnaant's words rang in my ears.*

*Finally, though, the torment ended. I had completed my degree. The land of the rising sun beckoned. I obtained a job, a three-year working visa and an air ticket. Eight years' study of Japanese were about to be sorely tested.*

# 1

# Endless day

*One-thirty in the afternoon.* I am standing halfway up a small flight of steps that leads to a concrete fishing pond where some young boys are idly fishing. The pond is a stagnant oasis, away from the main road and surrounded by green rice paddies. Nearby, crickets are competing with cars and trucks as to who can produce the loudest racket.

The humidity is stifling. The neck of my business shirt is soaked in sweat and my black leather shoes are radiating heat. All of my personal belongings are packed into my near-to-bursting suitcase, whose handle has cracked under the strain and is now digging into my swollen left palm.

I wipe my sweaty brow with my free hand. I have never been so hot in my life.

I am in Japan, or more precisely in Kanan Town in the southeast of Osaka Prefecture. It is mid July, the height of summer. I have just stepped into a blind date with a country I have been studying for eight years. I am about to meet my new employers, set foot in my new apartment, and start a three-year chapter of my life in a new world.

The day had started at a relaxed pace in a five-star, air-conditioned Tokyo hotel room. The Japanese government had bought me a business-class air ticket to Japan, put me up in the hotel and treated me to a massive buffet breakfast. I had then been chauffeured to Tokyo train station and ushered aboard a sleek, comfortable bullet train for a leisurely three-hour trip to Osaka. I had even been provided with a tasty eel-sushi lunch-box and a bottle of iced tea to enjoy during the journey.

Unfortunately, this lavish lifestyle was about to end. I was now out on my own, and the responsibility of the Kanan Town Board of Education.

The board's representative, Mr Tokunaga, was waiting nervously for me at the Osaka Station ticket barrier. He coughed a hoarse smoker's cough and shyly welcomed me to Japan. After taking great care to pronounce my name correctly, he announced that I should follow him.

With that he took off, weaving through a confusing labyrinth of train station shopping arcades and corridors. He seemed impatient, constantly checking his watch. Every 50 metres or so he paused, nervously checking that I was still following him, and that he had not lost Kanan Town's new English teacher.

We eventually arrived at the underground line, where Mr Tokunaga, gesturing and waving his right hand, pointed out our position on the railway map. I managed to decipher that we were to go on a purple train and head south. Although I had studied Japanese for several years, the place-names made little sense. I had lost all sense of bearing.

Mr Tokunaga opened his briefcase and proudly displayed a comprehensive train timetable. He pointed at several highlighted sections, explaining that we were to catch the 12.06 train south, disembark at 12.25, transfer to another train at 12.28 and disembark at 1.16, just in time for the 1.20 bus.

He seemed worried. The bus would get us to the Kanan Town Hall at 1.28, so I would be cutting it fine for a 1:30 meeting. I was sceptical anyway: there was clearly no way the trains could possibly get us places at such exact times.

We stood silently on the empty platform. Mr Tokunaga checked his watch again. I glanced curiously at mine, wondering how many minutes late the train would be. 12.05. Hmmm, I thought, it would probably be at least ten minutes away.

The digits ticked over to 12.06. A piercing whistle sounded and a purple Midosuji Line train rumbled into the station. I was astounded. A sheer fluke, I decided, and climbed aboard.

Exactly nineteen minutes later Mr Tokunaga was nudging me to my feet. We had crossed downtown Osaka with precision timing and arrived at our first stop. I staggered after my guide as he took off through yet another maze of corridors, escalators, newspaper kiosks and convenience stores. I was dazed and disorientated. I wanted to pause and take in my new surroundings. I wanted to stick my head into one of the blue-neon convenience stores and see what sort of food was on sale. I wanted to leisurely peruse the newspaper kiosks, and take my time exploring this enormous station.

Meanwhile Mr Tokunaga was up ahead, putting coins into a machine. He beckoned me over and pointed at the coin slot. 'This is a ticket machine,' he said wisely. 'Use it to buy tickets. This is an important station. You should remember your way. You will need to come back here. Don't forget where things are. Our next train is this way.' He thrust a new train ticket into my hand, clutched his briefcase to his chest and raced away.

I had forgotten where our last train had been, and at what platform we had disembarked. I had no idea what station I was standing in, or to which station we were travelling. There was no time to pause—Mr Tokunaga was quickly disappearing into the sea of heads. I took off after him, banging my suitcase against my left calf and snapping the handle in the process. Blood oozed out of a cut on my finger.

True to schedule, the next train departed at 12.28. Mr Tokunaga found us seats. He now seemed more relaxed. 'We are on the train to Tondabayashi,' he said calmly. 'You will live in Tondabayashi. I live in Tondabayashi also, but our job is in Kanan Town. Tondabayashi is a little big city. Kanan Town is a very little country town. Very very countryside.'

He said the last two sentences in English and coughed loudly when he finished. He asked if I were from a big city or a small town. We chatted about the differences between the populations and cities of New Zealand and Japan. Mr Tokunaga was excited to hear that I enjoyed camping, and exclaimed that he liked camping very much.

His wife, he said regretfully, did not share his enthusiasm. His specially imported German campervan had sat neglected in his garage for several years. He inquired if I would like to go camping at some stage. I hesitantly replied that I would, and he rubbed his hands together in delight. He would start work on repairing the campervan immediately and order new parts from Germany.

I asked him about his background. He said he had been a science teacher at a primary school in Tondabayashi, but the local government had transferred him to Kanan Town. He was married, with one son. He liked going to barbecue restaurants with his son, and he loved the countryside.

He had been born in a tiny mountain village in the Japanese alps, had moved to Osaka as a boy, and had lived in Tondabayashi ever since. He hated city life and loved skiing. His dream, he said, was to retire to the country and live out his days in a home-made log cabin. He had never stayed in a log cabin, but had seen them in magazines. He asked if there were many in New Zealand.

Mr Tokunaga exuded quietness. Apart from his heavy cough, which wracked his body every few minutes, he was softly spoken. His thick hair was flecked with grey, and his coughing made his hair fall over his thick-rimmed glasses. I liked him instantly. His big glasses, short stature and thick mop of hair made him look remarkably like the smaller of the two Ronnies.

The train rumbled slowly on, and the dense buildings of Osaka City gave way to plots of land filled with rice paddies. Mr Tokunaga announced that we were now in the countryside. I was yet to see any cows, sheep or barbed-wire fences, but there were distinctly more green patches in the concrete grey landscape. The buildings were more rickety than those in the city, and the houses more spacious. We passed concrete-lined rivers, motorcycle dealerships, convenience stores, vending machines, neon-lit casinos, roads lined with cars, massive apartment blocks, ancient Buddhist temples and intriguing-looking shops and stores. There seemed an endless amount of places to come back and explore.

Mr Tokunaga pointed ahead. 'We get off at the next stop.'

I strained to see my new home town. More rice paddies dotted the landscape, but the scenery was little different from the rest of suburban

Osaka. Large apartment blocks lined the horizon, and a massive unfinished highway on-ramp sat on the outskirts of the city.

A large white spire loomed into view above the apartment blocks. It seemed to be made of white plastic, like something from Disneyland. Five struts at the base merged to form a bulbous white body, which gradually tapered into a large tower in the shape of a melted candle.

I asked Mr Tokunaga what it was. He seemed embarrassed. 'Ahhh, that's Tondabayashi Tower. It's the tallest tower in town.'

'But what's it for?' This was not Japan as I had imagined it.

Mr Tokunaga coughed. 'I'll tell you later,' he said. 'This is our station. We get off here.'

The train stopped. I checked my watch: 1.16. I stepped out of the pleasant confines of the air-conditioned train and nearly fell over. For the first time since arriving in Japan, I experienced the country's notorious summer heat and humidity.

Tondabayashi Train Station was a humble building with two platforms and no air-conditioning. It opened into a large chaotic bus terminal that stank of diesel and exhaust fumes. Mirages leapt and danced on the concrete. A row of green buses seemed to slump in the heat.

Mr Tokunaga had exited the ticket barrier and was waiting impatiently, waving and signalling that we needed to get on the number three bus. I climbed aboard, hoisting my suitcase and banging it against my ankle. Mr Tokunaga checked his watch again: 1.18. We were still on schedule.

I surveyed the bus terminal. There was an orange and yellow doughnut shop in the far corner, opposite what appeared to be a bank. Row upon row of cycle racks lined the side of the station and a gaudy casino sat across the road, its flashy silver and gold frontage faded and peeling.

The bus's air-conditioning did not seem to be working. I could feel sweat patches appearing in the armpits of my suit and rivulets poured down my face. After five minutes we crossed a wide river and entered Kanan Town. Old wooden farmhouses stood in fields. A tree-clad mountain range loomed ahead. I was, at last, really in the countryside.

Mr Tokunaga rang the bell and the bus stopped. We seemed to be in the middle of the rice paddies. Mr Tokunaga pointed at a large grey building in the distance. 'That's the town hall. That's where I work. That's where we're going. You have a meeting there, now. We must hurry.'

He walked off down the main road. I noticed a footpath on the opposite side, but Mr Tokunaga seemed intent on walking head-on into traffic. Trucks of all shapes and sizes roared past. Despite being a sleepy little country town, Kanan Town appeared to be host to a major thoroughfare.

Why the bloody hell was I wearing a suit? The heat beat down. A smoke-belching concrete mixer roared past, missing me by centimetres.

Mr Tokunaga pushed on, regularly looking back to see if I were keeping up. My 30-kilogram suitcase crashed painfully against my shin. I braced myself, terrified of toppling under a speeding truck. Suddenly, Mr Tokunaga climbed a flight of steps that led up and away from the suicidal road. As I followed him up the steps on my rubbery legs I felt giddy and paused to steady myself. I was close to fainting.

Finally reaching the top, I surveyed what appeared to be a concrete fishing pond. Two boys absently toying with fishing lines stared up at me. I waved and wiped my sweaty brow again. The chirping crickets were driving me crazy and I felt ill. My left ankle and shin and my right calf were bruised and throbbing. My palms were scratched and swollen, and my suit was a bedraggled mess. The shimmering heatwaves were so close I could almost taste them. The town hall seemed a mile away.

Mr Tokunaga beckoned me to keep up my pace. He pointed and gestured at our destination. We were five minutes late. No doubt I was about to be fired. I limped after him, summoning my last few ounces of strength. At last, the automatic doors of the Kanan Town Hall opened with a hiss, and a cool breeze descended from heaven.

'We need to go to level three,' Mr Tokunaga said. 'Everyone will be waiting.'

The twelve staff members of the town's Board of Education and Social Education Department stood expectantly. The men were dressed identically, in dark trousers, starched white shirts and nondescript ties.

Mr Tokunaga coughed and I bowed. There was confusion. Several bowed back hesitantly. No one spoke.

Mr Tokunaga pushed ahead and beckoned me to follow. 'First you must meet Mr Fukumoto,' he whispered. 'He is the big boss, the education superintendent. Then you can meet the other people.'

Mr Fukumoto had his own office. He was a stern old man with a powerful air. I immediately decided not to trifle with Mr Fukumoto. He looked like a man who would not take kindly to incompetence or idiocy.

He shook my hand and told me that he was over seventy-six years old. He asked if I liked playing golf and was enjoying Japan. I stammered about being hot but he appeared not to hear. He turned to Mr Tokunaga. 'You are late. The meeting with the mayor has been postponed for ten minutes.'

Mr Tokunaga blanched and hung his head. 'I'm very sorry. I'm so sorry for keeping the mayor waiting.'

Mr Fukumoto was unimpressed. 'That will be all.' Our meeting was at an end.

I was now allowed to meet the rest of my co-workers. Again, this was to be done in order of social importance. Mr Muramoto was the division chief and sat in the centre of the room. Mr Fujimoto was the section chief of the Board of Education and sat on the right side of the room, at the head of his team. His team members sat next to him in order of rank, with Mr Sumitani the most senior. Mr Sumitani was completely bald, very slender and a little effeminate.

Mr Tokunaga sat between Mr Sumitani and the next man to greet me, Mr Tsujimoto. Mr Tsujimoto had a huge bristling moustache and his face creased when he smiled. He grasped my hand and announced that I would make a perfect drinking buddy. The office erupted in laughter—it seemed I had met the office clown. Next were two office ladies, who bowed deeply and, looking at their feet, hesitantly shook my hand. They offered to make me a cup of tea and shuffled meekly away.

I was now ushered to the left side of the room and introduced to the five members of the Social Education Department. The list of names, social ranks and job titles was becoming overwhelming. By the time tea was served I had forgotten nearly everyone's name. Only Mr Tokunaga and his likeness to Ronnie Corbett were firmly imprinted in my brain.

It was time to assign some nicknames as an *aide-mémoire*. Mr Tsujimoto, the office clown, became Magnum PI. Mr Sumitani was a dead ringer for the Australian rugby player George Gregan, so I decided to call him George. Mr Fukumoto was a lot less scary when I thought of him as 'the old boy', while Mr Muramoto, the division chief, became Mr Smiles.

. I refrained from nicknaming Mr Fujimoto: he seemed a quiet and kindly soul, and had come to work specially armed with a travel brochure about New Zealand so he would have something to talk to me about.

My initial meeting with the Board of Education was cut short when Mr Fukumoto stormed out of his office and ordered Mr Tokunaga to escort me to the mayor's reception room at once. Everyone fell silent, and I was whisked away.

When we met Mr Kitahashi, the mayor, Mr Fukumoto spoke haughtily in formal Japanese, pointing at Mr Tokunaga and shaking his head scornfully. Mr Tokunaga hung his head in shame and blushed. The mayor, though, appeared unconcerned, and sat me down for a good question and answer session about New Zealand vegetables and golf courses. We hit it off immediately.

Mr Kitahashi was a sprightly man and very skinny. When he spoke, he bobbed his head, wobbled like a string puppet, and arched his thick bushy eyebrows. He proudly showed me a desk calendar of New Zealand mountain scenes and I presented him with a silver-fern pin. He clapped his hands, and with a flourish attached the pin to his suit lapel.

The town photographer was summoned and ordered to take formal photos of the occasion. I smiled, the mayor beamed, Mr Tokunaga coughed and Mr Fukumoto frowned. Another hasty round of tea was served and I was ushered out of the office by Mr Fukumoto, who was determined not to take up any more of the mayor's time.

Mr Tokunaga breathed a huge sigh of relief. It seemed the day's formalities were at an end. Carrying my suitcase, Magnum PI escorted us to the town hall car park. He was impressed with the suitcase's weight and flexed his muscles, saying again how much he was looking forward to going drinking. He bade us farewell and Mr Tokunaga started the car. This turned out to be the Board of Education's 'number one vehicle', which Mr Tokunaga seldom drove. He apologised as he crunched gears and bunny-hopped out of the car park. We spluttered slowly down the main road, crossed the bridge and were again in concrete-grey Tondabayashi, with its skyline of Stalinesque apartment blocks and ever-present Disney tower.

I was becoming concerned that we were heading back towards the bus terminal and feared that my apartment might overlook the hustle and bustle of Tondabayashi Train Station. My fears were allayed when Mr Tokunaga veered down a small side-street and the scenery changed dramatically. We were now surrounded by ancient wooden temples, warehouses and ornate seventeenth-century buildings.

I had read about this place in a dusty, twenty-year-old Osaka guide-book I had tracked down in my local library before I left New Zealand. An historic suburb in the heart of Tondabayashi, Jinaimachi had started life as a monastic settlement, and developed into a sizeable and important point in the Buddhist pilgrim trail to the Koya-san temple complex in neighbouring Wakayama. Very little had changed in the four hundred years since. The intricate labyrinth of winding, single-lane streets de-signed for horse and cart was proving a nightmare for Mr Tokunaga. He sweated, coughed, and at narrow corners slowed to a crawl. Several times, oncoming traffic forced us to back up around a corner and wait our turn.

My new home was, apparently, smack bang in the middle of Jinaimachi. I was ecstatic—there were no ugly concrete buildings, smelly highways or diesel-soaked bus terminals. I would be free to wander the cobblestoned streets, visit temples, poke around in ancient cemeteries, and meet a Mr Miyagi who would teach me karate. Yes, I thought, this should work out just fine.

Tokiwa Mansion was a square building with only ten apartments. Mr Tokunaga sped up the stairs. Dragging my suitcase, I trailed behind him to the third floor and nervously entered my apartment. My immediate reaction was surprise. I had been led to believe by previous English teachers in Japan that I would be living in a small, sunless, grimy shoebox. This could not be further from the truth.

Mr Tokunaga coughed and began a lightning-fast tour. Inside the front door there was a typical genkan area, where shoes were to be removed before you stepped up on to the lino-covered hallway. This hallway led to a bedroom on the left, a bathroom and toilet on the right, and a kitchen straight ahead. I followed Mr Tokunaga through the kitchen into the living area. A large television set sat in the corner. Other than this, the room was completely empty.

Mr Tokunaga coughed and apologised for the smell. The walls, he explained, had just been repainted. The room looked brand new. New tatami mats covered the floor, and the walls were a fresh shade of olive. The bedroom, too, had freshly painted walls and new tatami mats. It was also empty, except for a thin pink futon mattress and some carefully folded pink flowery blankets.

This, Mr Tokunaga explained, was my bed. Western beds were forbidden in the lease as they would damage the precious tatami mats. I shrugged; apart from the girly colour, things didn't seem bad.

Back in the kitchen, Mr Tokunaga was busy explaining how to use the kitchen taps, power sockets and light switches. I was not paying much attention. I had spied a balcony through the living-room window. I stepped outside. The heat and humidity were sweltering but I barely noticed them: the view was breathtaking. Immediately in front stood an old wooden temple with a steep tile-covered roof and an ancient cemetery. Beyond lay a panorama of warehouses and monuments, and on the horizon loomed the Kanan mountain range.

Mr Tokunaga, however, did not have time for temple-gazing. He had the bathroom to explain. The washing machine stood on cinder blocks in the corner. Mr Tokunaga pointed out the on/off button and where the clothes and washing powder should go. Next came the extractor fan, bath taps, shower taps, shower nozzle, toilet flush, and bathroom cabinet door—and then he announced it was time for us to leave.

I was shocked. 'Ummm...I've only just arrived,' I said. 'Surely I should unpack and freshen up a little?'

Mr Tokunaga pondered this request for a few seconds and then agreed that I could change my clothes. Time, though, was of the essence: we still had much to do. I raced into the bedroom and rattled through my suitcase. I had no idea what lay ahead of me for the rest of the day, but if I were scheduled to meet the Emperor of Japan, he would need to make do with my wearing shorts and a T-shirt.

It felt great to be out of my suit and tie, but Mr Tokunaga did not intend to let me relax and enjoy my new-found freedom. It was time to go shopping.

Daiei Supermarket was a massive white three-storey building only 300 metres from my apartment. If I leant dangerously over my balcony railing and stood on tiptoe, I could just make out its large flat roof, and the two bright orange circles that were the chain's emblem. It was, in fact, more than just a supermarket. The ground floor was devoted to women's clothing. The first floor contained men's clothing and a video arcade. The third floor had appliances, furniture, electronic goods and a pet store; in the months that followed I would often spend time perusing the stereo section, with its distinctive odour of dog hair and kitty litter.

My maiden shopping trip with Mr Tokunaga, however, was spent underground—the basement of Daiei Tondabayashi was a massive food store. From the moment I stepped off the escalator, foreign smells, sights and sounds scrambled for my attention. A pair of elderly kimono-clad women with bright pink plastic buckets happily welcomed shoppers, bowing obsequiously and joyously thanking everyone for having entered the store. It all felt very religious.

Mr Tokunaga had no time to spare for such pleasantries. It soon became clear that he had been charged with setting me up with the necessities I would need until I figured out how to shop for myself. We raced through the vegetable section, thankfully avoiding strange-looking radishes and chilled pickles, to rows of brightly coloured bowls of instant noodles. I was unable to figure out any of the flavours. The red bowl displayed a devil's pitchfork, the yellow bowl had a one-eyed ghost, and I was puzzled and concerned as to why the brown bowl was decorated with a cartoon of a fried egg. Mr Tokunaga chose one of each.

The canned-food section was completely devoid of baked beans or anything else familiar. Instead, the shelves were lined with cans of eel and mashed salmon that looked, on the labels, remarkably like cat food. Mr Tokunaga gave me several cans, assuring me they were a particular favourite of his son.

A giant sack of rice landed in my trolley, crushing my spicy prawn-flavoured chips. It was followed by plastic buckets, and a green bottle that I guessed was dishwashing detergent.

I was becoming dizzy. In a few blindingly short hours I had experienced a three-hour train ride from Tokyo, a lengthy train ride across Osaka, a sweaty walk along a murderously busy road, a meeting with a mayor and a hasty attempt at making up nicknames for all my new co-workers, and now I was shopping for food whose names I could not translate. Large fish with bulging eyes and gaping mouths filled the frozen food chiller. I felt faint.

My first-ever grocery bill in Japan had managed to consume a large chunk of my small stack of Japanese yen. Mr Tokunaga, though, was not ready to stop just yet. It was suddenly imperative that we purchase enough plates, bowls, cups, glasses, mugs, knives, forks, spoons, chopsticks and saucepans to fill the cupboards in my kitchen. Before I knew it, I was the proud possessor of a swag of greenish-brown crockery and more cutlery than I could ever need. Mr Tokunaga thoughtfully added a large frying pan to the pile, and I blanched as my yen whittled down even further.

We staggered back to my apartment. I checked my watch: it was nearly four o'clock and I was exhausted. In the nine hours since I had left the Tokyo, my eyes had absorbed countless new sights, my nose had experienced both pleasant new smells and overpowering traffic fumes and fishy odours, my ears had been assailed by piercing train whistles and honking traffic, and I had been completely immersed in Japanese language. My body was coated in sweat, and my legs were battered and bruised. I fancied nothing more than a cold shower and a lie-down.

I smiled politely at Mr Tokunaga as we finished unpacking my groceries and placing my new crockery in the cupboards. I mentally prepared myself to say my goodbyes for the day, and tried to remember some formal Japanese words of thanks and gratitude.

Mr Tokunaga looked at his watch. 'Hmmm,' he muttered, 'we do not have so much time. My family will be waiting.'

I was confused. Surely his family wasn't coming for dinner?

'Tonight is a festival,' he went on. 'Very, *very* big festival. We will go with my family. The festival is very far though. In Osaka City. We must take a train soon.

'We do not have so much time,' he repeated.

The Tenjin Matsuri festival, I learnt, took place every year along the banks of the Okawa River and was one of Japan's biggest festivals. Over two consecutive summer evenings, nearly a million people lined the river to watch fireworks displays and festival barges, parade in bright summer kimonos, eat food and play carnival games.

Mr Tokunaga's wife and son were waiting patiently at Tondabayashi Station. Kenji was a large high-school boy, who looked shyly at his feet and seemed to want to hide behind his mother. Mr Tokunaga had prepared another detailed train timetable; his wife sighed as he pointed where we would need to disembark and change trains. He had cleverly purchased our return tickets earlier in the day. He smiled proudly and tapped his nose. There would be many, many people at the festival, he explained, and on the way home they would all queue for train tickets. This would take time, and he had saved us valuable minutes so we would not miss our trains.

The train was filled with festival-goers. Teenage girls in pink and green kimonos tittered, chattered and posed for cellphone photographs, beaming and displaying the 'V for Victory' sign. The carriage was immaculately clean, without a sign of graffiti, broken light bulbs or punctured seats.

When we arrived on schedule, Mr Tokunaga visibly relaxed. His busy, precise day was at an end. His wife was now in charge of getting us home on time so he was allowed to eat, drink and be merry. He would, he insisted, treat me to every kind of festival food on offer, and we dived into the mass of people in search of Korean pancakes.

I had never before seen so many people in one place at one time. The crowd stretched for miles. Once you had joined it, you could only be swept along: there was no place for idle gazing and standstill moments. If you wanted to escape, you had to push and shove your way to the side. Despite my colossal height, I was shunted, bumped, poked, prodded and stepped on. The worst offenders were bent-over elderly women, who viciously barged into people with their shoulders and elbowed their way to the front of food-stall lines.

I was doing poorly at navigating my way through the crowd. Mr Tokunaga, however, seemed to be a veteran. Still clutching his briefcase to his chest with his left hand, he returned, triumphantly carrying four plates of Korean pancakes and two cans of chilled beer. When I announced that I had never sampled Japanese beer, he was aghast. After scoffing his pancakes, he sped off to find me a selection of beers, some fried chicken and a punnet of octopus balls.

Kenji and I slowly ate our pancakes at the edge of the crowd. Mine seemed to comprise chillies and spinach baked in a thin batter. Kenji finished his pancake quickly and looked around hungrily. Like a mother bird, Mr Tokunaga hastened back and handed him a plate of fried chicken wings. My first beer was replaced with a second.

Mr Tokunaga was now red-faced and beaming. He had managed to purchase some very good octopus balls. These, he claimed, would be a good experience for me. They were typical festival food, and a trademark dish in Osaka.

Slices of octopus tentacle were encased in thick fluffy balls of fried batter. The balls were coated in a sweet brown sauce, and dusted with dried bonito and seaweed flakes. I regarded them suspiciously. Apart from not being the world's biggest octopus fan, I was unsure how to go about eating them. They were the size of golf balls and I doubted I could handle them with my small pair of chopsticks.

Mr Tokunaga proceeded to stuff an entire octopus ball in his mouth. His cheeks swelled to freakish proportions, his eyes lit up, and he gave me a satisfied thumbs-up. With an adventurous gulp, I mimicked my new boss and stuffed one of the largest balls into my mouth.

My head nearly burst into flames: the octopus balls were straight out of the fry-pan and scorching hot. I gagged and coughed. Tears leaked from my eyes. My taste buds felt as though they'd been seared from my tongue. I gulped down a can of beer to douse the third-degree burns, while Mr Tokunaga cheerfully sped off into the crowd to buy us some okonomiayaki, which he claimed was Osaka's most popular meal.

Okonomiayaki, which roughly translates as 'as you like it', turned out to be savoury pancakes, but quite different to the Korean ones. The batter was thick, and enhanced with shredded cabbage. Strips of bacon, shrimp and octopus were embedded on the top, and the whole affair was lathered with the usual sweet brown sauce, bonito and seaweed flakes—and topped with sweet mayonnaise.

Mr Tokunaga took photos of me as I messily cut up my pancakes with chopsticks and eventually managed to get a chunk into my mouth. Once I had finished, he shyly asked if I would have a photo taken with him. Kenji received detailed instructions on how to use the camera, and Mr Tokunaga fussed around making sure the flash was adjusted to the right setting.

With our evening out now safely documented, Mr Tokunaga announced it was time to go home. After managing to locate his wife in the crowd, he pushed a path through the throng and we suddenly emerged outside the train station, where, true to his predictions, people were already queuing to buy tickets. An hour and half later we stepped out on to Tondabayashi Station. My watch read 11.30 p.m. and the station thermometer recorded the outside temperature as 30 degrees. The Tokunaga family escorted me to my apartment, where Mr Tokunaga finally bade me goodnight.

Alone at last, I took a leisurely cold shower, unfolded my pink futon and settled down for my first night in Japan underneath a pink blanket decorated with flowers.

# 2

# Summer holidays

*I had come to Japan to work* as an English teacher in the government-sponsored Japan English Teaching programme—JET. My application had been lodged nine months before my departure, but it was only two months before arriving in Japan that I had learned where I would be working. There was a vacancy at the Kanan Town Junior High School, and I had been selected to fill the position.

I was the only foreign teacher in the school. In fact, I was the only foreigner, or gaijin, in the town of 16,000 people. I would be teaching seventeen classes a week of students aged from twelve to fifteen. Their English abilities would range from poor to non-existent. I had never before stepped inside a classroom as a teacher, and apart from being a native English speaker was completely unqualified for the job.

I would not be teaching alone though. Rather, I would be an assistant to the Japanese teachers. My role would be to provide correct English pronunciation, explain colloquial expressions, and provide a novelty factor that, it was hoped, would inject some entertainment into the classes.

I was looking forward to my new job, and eagerly awaiting the start of the school term. I would have to wait though, as I had arrived in Japan at the beginning of the eight-week summer holiday period. This had not been a miscalculation on the part of the Japanese government, but an attempt to give me and my fellow JET teachers time to acclimatise to our new homes.

The Kanan Town Board of Education, however, was keen for me to get set up and ready. I was requested to spend my weekdays in the board's office, studying Japanese and preparing lesson plans. I was welcomed warmly by people throughout the town hall, and affectionately dubbed 'Mr Hamish' by my new colleagues.

An English-speaking assistant, Mrs Isoi, was assigned to help me sort out the logistical necessities of my new life. She, Mr Tokunaga and I spent a week setting up bank accounts, pay accounts, tax accounts, electricity accounts, gas accounts, telephone accounts and the all-important gaijin card. This photographic ID is essential for any foreigner living in Japan and I was required to carry it with me at all times.

I was now 'set up' brilliantly—a fully functioning member of society with a job, an apartment, an ID card, a personalised wooden stamp and automated bill payments. It was time for me to kick back, relax and enjoy the holidays.

My weekday routine quickly fell into a pattern. I would wake every morning at 7.20, sweaty and dehydrated. The sun would have been baking Tokiwa Mansion for two hours, reducing my apartment to an oxygen-deprived oven. I would take a cold shower and swig an entire litre of chilled water. I would then fold away my pink futon, get dressed, and pack my bag for work.

Breakfast consisted of toast covered in Japanese peanut butter, a gooey golden spread that tasted nothing like peanuts. I would then watch television, and leave the apartment no later than 8.23, waving goodbye to my landlady and her two pre-school children, who were usually playing on the front steps of the building, and chatting with Mrs Okuda, the old woman across the road, about the weather. She would tell me it would be hot and that I should take care.

I would then walk eight minutes to the smelly, diesel-stained Tondabayashi Bus Terminal along narrow, twisting cobblestone streets that felt as though they had emerged straight out of mediaeval Japan. On the numerous days when I overslept or watched too much television,

I would be forced to skip the scenic route and sprint like a maniac along one of the ugliest roads in the world, Tondabayashi main street.

My bus invariably departed at 8.33 on the dot. There were always the same passengers sitting in exactly the same seats. An intellectually handi-capped man with crossed eyes sat in the front row reading the newspaper. A gaunt old man with a tattered baseball cap sat in the seat behind him, staring out the window. A chatty trio of elderly women sat behind him, having the same conversation every morning:

'Good morning, my dear!'

'Oh, good morning!' (They act surprised to see each other.)

'It's hot today, isn't it?'

'It sure is.'

'How are you?'

'Hot.'

'What did you have for dinner?'

The bus ride would take thirteen to fifteen minutes. I would get off near the town hall, walk through the rice paddies and past the concrete pond, and arrive at the Board of Education at the same time as everyone else. Mr Tokunaga would eagerly check that I was all right and had managed to cook dinner for myself. Mr Smiles would try to teach me a new Japanese word and George would comment on my choice of clothes. Magnum would ask if I'd been to any pubs the previous evening. The timid office ladies would serve me a cool glass of Coca-Cola, which they had apparently started purchasing especially for me.

I spent my days at the Board of Education reading novels and studying Japanese. Mr Fukumoto, the superintendent, had sternly stated that he expected me to spend the summer creating lesson plans and curricula for my students. Mr Tokunaga, however, quietly took me aside and confided that this would not be necessary as the Japanese teachers whom I would be assisting had already prepared the entire English syllabus for the year. I should wait until school started and work things out with them then.

This lack of meaningful duties left me with eight weeks to kill. My colleagues at the board seemed to be aware of my situation, and did their best to distract me and help me pass the time. From time to time, my novel-reading would be cut short by Magnum or Mr Fujimoto.

Mr Fujimoto would casually glance at my book and ask what it was about. He would make a token appearance of being interested in my reply, and then produce his own reading material—usually New Zealand travel brochures—and ask me to pronounce place-names and give my opinion on certain tourist destinations. Magnum, on the other hand, would lean over my shoulder and laugh loudly, before announcing that he didn't understand a single word of English.

Attempts at study were equally short-lived. Mr Smiles and Mr Tokunaga reacted joyously whenever I opened one of my Japanese dictionaries. Mr Smiles would be at my side within seconds, eagerly peering over my shoulder. He loved to voice his own translations of words and mime some of the more random connotations. Mr Tokunaga, meanwhile, would cough and provide me with a detailed history of the meaning and origins of a particular Japanese character.

On occasion, Mr Smiles would race off into Mr Fukumoto's office to inform the superintendent of the latest word I was studying. The office ladies would giggle and Magnum would announce that he had never heard the word in his life before, and that Mr Hamish spoke better Japanese than he did.

Any visitors to the office would be paraded over to my desk and introduced. On one occasion I had just opened my Japanese language textbook when Magnum escorted a middle-aged woman to my desk. 'This is Mrs Hashimoto,' he explained, a big smile building beneath his moustache.

Mrs Hashimoto bowed and looked at the floor. I bowed in return and introduced myself. 'That will be all,' announced Magnum, and ushered Mrs Hashimoto away.

I found out later that the hapless Mrs Hashimoto had simply come to the Board of Education to request a form giving school uniform requirements for her eldest son, who had to purchase a short-sleeved shirt for Junior High.

Such interruptions rapidly became the highlight of my working day. I enjoyed chatting with Mr Fujimoto about maps and mountains. Mr Smiles was teaching me useful words, and I was learning more about Japanese kanji characters from Mr Tokunaga than I ever had at university.

Many of these interruptions developed into excursions away from the office. On one particularly hot day, Mr Ohashi from the Social Education Department approached and asked if I liked baseball. I had neither watched nor played a game of baseball, believing it an inferior sport to cricket. However, I smiled politely and replied, 'Yes, I enjoy baseball.'

Mr Ohashi clapped his hands. 'Follow me' he instructed. I followed him to the car park, assuming he had a baseball bat and ball in the boot of his car. 'We are going to watch baseball,' he announced, opening the car door.

Mr Ohashi's son, it turned out, was a member of Kanan Town's junior league baseball team. This feisty bunch of fourteen-year-olds were the pride of the town as they regularly won the prefecture-wide competition. The players' summer holidays and weekends were crammed with baseball practice and Mr Ohashi had decided we should go and watch so I could give critical feedback on the team's performance.

We sweltered on the sideline for an hour and a half in bright sunshine while Mr Ohashi's son and his team-mates practised catching and throwing. Mr Ohashi looked most uncomfortable in his suit. At the end, he eagerly inquired as to my impressions of the team, and whether I thought they would be able to win their upcoming tournament. 'Yes, most definitely,' I lied.

Word of Mr Ohashi's outing soon spread through the office, and it became common practice for people to escort me on excursions. Magnum took me to the local convenience store, explaining where the beer fridge was located. George gave up a lunch hour to drive me to an historic temple. Mr Smiles took me to a prehistoric burial mound, and Mr Fujimoto took me to one of the local tea shops. A woman from the Social Education Department gave me a guided tour of the town's fitness and pensioner centre. Mr Tokunaga and I spent a leisurely afternoon driving through the local mountain range in the office car, and the following weekend we made a day-long trip to Kyoto with George to look at more temples. Another staff member arranged for me to visit a local monastery and meet some Buddhist monks.

Mrs Isoi, my English-speaking assistant, picked up on my curiosity about the rocket-shaped Tondabayashi Tower, and decided a special trip there would help me understand its background. It turned out that the tower had been built by the Perfect Liberty cult, a bizarre religious group from Brazil that had mysteriously sprung up in Osaka in the 1940s. For some reason, the cult had gained a large following, and one of its acolytes had had the idea of building a gigantic monument to pay homage to the cult's motto, 'Life is art'. The massive fibreglass construction was visible from everywhere in Tondabayashi and the surrounding countryside.

Mrs Isoi had never visited the tower before, and as we entered the visitors' elevator she seemed nervous. 'I am a little afraid of the cult,' she whispered. 'They are very strange.'

The cult was certainly going to great efforts to keep to itself. The visitors' elevator was separate from the members' elevator, and stopped only at a special observation deck. Access to the rest of the tower was prohibited, and further information was limited to a pamphlet at the entrance. Surprisingly, it was available in English.

I was bemused to discover that the tower was supposed to represent the passage of life. The five slim struts at the bottom slowly merged into three fat struts, which then melded into a bulbous hub in the centre. From here the structure continued upwards into its melted candle form. This design, the pamphlet explained, resembled the maturity of mankind. We were all born as individuals (skinny white struts), but were brought together by society until we became one united entity (fat and bulbous). This did nothing to dispell the impression that the tower looked like a toy rocket ship that had been put in a microwave by accident.

The visitors' observation deck was also an aesthetic disaster. Because of the tower's ridiculous shape and firmly sealed windows, it was obviously impossible to clean its exterior and small glass peepholes. I peered through the grubby apertures but could see nothing of the city below.

And so my summer holidays at the Board of Education soon lapsed into a lazy and happy period of sightseeing and time-wasting. Shortly after four o'clock every day I would stop work and catch the bus home, stopping in at Daiei to buy bread and something for dinner. Mrs Isoi had bought me a Japanese recipe book and I was making good use of it.

During my first shopping expeditions, I was surprised to find that many of the items I had expected to be expensive were, in fact, reasonably priced. Chicken was cheap, as were vegetables. Rice, on the other hand, was very expensive, and seemed to be sold only in packs that catered for families of twenty.

After shopping, I would trudge home in the afternoon heat. As I passed the gaggle of elderly neighbours who seemed to spend their afternoons gossiping on the street outside Mrs Okuda's apartment, they would wave back, pointing and remarking on the amount of groceries I was carrying.

It was my grocery bags that eventually enabled me to get to know Mrs Okuda. A sprightly woman of over seventy, Mrs Okuda lived with her mother and father in a large, 400-year-old house on the other side of the road. She spent her days caring for her wheelchair-bound mother and tending the family's vegetable garden. Her mother would sit quietly on the back step while her daughter watered their large tomato plants and weeded their latest zucchini crop.

Mrs Okuda had initially regarded me with suspicion, and scurried away whenever I walked past. As the weeks went by, however, she and her circle of lady gardeners became intrigued with the contents of my shopping bags. I would stop and chat about the weather, and explain how much hotter Japan was than New Zealand. The women would nod in agreement, all the while nosily eying my latest purchases.

As my dietary routines and limited cooking skills slowly became apparent, they were able to predict and comment on changes in my shopping list.

'Oooh, that's a new flavour of juice. Didn't you like that other flavour?' remarked the woman with the amusing glasses.

'He likes apple juice,' Mrs Okuda would answer on my behalf.

'I saw him buy bread the other day,' the skinny woman remarked.

'Yes, he likes bread.'

'Do you live by yourself?' Mrs Okuda's mother piped up from her wheelchair, peering earnestly at me. 'Do you live by yourself?' she repeated.

'Yes.' Everyone nodded in agreement.

'Do you cook by yourself?'

'Yes.' Everyone nodded again.

Mrs Okuda's mother asked the same questions every day, and her delighted response was always the same.

'That's great. That's great. Oh my, a young man who can cook for himself. That's great. Do you clean for yourself?'

The younger women would answer on my behalf, and the nodding and head-bobbing would continue.

These grocery-bag conversations often lasted for up to quarter of an hour, and would eventually come to an end with Mrs Okuda rushing off to her kitchen and returning with fresh vegetables. She would apologise profusely for their quality, promising that next year would be a better season and she would be able to offer me better specimens. On the days when she couldn't find anything in her garden, she would give me a carton of my favourite apple juice or something else she believed I needed.

Overwhelmed by this generosity, I took to bringing Mrs Okuda and her mother cakes and savouries from the supermarket.

I was beginning to think that everyone in Japan was incredibly kind and generous. My landlady, Mrs Fujita, was no exception. The Fujita family lived downstairs, on the second floor. Mr Fujita was a chiropractor and operated a clinic on the ground floor, opposite Mrs Okuda's vegetable garden.

Mr and Mrs Fujita had two small daughters, Fumiko (Fu-Chan) and Mikako (Mi-Chan). The girls spent their days playing in front of the apartment block, squirting each other with Mrs Okuda's garden hose and speeding around on their tricycles. Never shy, they always ran to welcome me home. Fu-Chan celebrated her fifth birthday shortly after I arrived in Japan, and I gave her some New Zealand stickers and kiwi-fruit chocolates. These were shared with her sister, and I soon became a favourite member of the apartment block. The girls drew scribbly pictures of me with bright yellow hair and neon-green shirts and I was invited to join games of jump-rope and spinning top.

I had obviously not paid close enough attention to Mr Tokunaga when he explained how to use my washing machine, as on my first attempt I flooded the apartment. Fortunately, the water had not made it to the precious tatami mats, but the hallway and kitchen floors were completely submerged. I danced around in a panic, terrified the water would seep through the floor and drench the apartment below. What could I use to soak up the spillage? I possessed only a thin bath towel and a tea towel, and using the pink futon and flowery blanket did not seem advisable.

I raced off to find Mrs Fujita, who instantly sped to my rescue, and using her family's entire bath-towel collection we had the mess cleaned up in minutes. Instead of scolding me, Mrs Fujita apologised for not having explained the washing machine's strange drainage function, and despatched Fu-Chan to get me a bunch of grapes.

My close shave with the overflowing washing machine had highlighted two areas of concern. First, I had only one towel and very little linen. Secondly, I had no furniture. All my belongings were sitting around in piles in the living room. I sat on two wooden chairs that I had inherited from Mr Tokunaga and ate my dinner on a cardboard box. I watched TV on the floor, surrounded by stacks of books and CDs.

It was time to go shopping again. My dwindling supply of yen led me to Daiei, where prices were cheap—except for bed sheets: a replacement for my pink futon would have to wait until pay-day. In the meantime, blue pillowcases were purchased to help me feel more masculine.

A blue sofa soon followed. It was a soft, spongy contraption that sat close to the ground and seated one and a half people. A matching blue glass coffee table added a summery feel, and soon afterwards I purchased a couple of bookcases.

The *pièce de résistance*, though, involved a trip further afield. I was growing tired of Japanese television and was desperate to hear some English music. My CD collection, which I had taken great pains to bring to Japan with me, was gathering dust. I counted my yen and made the daring decision to buy a stereo.

Mr Tokunaga applauded my decision the minute he overheard me talking about it. He was, it turned out, a frequent shopper in Osaka's electronics district and a self-proclaimed expert haggler. We took an afternoon off work and drove north in the office car. Mr Tokunaga dithered through city traffic and found a park close to the main street.

The Nipponbashi strip of electronics stores was a riot of flashing neon. Multi-storey places with names such as Yodobashi Camera and Bic Camera displayed huge banners and blasted jangly tunes on to the street. Each stocked an overwhelming range of cameras, television sets, DVD players, computers, laptops and stereo equipment. For several hours Mr Tokunaga and I wandered from shop to shop. I had never seen such flashy gadgets. There were petite pink and white stereos, large silver stereos, bright green boom-boxes, red cassette players and orange portable CD players. Sliding panels swivelled noiselessly at the touch of a button, revealing panoramas of buttons and knobs. On blinking display screens, dancing cartoon characters helped the listener choose the volume level.

I was captivated by a medium-sized system. Large blue speakers were set into a sleek silver body. CDs were inserted vertically, locked in place by a magnetic disc. Half the front panel of the system would then slide up, enabling the CD to be played. It looked and acted like a robot. I was determined to purchase it.

Mr Tokunaga nodded in approval. 'Yes, yes, good model, good price. But I think you need to get a reduction. I know how to haggle for a reduction. Let me do the talking.'

With that, he strode up to a salesman and began to complain that the stereo was overpriced. I should be given a ten percent discount. The salesman politely assured him the stereo had already been reduced and was at the lowest possible price.

Mr Tokunaga shook his head and coughed. 'No, no!' he stated loudly. 'We have just seen this stereo for ten percent less down the road, and hoped you would do us a deal.'

The salesman's manager overheard this remark and joined the debate. 'Sir, please accept our humble apologies. My clerk here did not realise our competitor's price. We will match it immediately. Please, you are most welcome to a ten percent discount, and would you like some mini discs thrown in for free?'

Mr Tokunaga's smile of triumph lasted only a split second before being replaced by a look of serious contemplation. 'Hmmm, that sounds acceptable. I don't know though. I do need some new batteries.'

The store manager nodded and clicked his fingers. The salesman, now bowing and blushing with shame, rushed away to arrange the sale and find AA batteries and a pack of mini discs.

Mr Tokunaga was on top of the world. He floated happily around my apartment, and in no time had my new toy set up. He then called his wife to inform her that he was on his way home for dinner, and eagerly filled her in on my discounted purchase.

An angry buzz of a reply made him wince and hold his cellphone away from his ear. 'No, no!' he pleaded. 'Mr Hamish *wanted* to buy the stereo. I didn't talk him into it … No, no! He *wanted* to buy it … No, I'm sure.'

He paused and turned to me. 'You wanted to buy that stereo, didn't you?' He looked close to tears. I nodded enthusiastically and stammered out my best assurance in Japanese.

'See, see. Did you hear that? He wanted to buy it.' Mrs Tokunaga was seemingly still unconvinced, and Mr Tokunaga was scolded again and ordered to come home. He bowed sadly, coughed and bade me good-night. I thanked him sincerely for taking me shopping, getting me a discount and setting up my stereo. He smiled slightly, recommended that I refrain from playing the stereo too loudly as it might disturb the neighbours, collected his bag of AA batteries and departed, leaving me alone with the familiar comfort of English music.

The incessant summer heat prevented any decent daytime exploration of my new home town, so I limited my forays to the evenings when it was cooler. I enjoyed wandering the cobblestone backstreets of Jinaimachi. The town council had thoughtfully done away with the usual glaring street lights and winking neon signs. Instead, subtle pavement-level lamps illuminated the streets with a soft orange glow.

My intrepid scouting unearthed a wealth of interesting places. I bought ceramic chopstick holders at a small pottery shop, and regularly drank green tea proffered by the two old women who sat behind the counter. A wooden house down the road from my apartment doubled as a pub during the evenings: two small red lanterns signalled when it was open for business. Inside, a woman served large savoury pancakes to an assortment of toothless old men. There was a former warehouse that had been converted into a museum of artefacts from Jinaimachi's glory days, and a brick building I dubbed 'the old mill'.

I enjoyed getting lost and then emerging somewhere new and unexplored. One nondescript alley brought me first to a small park, and then, after several more twists and turns, to a toy store specialising in plastic kitset aircraft and tanks, and a hair salon providing 'ladies' perms'. After several more twists and turns I encountered a florist and a fruit market. Soon afterwards I discovered several more short cuts to the train station, and a completely new train station I hadn't even known existed.

My adventures became more daring, and I began to test the boundaries of my new world. The mighty concrete-lined Ishikawa River surrounded Jinaimachi to the south and east, and formed the border with Kanan Town. On a slightly cooler than normal day, I decided to follow a path that started behind the pottery shop and disappeared into some undergrowth. After bashing through the scrub, I followed the path through a vegetable patch and on to the banks of the river, where families were picnicking and teenagers playing soccer on a dry brown pitch.

North of Jinaimachi proved a fruitless destination—Soviet-style apartment blocks and the absurd PL Tower lined the horizon, and multi-lane highways killed any hopes of a peaceful walk—so I turned my attention west. I had caught glimpses of rice paddies and scenic views from the train and I was determined to find them.

One evening, walking due west from my apartment, I crossed Tonda-bayashi's main street and continued past Daiei. I was now in uncharted territory, amidst rotating sushi restaurants, barbeque-beef barns, gaudy casinos, hardware stores, car yards, video stores, karaoke bars, more sushi restaurants and more barbecue restaurants.

Suddenly I spied the field of rice plants. It was tucked away behind a second-hand CD store, and nowhere near as romantic as I had imagined. My search for a scenic oasis had failed. I contented myself with a visit to the CD store, where the stock consisted largely of tragically bad rock albums from the '80s. I then purchased a chocolate bar from a vending machine and set off for home.

As I walked down the road, I studiously fumbled with the wrapper. The seal opened and I licked my lips, ready to take my first bite. Suddenly, the ground beneath me evaporated and I plummeted headlong into a pit of mud and slime.

Bang! I had landed heavily on my stomach. I lay still for a moment, unhurt but mortified. I had just fallen into a drainage channel. Japanese rice paddies were often ringed with these deep channels, which usually ran alongside footpaths and were seldom fenced. Luckily, my perfect dive had saved me from serious injury. If I had toppled sideways or on an awkward angle, I would probably have smashed my chin and teeth on the channel's concrete sides. Instead I had merely dented my knee and sustained a small cut on one elbow.

I pulled myself out and limped home. My mud-stained clothes smelled bad, my elbow was bleeding and I started to worry that I may have actually fallen into a sewer. Never again, I swore, would I attempt to multi-task while walking in the Japanese countryside.

'Futsukayoi,' explained Mr Smiles, 'is Japanese for hangover.' He laughed. 'Too much beer equals too much tension. High tension. Ha ha— you are very high tension. I am high tension too. Ha ha.'

He drank an imaginary glass of beer, and mimed an electric shock. 'Ha ha. High tension. Ha ha.'

He was right though. I was certainly high tension. My head felt as though it were full of cotton wool, my eyelids were heavy and I couldn't stop yawning.

Mr Smiles and Magnum PI looked on encouragingly. 'You like beer. That is very good.' Magnum still considered me his drinking apprentice.

It was Monday morning and I was sitting at my desk, still hung-over from Saturday night. I had spent Sunday in bed, surfacing at five in the evening to heat a supermarket pizza before crawling back into my pink and blue bed. This was my second hangover in as many weeks, and possibly the worst I'd suffered in my life.

I had spent the previous two Saturday evenings enjoying a newly discovered pleasure—Japanese beer gardens. These outdoor garden bars were usually situated at the top of high-rise department stores. Once you had paid a tiny entrance fee, you had full access to an extensive buffet of food and a bottomless pint of beer. They were open only during the summer months, when the warm evenings induced thirst. Fairy lights twinkled and soft elevator music played from small concealed speakers.

I had joined a small band of foreign English teachers, all of us newly arrived in Japan. Justin and Matt were both from New Zealand. I had met Justin on the train from Tokyo to Osaka; he was living in a town twenty minutes' drive north from Tondabayashi. Matt also lived close by, in Sakai, a large industrial suburb. His ghastly twenty-storey apartment block could have stepped out of the streets of East Berlin. Blake and Wij lived downstairs from Matt. They were both from the UK, and I had met them during my short stay in Tokyo.

We had all arranged to meet up in downtown Osaka on our first free Saturday night.

Wij had heard about the Namba Station beer garden from a Japanese co-worker, who had recommended it. Namba was the second biggest train station in Osaka and, as well as its maze of underground platforms that stretched for several city blocks, it was famous for its sprawling department store.

Finding an elevator that would take us to the beer garden on the roof had proved to be anything but simple. Because it was open for only three months of the year, direct access was clearly not a priority for the management of the department store. After half an hour, we found a route through the twelfth-floor toy department, up a discreet escalator, down a deserted corridor, and then up two flights of what appeared to be emergency exit stairs.

Eventually we stumbled upon the twinkling entrance, paid the miniscule entrance fee, and were presented with refillable beer jugs and reheapable dinner plates. Scottishness reigned: we three New Zealanders had proud Scottish heritage, Wij was from Edinburgh and Blake was practically Scottish, coming from Newcastle. We were, therefore, intent on making the most of our entrance fee.

We had each paid 1500 yen. A pint of beer in a pub usually cost around 400 yen and a plate of fried noodles 500 yen. Four beers, two helpings of fried noodles, two steamed buns, a plate of fried beef, and an assortment of sausages, squid rings and fried dumplings later I was confident I had comfortably made back my money.

There was, however, still an hour before the beer garden was scheduled to close, so there was no time to waste congratulating myself. There was still plenty of food and drink to be consumed. My friends seemed to be streets ahead, and I realised I would need to develop a drinking addiction in order to keep up with Wij.

Forty minutes later, I had lost all track of the beer I had consumed. Things had become shambolic. Blake and Justin were throwing beans at each other. Wij was joking crazily with an equally plastered man next to him. I was giggling to myself like a simpleton.

The elevator music changed to 'Auld Lang Syne' and a bell chimed, signalling the last drink. It was suddenly apparent that we were in no fit state to travel across town on unfamiliar railway networks. Justin noticed some young women nervously sipping bright orange and yellow liquids, and inquired of the bar staff what they were. They were, he was informed, soft drinks called chuhai. They were available free of charge and came in a variety of flavours, such as orange, lemon, grape, apple and lime.

We unanimously decided this chuhai would make an excellent way to end the evening; a non-alcoholic beverage would dilute the beer and sober us up for the ride home. We each ordered three pints and lined them up on the trestle table, keen to drink the lot before we were ejected from the premises. I downed an entire pint in one go, and the others were suitably impressed.

The route we needed to find to get out of the department store was now a blur. My eyelids felt leaden and I leaned on Blake to stay upright. By the time we reached the street, I was in an even sorrier state. As I was now unable to open my eyes, Blake and Justin all but carried me to the platform of my train. Wij, meanwhile, had disappeared.

The others left to catch their own trains and I slumped pitifully against a wall. Quite how I managed to find my way home is a mystery. I must have staggered aboard the southbound train from Namba Station, somehow remembered to get off two stations later, and then transferred to the Tondabayashi express. This would have involved navigating the entire length of Abenobashi Station—another major train station—and purchasing a new ticket. I seem to have accomplished all of this with my eyes closed.

At Abenobashi, a distant voice in my head told me to choose the green train. I hopped aboard, not even checking its destination. My eyes were now firmly shut. I stood swaying in the middle of the carriage, arms draped through a handrail in a desperate attempt to stay upright.

The train started and I lurched sideways. I muttered drunkenly to myself, wondering where I was, and where my friends had disappeared to. I could hear concerned gasps from passengers around me, but could not open my eyes to see them.

The train rumbled on, and I grew sleepier and sleepier. After a long time, it stopped at an unknown station. 'This is it!' I boomed, untangling myself from the handrail and bouncing out the door. My eyes opened for a split second, long enough to tell me I was still far from home. The station platform was pitch-black—and completely unfamiliar.

Ooops! I lurched back on to the train just as the doors snapped shut. The ride seemed to be getting increasingly bumpy. I leaned against a skinny metal pole. My greasy dinner gurgled ominously in my stomach. 'Where am I? Am I home yet? I don't feel so good.' I took a deep breath to steady myself. The train braked suddenly. I banged my head against the pole and nearly lost my footing.

What followed was one of the most embarrassing and depraved moments of my life. My stomach heaved, and I vomited its contents on to the floor of the train. I was still unable to open my eyes, but I could hear a woman screaming. Someone thrust a newspaper into my hand to clean up the mess, and I wiped my vomit-covered lips on it. The train stopped and I threw the newspaper out the open door. I lurched off the train to retrieve my 'napkin', blinked and discovered that I had somehow arrived at Tondabayashi Station.

I took stock. I still had my wallet in my pocket. My clothes were still clean, although my right shoe had vomit on the toe. I was, under the circumstances, in remarkably good shape.

The next day, however, was not enjoyable. My head hurt, and sported a deep bruise where I had banged it on the pole. I felt nauseous when I relived the events of the previous evening, and burned with shame when I realised what I had done on the train. I was baffled as to what had brought about my blindness, and decided I must be allergic to the green beans on which we had been snacking during the evening.

My friends had all made it home safely except for Wij, who had woken up at ten o'clock the next morning in Kobe, a city an hour north of Osaka. Having missed his train home, he had spent the night sleeping at Osaka Station. First thing the next morning he had boarded the train home, fallen asleep, missed his stop, and travelled to the end of the line. The train had then turned around and travelled north for two hours until it reached Kobe, where a friendly passenger had decided to rouse Wij from his drunken slumber.

Sadly, my first Japanese hangover was not enough to put me off drunken escapades, and the following Saturday evening the five of us again merrily hit the town. This time, however, research had been conducted. Trains stopped running at midnight, and beer gardens closed around 11.30 so patrons could catch the last train. Being keen to make the most of our Saturday evenings and not interested in scuttling home at midnight, we had devised an itinerary to see us through until dawn when the trains started up again.

Justin had unearthed a new beer garden, Blake had heard of a promising-sounding bar that was open until three, Wij had come across a 24-hour karaoke bar, and I had scouted out an all-night internet café where we could recline on sofa beds and drink complimentary coffee.

The night began well: greasy food, lots of beer, more greasy food, more beer, and big glasses of chuhai to help dilute alcoholic intake. During some friendly games of pool at Blake's late-night bar, however, I started to notice the symptoms of yet another downward spiral. My eyes felt heavy and I was having trouble walking straight. I slumped down on a seat in the corner.

The bar closed and I clung to Justin and Blake's shoulders as they ferried me to the karaoke bar, where we were ushered into our own private booth. I immediately ordered an apple-flavoured chuhai to sober up, while Justin, a guitarist and former rock band member, took centre stage, crooning through some rocky ballads, and then croaking out a duet with Blake.

Wij, meanwhile, had fallen asleep and I was feeling very unwell indeed. Matt started singing but I had lost all comprehension of where I was. I passed out and fell off my chair. A few minutes later I was woken by Justin performing a rousing version of 'The Piña Colada Song'. My mind raced, my stomach churned, and I daintily projectile-vomited noodles and steamed buns into a puddle on top of the booth's coffee table. Justin gasped. Matt laughed. Blake leapt to his feet and quickly mopped up the mess using the five-centimetre-thick karaoke songbook. The crowd applauded and the singing resumed. I was shunted into the corner with Wij and fell asleep.

Four hours later, having somehow got back to my apartment, I had a shower and retreated to the loving embrace of my pink futon. Some time later I awoke. The room was spinning, my head was throbbing and my throat was on fire. I drank a bottle of water and passed out. This cycle continued until five in the evening, when I summoned the energy to grill myself a supermarket pizza.

Next day, co-workers were overjoyed to hear of my exploits at the beer gardens. Mr Smiles flipped through my Japanese–English dictionary, eager to explain why my head hurt. Magnum was keen to hear how many pints of beer I had been able to drink. He counted these on his fingers, with a stern look of concentration. 'Very good,' he proclaimed. 'But did you drink anything else? Sake? Whisky?'

'No,' I replied, sorry to disappoint my new mentor. 'Only chuhai.'

'Oh!' he exclaimed. 'How many chuhai did you drink?'

'I can't really remember,' I shrugged. 'Five, maybe six.'

Magnum's eyes bulged and Mr Smiles danced about excitedly. 'Oh, Mr Hamish, very good. You like chuhai?'

I shrugged. 'It's okay. I prefer Fanta though. Much nicer.'

Magnum looked confused. 'But Mr Hamish, chuhai is alcohol. Same as beer.'

I blinked in surprise. 'Pardon? I thought it was a soft drink.'

'No, no, Mr Hamish. It is alcohol. High tension!' Mr. Smiles did an impersonation of someone being electrocuted, clapped his hands and dispatched one of the office women to fetch a can of chuhai for scientific observation. She returned minutes later, having purchased one from a vending machine across the road.

'See see,' Magnum said proudly, 'chuhai is alcohol.'

I surveyed the white can. At the bottom were the words: 'Alcohol content: four percent.'

My drunken escapades had really struck a chord with my colleagues in the Board of Education. Magnum proudly informed anyone who would listen that I was a great fan of beer gardens. Mr Smiles eagerly questioned me each day as to whether I had had a beer with dinner the previous night. George politely inquired about the popularity of various drinks in New Zealand, while Mr Tokunaga coughed nervously and asked if I ever found it difficult to catch the train home.

This bewildering level of interest in my consumption of alcohol carried on throughout the week. I was constantly overhearing my name, and when I looked up I would see Magnum and other men in secretive conversation in the corner.

The next Tuesday morning, I was sitting at my desk when Mr Tokunaga quietly approached and asked whether I had any plans for the evening. Members of the Board of Education were keen to take me out for a meal. Touched by this generosity, I happily accepted.

It was not until Magnum arrived at work that I began to suspect all was not quite what it seemed. 'Aha,' he beamed, on learning I had accepted the invitation. 'We will go drinking tonight. Aha ha ha. We will drink many beers and eat lots of food. We will try many strange foods. You must challenge yourself.'

He lowered his voice to a conspiratorial tone. 'It is a test for you.'

After work, Mr Tokunaga picked me up from my apartment. 'We will go to a very small Japanese pub,' he said. 'It serves many—how do you say?—delicacies. You can try many interesting dishes.'

We arrived at a decrepit-looking building and entered by a back door. It looked as though we had wandered into somebody's home. Mr Tokunaga ushered me through the kitchen and into the restaurant. A few empty tables and chairs filled the smoky, dimly lit room. No one else from the Board of Education was present.

A bent old woman shuffled into the room and enthusiastically clasped Mr Tokunaga's hands. 'It's so good to see you again, sir. It has been such a long time. Come this way please, we have prepared a special room for tonight.' It seemed my ritual test of manhood was to be conducted behind closed doors.

The woman twisted her head to peer up at me. 'Oooh,' she rasped, 'so tall.' Cackling, she led us out of the room and up some stairs. A screen door stood closed at the top of the staircase. The woman knelt, and bowed as she pushed it open. Enthusiastic laughter and a round of applause erupted from within. All the men from the Board of Education and several mysterious new faces grinned up at me. I recognised some as the men with whom Magnum had been conspiring. Magnum himself was sitting in the far corner of the room. He laughed heartily and beckoned me to sit down in the centre next to Mr Smiles.

A beer had been poured for me, and Mr Smiles called out for the woman to bring a pot of sake. My co-workers were already red-faced and tipsy, and one of the men had his neck tie fastened around his forehead.

Mr Smiles stood and welcomed me formally, before thanking everyone for showing up. With that, another round of beers was ordered. I suddenly had two untouched pints of beer and a pot of warm sake sitting in front of me. I decided to sample the sake first. I noticed that whenever I took a sip Mr Fujimoto, who was sitting on the other side of me, would quickly top up my small ceramic cup.

Magnum sat quietly in the corner, watching me carefully. A small bespectacled man next to him studiously studied the menu, whispering in Magnum's ear and pointing eagerly. Magnum beamed, several mysterious dishes were ordered, and I was asked if I needed another beer.

We were soon tucking into spring rolls and fried chicken wings as if this were the last supper. A plate of sushi arrived and I was given first choice of the expensive-looking selection. I chose a tasty salmon roll, but Mr Fujimoto clicked his tongue in disapproval and heaped four of the largest pieces on to my plate.

'Mr Hamish,' he lectured, 'you must eat. You look hungry.'

Japanese hospitality dictates that a guest should never have an empty plate, bowl or glass. This protocol was being strictly observed, and I was made to sample every meal on the table, given the last mouthful of every dish, and if my glass of beer or cup of sake became empty they were replaced instantly.

Magnum stood up and left the room. When he returned, he nodded to Mr Smiles. There was an expectant hush. The screen door opened and the old woman entered the room. She was carrying a plate of writhing purple spaghetti. The plate was placed in front of me.

I had noticed a live octopus in a large tank when we had entered the restaurant. He had been swimming around happily. My manhood test, however, had required him to be plucked from his tank, laid on a chopping block, and have two of his finest tentacles removed with a cleaver. The two wriggling, squirming tentacles had been diced into smaller wriggling, squirming pieces and carefully laid out on an attractive serving platter.

The assembled company gasped. Live octopus tentacles, it seemed, were a rare treat, and a tremendous honour for the guest.

I looked down at the plate. One of the tentacle pieces had managed to crawl to the edge and drop on to the table cloth. The rest were squirming helplessly. Emboldened by the alcohol I'd consumed, I reached out with my chopsticks and grabbed a large piece from the middle of the plate. Magnum clapped and everyone cheered. The tentacle resisted and stuck fast to the plate. I tugged and it came free.

Its slimy coating was, however, difficult to grip with the chopsticks. The tentacle dropped to the tabletop and started to crawl away. I gripped it again and swooped it into my mouth.

There was another drunken cheer and the audience peered at me intently, eager to see how I would react to this delicacy. The tentacle squirmed madly and attached itself to the roof of my mouth. I gagged, and then proceeded to chew the demon tentacle until it gave up the struggle.

The taste was oddly refreshing. There was no oozing blood or ink, and no fishy after-taste. I gave a satisfied thumbs-up and got a pat on the back from Mr Smiles. Magnum slumped back in his corner, a relieved smile on his face. I had passed the first section of my test.

After the octopus tentacles had been devoured, the screen door slid open again and the woman shuffled in again with another dish. A live fish lay flapping on the plate. His mouth opened and closed in shock, and I tried not to look at his terrified face. Strips had been cut in the fish's sides and Mr Smiles demonstrated how to delicately peel these off with chopsticks. He then laid several on my plate and encouraged me to dip them in soy sauce before eating them. Everyone joined in, and the poor fish was soon reduced to a bare skeleton.

Eating the flapping fish had apparently been the final part of my manhood test. I was given another beer, my sake pot was topped up, and fried noodles and steamed buns were ordered.

The mysterious strangers introduced themselves and enthusiastically shook my hand. The man with the necktie around his head told me that he was interested in prehistoric artefacts. Kanan Town and the surrounding countryside were, he explained, famed as the site where archaeologists had unearthed a wealth of old arrowheads and cooking pots. Burial mounds and prehistoric tombs could be found if you knew where to look. He would take me sightseeing and show me his favourites.

Magnum sat sagely in the corner, a contented look on his face. He had found his new apprentice.

By the end of August, I had settled into my new home and was feeling well-established. I was smugly confident I would be able to handle anything that Japan could throw at me. Then the summer holiday bubble burst.

# 3

# Jun Fujita and the young minnows

*I met Jun Fujita for the first time* on the hottest day of summer. It was the middle of the holidays and Mr Tokunaga had decided to take me on an introductory tour of the school. The office thermometer had stopped working at 36 degrees, and during the short walk between the town hall and the school gate several sweaty haloes had appeared on my white cotton shirt. My shoes and socks were damp and grimy as I removed them in the locker bay, and my feet slid as I tried to insert them into the plastic hallway slippers that were five sizes too small.

My first impression of the school was, therefore, of intense heat. The buildings lacked any form of air-conditioning or ventilation. As we walked slowly through the hallways, I struggled to stop the tiny slippers firing off my feet like banana peels. Every time I retrieved them, I noticed an increasing number of sweat beads in the toe area, and pitied the poor soul who would inherit the slippers after me. I also noticed that since my feet could fit only halfway, my heels were dragging along the floor, collecting a thick layer of grime.

By the time I was shown into the staffroom, I was a bedraggled mess. The sweat stains on my cotton shirt had merged to form the map of Australia, and the heels of my feet suggested I had been working in a coal mine. Fortunately, the PE teacher was the only other staff member at school, and he was busy making a phone call.

The staffroom seemed even less ventilated than the school corridor. Heat waves accosted me from every direction. As I tried to stop fainting, the door swung open and a small boy burst through. He was about five foot tall, with a spiky crew cut that was long in the front but gradually became shorter until the crown of his head was practically bare. His face had the distinctive characteristics of Down's Syndrome.

The boy opened his mouth to call for the PE teacher, noticed me and turned to stone. I managed a smile and he continued to stare. I waved and he took to his heels and fled.

Mr Tokunaga seemed not to notice the small boy's dramatic entrance and exit, and we continued our tour of the school. I was thankful when we eventually staggered into the fresh air to survey the playing field. Two clubs, athletics and girls' softball, were practising in the sweltering heat, but on seeing me the students waved and cheered. I waved back and felt like a rock star.

As we walked back to the entrance to collect our shoes, I noticed a small spiky head with curious eyes peeping through a window in the hallway. I waved and the spiky head and curious eyes vanished.

My plastic slippers were now horribly slimy, and my soggy socks offered welcome relief. I hopped around on one foot, trying to put on my socks and shoes without overbalancing. Looking up for a second, I saw the small boy hiding behind a pot plant. I gave him a smile and waved. In doing so, I lost my balance, tripped and crashed into a locker.

The boy stood and stared. His open mouth cracked slightly to form a shy grin, then he turned and ran away.

A fortnight later, my glorious summer holiday was over. After six long hard weeks of sightseeing and reading novels at my desk in the Board of Education, I would finally make it to school.

I stood nervously to attention during the morning staff meeting while Mr Kazama, the owl-like principal, introduced me to my fellow teachers. His formal speech produced some hushed bows, a few smiles, a smattering of frowns and a couple of scowls. I then scuttled back to my desk. The schedule for the remainder of the day was completely bare.

One by one, the school's three English teachers approached my desk and introduced themselves. Mrs Takaoka was a kind-looking middle-aged woman whom I would be assisting during first-grade classes. Ms Domae, the second-grade teacher, who I guessed was in her thirties, seemed shy and unsure how to talk to me.

Mr Higo was twenty-four; until my arrival he had been the youngest teacher in the school. Chirpy and smiley, he asked if I would be interested in purchasing school lunches on a regular basis. He explained that the small handful of unmarried male teachers relied on these lunches as they were unable to cook for themselves. The lunches were not very appetising, he confided, but they were certainly better than anything we could make ourselves.

After a five-minute chat about octopus and squid, I was left to continue my efforts to look busy and productive. I spent an hour lining up my few dictionaries and English-language books and sorting and arranging my pen collection. I updated my diary and sorted out my schedule for the next few days. There were no appointments, and no tasks needing to be completed. I counted the change in my wallet: 256 yen, enough for an ice-cream and a can of Coca-Cola on the way home. I read a few chapters of *Harry Potter and the Philosopher's Stone* and caught myself nodding off.

Sadly, my students would not be as well rested. The Japanese education system demanded that summer holidays were filled with sports team practices and copious amounts of homework. The first week of term would be entirely devoted to serious exams, to test whether the students had spent their time reading about mediaeval Japanese history or playing PlayStation or baseball. Exams would then need to be marked and handed back. This meant I would have two more weeks to fill before I set foot in an actual classroom.

I was not overly concerned by this. I would be paid. In fact, by the time I actually started teaching in Japan I would have been paid for eight weeks of eating chocolate, reading *Harry Potter*, sleeping at my desk, getting drunk and throwing up on trains.

The school principal did, however, attempt to save me from sinking into a slothful void. I was called into his office and presented with my first ever task—to deliver a speech the next day at the school assembly, in front of five hundred people. I sat back in his plush leather sofa and nonchalantly asked what sort of speech he would like—a formal welcome, a self-introduction, or even my first impressions of Japan. He shook his head. He would, he said, prefer a song or dance.

Despite being gripped by an instant surge of panic, I put on a professional veneer and assured Mr Kazama he would enjoy my performance. I rose from the sofa, shook his hand and walked calmly back to my desk, where I collapsed into a nervous wreck.

I spent the next hour trying to concoct a theatrical performance that would not single-handedly destroy all my future credibility with the students. Dancing was immediately discounted. Apart from a mild ability to stay in time with techno beats at nightclubs, my dancing skills were non-existent. I would need to resort to song. This did nothing to calm my nerves: my singing was only marginally better than my dancing.

The next problem was what song to choose. The New Zealand national anthem had been my immediate choice, but I could remember only the first verse. My knowledge of Maori songs was poor at best, and I shuddered at the thought of having to translate the lyrics into Japanese. My last resort was the meagre list of English pop songs that I knew by heart. My brain churned away and the best it could come up with was the early '90s Guns and Roses hit 'Don't cry'. I tried humming it a few times, and could already imagine myself having an embarrassing accident while trying to imitate Axl Rose's hoarse shrieks and high-pitched whines.

Perhaps I could sing a Christmas carol? Any idiot can bash out a rendition of 'Jingle Bells' or 'Rudolph, the Red-Nosed Reindeer', I thought to myself. But given the time of year, a Christmas carol seemed wildly inappropriate. I slumped deeper into my chair.

It was then that salvation arrived. Ms Domae approached my desk and asked what I was doing. I explained that I was trying to come up with a song for the school assembly. She looked unimpressed. 'The previous English teacher sang a song *and* did a dance,' she trumpeted. I hated the previous English teacher immediately.

'That's very nice,' I said, 'but I'm very bad at singing and dancing. I speak English very well though.'

Ms Domae beamed. 'Maybe we can do your speech together,' she suggested.

'I thought Mr Kazama wanted a song or dance?'

'No, no, he won't mind. Just tell the students about yourself. They'll be happy, and then he'll be happy too.'

I was ecstatic with relief.

'You write your speech in English,' Ms Domae suggested, 'then give it to me and I'll translate it into Japanese for the students.'

'Are you sure this will be all right?' I asked again.

'It will be fine,' she replied. 'Mr Kazama will be pleased to see us working together so well.'

The day of the assembly dawned bright and hot. By the time I arrived at school, preparations were already underway. For some reason the hour-long ordeal was to take place outside in the full glare of the sun. The students were being herded on to the sports field and shepherded into alphabetical order according to class rolls. Once perfectly ordered they sat down, each one carefully measuring the distance to the student in front and to their left and right. Within seconds this had produced seamless ranks of boys' white shirts, making stark stripes next to the girls' navy-blue blazers.

The scene was set, the students were in place, and it was time for the first Kanan Town Junior High School term two assembly to begin. The principal and I climbed up on to the rickety tin stage. A hush fell over the already deathly silent crowd. I stood in front of the raised microphone. A lump of nervousness rose in my throat.

'Hello,' I shouted. There was a smattering of a reply. 'Hello,' I shouted again, more loudly. A bigger response. By the third time, I was sure that everyone had joined in.

I moved into a rendition of my newly learned Japanese comedy routine, 'Oha!' 'Oha!' was then the most popular comic turn in Japan. The performer started by forming a circle with the forefinger and thumb of each hand and pronouncing the syllable 'O'. He or she then flicked the hand open to show the audience the palm with all fingers and thumbs extended straight, at the same time completing the second syllable of the 'joke'—'ha!'—and the audience erupted into laughter, as if on cue.

The humour and meaning of this joke eluded me. I had been told its popularity was due entirely to the celebrity of its creator, a comedian and boy-band member called Shingo Mama. Shingo Mama had invented an *alter ego* for children's television programs, in which he paraded around dressed as a housewife, singing and performing his mystifying 'Oha!' routine. His performances were seemingly aimed at four-year-olds, with songs about the benefits of brushing your teeth and eating mayonnaise. For some reason, 'Oha!' had become a national phenomenon.

I had been very sceptical of 'Oha!' when I had first seen it on television. Soon afterwards I had attempted to recreate it at the Board of Education and received a mixed reaction. Finally, having embarrassed myself with several under-par performances, I had been taken aside by a well-meaning co-worker, who recommended that I work on the speed of my flick and the volume of my 'ha!' Before I knew it, I had people rolling in the aisles and exclaiming that I spoke fluent Japanese and 'knew so much about Japan'.

I delivered my fluent two-syllable gag to my audience of five hundred schoolchildren and received a huge round of laughter and a big reply. I repeated the routine twice, and each time received a loud and enthusiastic 'Oha!' back.

I then tried to get the audience to call out 'Gidday!' There were lots of giggles, and some of the louder boys yelled 'Gud dye!' to each other. It was then that I noticed how loud my voice was on the loudspeakers. What made it worse was that there was a slight time delay before several echoes of my voice made their way around the school, the town and the nearby mountain ranges.

I quickly moved on to the main part of my speech, pausing at the end of each sentence for Ms Domae to translate. Despite having gone over the speech beforehand, she missed vital words and the general meaning was distorted. I had wanted to tell the students a bit about myself, and that I wanted to play some Japanese sports and learn about their music and pop culture — and that they should not be too shy to come and say gidday and tell me a little about themselves. This was translated as: 'I like all sports, tennis, cricket, netball, baseball, basketball, martial arts etc. I like all music but don't know anything about Japanese pop culture. Please say hi to me if you see me.'

Mr Kazama applauded enthusiastically. 'Verrry goood speech!' he beamed in English as I finished. 'Nice Oha!'

I climbed down from the stage and stood in the searing heat while, for the next forty minutes, Mr Kazama read out the summer holiday sports results. It seemed that all five hundred students had done something remarkable, and it took quite some time for all the basketball scores, track and field times and volleyball results to be announced. At one point, a senior boy got up to make a speech on behalf of the basketball team. Students should not, he said, be shy about approaching him, and should feel free to say hello or 'Oha!' if they saw him around town. I had a quiet chuckle and made a mental note of the boy's face for later reference.

And so the second school term of the year officially began. The students were ushered away to sit their exams, and I returned to my desk to try the summer range of Japanese chocolates. The occasional curious thirteen-year-old would venture into the teachers' lounge during an exam break to catch a glimpse of the new foreign teacher, before giggling nervously, waving and racing off to tell their friends what they had seen.

As I arrived and departed, some third-grade boys would accost me at the bike stand or locker bay, keen to shake my hand, and to compare heights by standing back-to-back. As I cycled home every day past the town tennis courts, members of the boys' tennis team would wave and holler, and pretend to shoot me with their tennis racquets.

Finally the exam period came to an end and I was allowed into the class-room. Thus began a fortnight during which I delivered my introduction speech to each of my sixteen classes. I would start by asking the students where New Zealand was on a world map. A few of them would know, so I would get them to go up to the map and point to it. Then I would pull out my New Zealand map and show them where Christchurch, my home town, was. This would produce a mixed reaction of blank stares, bored expressions and nerdy nods.

From there I would talk about my family, showing the students en-larged family photos and telling them the names of close family members. Next, I would try to get them to guess my age. Answers ranged from six to one hundred.

I would then show them pictures of my home and garden. They reacted well to these, especially since I would lie and say that our garden was so big that I could play soccer, tennis and cricket in it. I would show them photos of my pet cats, Smudge and Bubbles, and ask them to raise their hands as to who liked cats and who liked dogs. Usually only two or three students responded.

Lastly, I would show them some baby photos and ask if they had any questions. After a long pause, one of the cheeky boys would ask how tall I was, or how long my feet were. Then a few others would inquire what Japanese food I liked, what music was currently in the charts in New Zealand, and what sports were popular.

At the end, if time permitted, I would wander around the room and ask the students one by one to stand up, say their name and one thing they liked to do. Half the class seemed to struggle to remember their own names, and had to ask their friends for help. 'My name is'—blank pause while he consults his neighbour—'Yoshi.'

Some boys took to approaching me in the corridor after class, asking me to make up English nicknames for them. Within days, I had created a loyal fan club of a Charlie, a Benjamin, a Nick and a Big Tom. Without realising it, I had won the admiration of the 'naughty group'.

Their ringleader would turn out to be one of my staunchest supporters. Hiroshi Nagata, or Nagachi as he preferred to call himself, consistently attempted to be the loudest boy in the second grade. He was well-known for interrupting class and trying to be the centre of attention. The girls thought he was cool, and the naughty boys misbehaved even more in order to impress him.

It was during my introduction speech to his class that Nagachi asked me to draw a picture of him on the back of his school book. Cheekily, I used my left hand and drew a wobbly head, big ears, scraggly hair and a huge mouth. Nagachi initially went quiet, but when the other naughty boys chortled with mirth he joined in and drew a cheeky picture of me in return. From then on, he would wait for me in the corridor, saunter over nonchalantly with his hands in his pockets like Fonzie from *Happy Days*, and give me a high-five as I walked past.

Having won over the second-graders, it was now time to work my charm on the first grade. I had expected this collection of knee-high twelve- and thirteen-year-olds to be shy and incompetent when it came to using the English language, but they responded even better than the second-graders.

A little girl with milk-bottle glasses turned up to escort me to my first class. During my introduction speech she giggled shyly and pointed at all my photos. As always, there were a couple of 'cool' kids. One had the ability to ask me in English if I liked the rock band Kiss, which was amazing considering the second-graders had hardly asked me anything other than the size of my shoes.

Another small boy shyly asked me to talk with him about rugby. I found out later that he was a slow learner, and the first-grade English teacher, Mrs Takaoka, was delighted that he had been so enthusiastic.

At last, only one muggy day remained before a relaxing weekend in which I would no longer need to ask whether people preferred cats or dogs, or answer questions about my height and marital status. I had two third-grade classes scheduled after lunch, but at 8.35 in the morning they seemed an age away. I chewed my pencil nervously and looked at the clock.

The first period of every Friday morning, I was scheduled to teach a class by myself. This was the waka-ayu, or 'young minnows', class of children with intellectual disabilities. I was filled with dread. I had never before had to communicate with people with significant mental or physical impediments, but in less than five minutes I was going to be confronted with a classroom of children who would no doubt be banging pots on their heads and eating faeces. I had no idea how I was going to keep them calm, communicate in Japanese if they acted up, or know where to send them if they soiled themselves.

I nervously packed up the props for my self-introduction class and walked slowly to the waka-ayu room. I had forgotten to bring my own hallway slippers and struggled along in the miniscule plastic visitor's ones. Outside the classroom I collected myself and took a deep breath. I knocked lightly on the door and waited. Nothing. I knocked again and could hear some nervous hushing and shhhing from inside.

I opened the door. Three cheerful faces stared eagerly up at me.

One of them was an adult. Mrs Hotta was the students' minder; I had not known that she would be present. She rattled off a brief introduction, pointing out that she would be sitting back and watching, not teaching, as she could not speak any English. She was just present in case I needed— how could she put it?—some assistance.

I resisted the urge to bound over the table and kiss her. A huge weight lifted from my shoulders. In my relieved state, I was able to notice that there were no pots scattered around the place, and no one had faeces smeared on their faces.

I bowed to my students, and they instantly leapt to their feet and bowed in return. They then stood awkwardly fiddling with the buttons on their jackets. They glanced nervously at Mrs Hotta and she nodded at them. They sat down immediately.

The two boys had scribbled their names on name badges and were displaying these proudly on their shirt lapels. One had missed a vital stroke on a Japanese character, but I was able to decipher his true identity. Hirokazu was of medium height, with scruffy hair and thick glasses. From outward appearances he seemed perfectly normal, if perhaps a little messy. This was, however, until he opened his mouth to speak. Hiro slurred his words and was difficult to understand. He smiled a lot though, and laughed to himself whenever he said anything. I liked him at once.

Next to Hirokazu was a boy I instantly recognised as the one who had raced into the staffroom during my introductory tour of the school. I smiled, introduced myself in Japanese and bowed. Jun Fujita's wide flat face broke into a grin and he grabbed Mrs Hotta by the arm. Shielding his mouth with his free hand, he leant forward and whispered confidentially in her ear.

Unfortunately, in his agitated state he was unable to control the volume of his voice. 'We've met before,' he was saying. 'I told you. I told you. I met him before. Tell him, tell him.'

Mrs Hotta smiled and relayed Jun's message. She added, 'He's very excited and has been telling us about you all week.'

Jun blushed and hid behind his hands. Hirokazu cackled and rubbed his stomach.

Introductions out of the way, it was time to get down to business. I put my props beside the blackboard and launched into my by now well-rehearsed speech. I started by showing them pictures of my home and family. Jun clapped himself on the head. He squealed with excitement when he saw our garden. The pictures of my cats made him giggle, and he had to cover his eyes. I showed them pictures of Christchurch and New Zealand and they both announced that they intended to travel to New Zealand. Next I showed them my cricket book. They oohed and aahed, and Hiro tried to bowl. He hit his arm on the desk and went momentarily quiet.

This had all taken about twenty-five minutes—half the class time. I had brought along a game of *Snakes and Ladders* and decided it was time to play. I had made up several pieces for them to choose from, printing pictures from New Zealand-themed rubber stamps on to pieces of cardboard, and taping these to magnets. Jun chose the Maori warrior, while Hiro managed to break a sheep and a kiwi. Luckily I had plenty of spares. Hiro ended up being a kiwi, I was a sheep, and Mrs Hotta, whom Jun coaxed into playing, was a sheep too.

Jun became extremely excited and threw his dice wildly. I tried my best to lose but kept throwing sixes and landing on ladders. Hiro quickly caught up, and we battled our way towards the top of the board. He was having a great time, and danced and clapped. Jun hit himself on the head and giggled, even though he was coming dead last and continually rolling the number one. Seconds before the bell rang, Hiro landed on the big snake and came last. He went quiet again.

We shook hands, Hiro using his left hand upside-down, and I went on my way. My first young minnows class had been a lot of fun, with not a clanging pot in sight.

# 4

# The Okis

*Toshio and Miyoko Oki appeared* on my doorstep in the middle of a scorching Saturday morning. Mr Oki, wearing his trademark tweed jacket, smiled quietly as I opened the door. Mrs Oki, on the other hand, was fidgeting and blinking and adjusting her glasses with trembling hands. She peered up at me inquisitively and, without wasting any time on hellos, enquired 'Heymishi? Heymishi? Are you ready to go?'

I had prepared myself to give a polite Japanese greeting to these old friends, but it was now caught in my throat as Mrs Oki bowled past me and bustled into my living room.

'Heymishi, Heymishi, is this your apartment? Is this your table? Where do you sleep? Do you cook for yourself, Heymishi?'

Mrs Oki disappeared to inspect my bathroom. I turned to greet Mr Oki. Chuckling to himself, he slapped me on the shoulder, slipped off his shoes and stepped into my apartment, bowing slightly and welcoming me to Japan. 'It's been a long time,' he said.

I had first met Mr and Mrs Oki in New Zealand, when they had stayed with my family for three weeks as part of a sister-city visit set up by my father's Rotary Club. At the time I was sixteen, and had spent an eventful three weeks acting as translator, interpreter and tour guide for the elderly couple.

The Okis were one of the most unusual couples I had ever met. Mr Oki was calm and polite and thought the world of my father. He had a quiet noble air, a thick head of silver hair, a deep voice and a gravelly laugh. His wife was the complete opposite. Short, boisterous and incredibly talkative, she was constantly chattering and readjusting the large Elton John-style glasses that balanced precariously on her tiny nose and dwarfed her face. She adored our pet cats, was enchanted by my mother's clothing and cookery skills, and tested my beginner-level Japanese to its absolute limits.

When the Okis had learned that I would be coming to live in Japan, they had insisted I live with them. As I had declined this kind offer, they had settled for visiting me at the first available opportunity to make sure I was settling in all right.

Back in my apartment, Mrs Oki was now examining my kitchen and the insides of my cupboards. 'Your bath is very nice. Do you use the bath?' she asked.

'Unfortunately I can't fit into my bath,' I replied. 'My legs are too long.'

Mr Oki found this hilarious and burst out laughing. He slapped me on the shoulder again, and had a coughing fit. Mrs Oki, however, was unimpressed. She adjusted her spectacles and peered up at me. 'Heymishi! How do you get clean then?'

'I use the shower,' I volunteered, but Mrs Oki was no longer listening. She was now fossicking in my living room.

'Heymishi! Is this your television? Heymishi! Where is your bed?'

There was a crash and the sound of several small objects falling on to my tatami mat.

'Heymishi, what's this?' I hurried into the living room from the kitchen, where I had been closing the cupboard doors left open by Mrs Oki. Mrs Oki had knocked over a stack of books and was now looking through my wardrobe. Mr Oki was laughing and looking intently at my television set.

'Heymishi, what clothes do you wear to work? Your mother had nice clothes. She's so beautiful. I had such a lovely time in New Zealand. Are you ready to go yet?'

'Yes,' I replied, somewhat confused. 'Where are we going?'

'Shopping,' said Mr Oki suddenly. 'What do you want?'

'Oh, thank you,' I replied, 'but I did my grocery shopping yesterday. There's a big Daiei just down the road and—'

'No no no,' he said, 'what do you want? I was going to buy you a TV, but you already have one. It's very big.'

I paused, unsure what I should say. Mr Oki frowned. 'You can decide in the car then.' He slapped me on the shoulder again. 'Let's go.'

Mrs Oki had finished her inspection and was now waiting impatiently at the front door. 'Heymishi! Put your shoes on. Come on, Heymishi.'

I was bustled down the stairs and into Mr Oki's waiting car. He had parked in my landlady's parking space. Mrs Fujita was examining the car with a baffled look. Mrs Oki swept by and introduced herself. 'Hello, I stayed with his family in New Zealand. Oh, I had a lovely time. His mother wears lovely clothes and is very beautiful. Heymishi is very tall. He can't fit his legs into the bath.'

And with that we disappeared. I waved goodbye to Mrs Fujita and she looked back with concern, perhaps wondering if she should contact the police and file an abduction report.

I sat in the back seat while Mr Oki drove. In the passenger seat Mrs Oki was completely hidden. From behind, I could not even see the top of her head. I could, however, hear her. Now that Mrs Oki was constrained by her seatbelt, her overactive brain had nothing to do but think aloud and create verbal mayhem.

'Mr Oki, there's a cat!'

'A car is coming the other way.'

'Traffic lights are red, we should stop.'

'Green, go.'

'There's a supermarket. I bought some noodles the other day.'

'There's a bicycle in front of us.'

'Heymishi, what clothes do you wear to school?'

'Stop sign.'

'I had a lovely time in New Zealand. Your mother wears lovely clothes. She's very beautiful.'

'Oh, I must feed the cat when I get home.'

'Mr Oki, a car is coming the other way!'

With all the commotion in the front seat, I was still undecided as to what I wanted Mr Oki to buy me. It seemed, however, that he had kindly made this decision for me, and we parked outside an appliance store.

'Mr Oki and I have decided that you need appliances for your kitchen,' Mrs Oki announced. I was surprised as I had been completely unaware of any coherent conversation taking place during the car journey.

Mrs Oki's telepathic abilities aside, the Okis then proceeded to buy me a microwave oven, a toaster, a jug and a set of pots. Grateful, I managed to give them a heartfelt thank-you speech, using leftover bits of the greeting speech I had been unable to deliver earlier.

Mr Oki smiled and Mrs Oki blinked. 'Don't be silly,' Mr Oki said, slapping my arm. 'Your family looked after us for three weeks. It's the least we can do. I wish I could have bought you a TV. If you think of anything else you want, let me know.' And with that, I was driven back to my apartment.

Mrs Fujita gave me a relieved wave as we pulled up. Mr Oki parked on the street and kept the car running. 'Keep next Sunday free. We'll go sightseeing together.'

Mrs Oki peeped round from the front of her seat. 'Thank you for looking after us in New Zealand, Heymishi.'

And so my first encounter with the Okis was at an end.

Mrs Oki called the following Wednesday evening.

'Heymishi! We'll come and pick you up on Sunday morning. We're going to go sightseeing up Mount Kanan. It's the mountain in your town. We'll ride a cable-car. We'll see a nice view. Be ready to leave at 6 a.m.!'

I started to explain that this was a little early, and to ask why we needed such an early start, but the line was already dead. Mrs Oki had hung up.

I went to bed early the following evening, and was just drifting off to sleep when the phone rang. This time it was Mr Oki. 'Don't forget about Sunday,' he stated.

'No, I'll be ready. Six o'clock, isn't it?' I replied.

'Yes, that's right. You sound sleepy. Were you asleep?'

'Yes. I was trying to get a good night's –'

Mr Oki laughed and hung up the phone.

On Saturday night I went to bed nice and early. I had prepared my clothes for the next day and set my alarm clock for 5.45. This would give me enough time to have a shower, get dressed and wait for the Okis to arrive.

The Okis, however, had been using their telepathic powers to thwart my good intentions. The phone woke me up at 5.30. Mrs Oki asked why I was still sleeping. She assured me that 'someone' was on their way and that I had best get ready. I got dressed and was toasting some bread when Mr Oki arrived at 5.45.

I welcomed him in and made a big fuss of showing him how my computer had to sit on the floor, and how I desperately needed a computer desk. Sadly, he didn't seem to have his hearing aid turned on and didn't hear a word I said. He ordered me not to waste time packing a jacket or sweater as I wouldn't need them.

Okay, I thought. After all we're just taking a leisurely ride up a mountain in a cable-car.

Wrong! Mr Oki and I spent two and a half hours briskly hiking up Mount Kanan, all 1020 metres of it. The ascent was done under the cover of darkness, and it was raining and cold. Mrs Oki was nowhere to be found: she was apparently at home making lunch. When we eventually made it to the summit, we couldn't see a thing because of mist and cloud. We stopped for five minutes to drink beer, which we bought from a quintessential Japanese mountain-top vending machine, and then hiked back down.

I was speedily driven back to my apartment for a change of clothes and we then sped off to the Okis' house for lunch. It was still not quite midday.

Upon arrival, I was immediately told to have a shower. I had only just started to wash my hair when Mrs Oki burst in to check if the water was okay. I managed to hide behind the soap rack and told her the water was fine and that I was quite capable of operating a shower.

Lunch was waiting when I emerged, and I was finally allowed a chance to sit still and relax. I soon came to the conclusion that Mrs Oki had taken far too many drugs at some previous time in her life. Between mouthfuls of fried chicken wings and miso soup, she mumbled and hummed to herself and seemed to repeat the same thing over and over again. She continued to thank me for letting Mr Oki and her stay at my home in New Zealand, and ranted on about how beautiful my mother was.

Mrs Oki seemed to consider my Japanese to be fluent, and made absolutely no effort to differentiate between the way she spoke to me and to Mr Oki. As she never referred to either of us by name, it soon became impossible to figure out whom she was talking to, or about. To complement this, Mr Oki took his hearing aids out during the meal in order to clean his ears, and subsequently couldn't hear a thing.

After lunch we all went for a drive in Mr Oki's car. He was very keen to point out his office.

I asked him if he drove to work every day.

*Mr Oki*: 'Eh?'

*Hamish*: 'Do you drive to work every day?'

*Mr Oki*: 'Who?'

*Mrs Oki*: 'Do YOU drive to work?'

*Mr Oki*: 'What?'

*Mrs Oki*: 'Do you drive to work?'

*Mr Oki*: 'Who's asking?'

*Mrs Oki*: 'Him!'

*Mr Oki*: 'Who's he asking about?'

*Mrs Oki*: 'You!'

*Mr Oki*: 'Oh yes, I drive to work.'

Needless to say, after several hours of this I was fairly tired. During the drive, the Okis suddenly announced that we were going out to dinner. The restaurant in question was apparently quite far away, and the drive would take some time. I took the opportunity to try and fall asleep in the back seat, but Mrs Oki wouldn't have a bar of this, and kept bombarding me with the same questions that she'd asked during lunch. 'Heymishi! What do you wear to school? What grade classes do you teach?'

Despite my exhaustion, dinner turned out to be a hilarious affair. The entire Oki clan had turned up to a Korean barbecue restaurant, and it seemed that I was the guest of honour. The Okis' two middle-aged sons, their wives and respective children were waiting patiently, and bowed politely as I sat down.

Everyone sat quietly with clasped hands and serious faces during the formal round of introductions. The Oki gene, however, did not allow such tranquillity to exist for long. As soon as dinner had been ordered, the gathering abruptly degenerated into chaos. The children began to cry, one fell off his chair, the three-year-old girl screamed, and the baby boy did poos in the corner and then vomited on the floor. In the midst of all this, the two Oki sons had an argument and then apologised to me for making a scene. Mrs Oki mumbled to herself happily and Mr Oki appeared not to hear a thing. I was served raw meat and felt sick.

I was finally driven home at nine o'clock, and after disconnecting my telephone from the wall I fell fast asleep.

I had been in Kanan Town about two months when Mr Kazama, the school principal, invited me into his office and asked if I would do him a favour.

'Mr Hamish,' he began as I sank into his plush leather sofa, 'one of the third-grade students, Hiroshi Yamaguchi, will graduate soon. He very much wants to go to high school in a foreign country. Hiroshi likes you very much, so he wants to go and live in New Zealand.'

He paused and I blushed. 'His mother is very worried about this. She is worried that his English is not very good and he will not be able to do well in New Zealand. She wants you to give extra English classes to her son. What do you think?'

I was delighted with the proposal. 'Sure,' I agreed enthusiastically, 'I'd be happy to help out.' Being invited into a Japanese home was not an opportunity to pass up, and Hiroshi was one of the more cheerful and capable English students I'd come across. He was always keen to greet me in the hallways, and eagerly asked about life in New Zealand and the differences with Japan.

Mr Kazama was equally pleased. 'Excellent. You can start on Wednesday. Mrs Yamaguchi will pick you up after school.' Thus began my weekly English tuition of Hiroshi Yamaguchi.

Mrs Yamaguchi was waiting patiently outside the school gates when the bell chimed on Wednesday afternoon. A well-dressed, pleasant woman, she greeted me politely and thanked me profusely for agreeing to her request.

During the short drive to the Yamaguchi home, she inquired as to my preferences for snacks and junk food. She had seemingly purchased a healthy assortment of chocolate, cookies, potato chips, popcorn, pretzels, soft drink, instant noodles and mixed nuts in anticipation of having to satisfy the barbaric appetite of her foreign guest. I opted immediately for chocolate and cookies, while Hiroshi maintained that he would require potato chips, popcorn, pretzels, soft drink, instant noodles and mixed nuts.

Mrs Yamaguchi went straight to work preparing our banquet, while Hiroshi and I were allowed full use of the Yamaguchi's living room. The proposed English tuition soon degenerated into a junk-food overdose and fierce PlayStation battle. Forty minutes later, after being soundly defeated at several games, I announced the English lesson would begin. I was looking forward to getting revenge on Hiroshi by making him pronounce as many long 'r' and 'l' words as I could come up with.

It was then that the door opened, and in walked a vision in tight jeans and a lemon-yellow T-shirt. Hiroshi's older sister, Aki, had just finished university for the day, and from where I was sitting she looked remarkably radiant. I frantically tried to brush the potato-chip crumbs from my shirt front and sweep away the chocolate wrappers that seemed to have mysteriously gathered on the tabletop in front of me.

I stammered out the most charming introduction I could muster, and offered Aki one of the few remaining pretzels. She giggled and blushed shyly. Hiroshi, however, was not keen for his sister to share in his hoard of junk food; he swatted away her hand and shooed her from the room. Less than impressed, I mentally added the words 'railway', 'radiation', and 'larium' to Hiroshi's vocabulary practice.

I spent the remaining hour of the lesson paying only scant attention to Hiroshi and hoping feebly that Aki would return. My hopes crumbled when at six o'clock Mrs Yamaguchi entered the room and announced it was time for me to go home. She bowed deeply and thanked me again for teaching her son English. I nodded sheepishly, suddenly realising that I had done little but eat junk food and laugh inwardly as Hiroshi lisped his way through my fiendish labyrinth of tongue-twisters.

Mrs Yamaguchi bowed again, and produced a large bag of groceries from the kitchen. 'Here,' she said. 'Mr Kazama said I was not allowed to pay you in cash, so I decided to give you a week's worth of groceries at the end of every lesson.'

I had not been expecting this at all, and cautiously examined the bag, fearing that Mrs Yamaguchi had assigned me a diet of Brussels sprouts and lentils. However, it seemed she had been listening carefully when I outlined my junk-food preferences. My shopping bag contained a token helping of lettuce and bread, and was then filled to the brim with candy, chocolate and cookies.

I was escorted to the door, and was preparing to step out into the muggy summer air when Aki breezed back into the living room to say her farewells. I stammered out a flustered goodbye, and she told me that she was looking forward to seeing me again. I decided to continue my Wednesday lessons with Hiroshi, no matter how many Brussels sprouts I received in payment.

I was still in a love-struck mood as the Friday first period rolled around, and I strode confidently to the young minnows' room well before the bell had chimed. I had devised an 'English passports' project for the team, and we spent most of the time gluing pictures into little cardboard booklets and colouring them in.

As well as a huge sticker book full of animals and birds, I had taken along a *TV Hits* magazine that included glossy sheets of celebrity stickers. The boys instantly fell in love with the stickers, and had a lot of fun choosing pictures of pretty girls. Hiro chose three stickers of scantily clad female singers and seemed about to throw a tantrum when Mrs Hotta teased him about having so many girlfriends. When he calmed down, he contritely chose a handsome male actor for Mrs Hotta. He selected a pretty blonde girlfriend for me as well.

Jun, meanwhile, was in heaven. He clapped himself on the head, and kept saying 'Great!' in Japanese. He preferred the animal stickers and adorned his passport with pink birds and grey hippos.

Work on the ambitious 'English passports' project continued enthusiastically the next Friday, and I spent the first half of the lesson teaching basic family nouns such as 'father', 'mother', 'brother', 'sister' and 'pet'. However, it soon became apparent that a considerable ability gap existed in the class. Jun was in the third grade, had been studying English for three years, and could already pronounce these words, although he could not spell or write any of them without assistance. Hiro, meanwhile, was in the first grade and had come into contact with the English language only two months earlier. He was still unable to count to ten and struggled to pronounce even Japanese words properly.

Nevertheless, the class flowed along merrily as the boys diligently tried to fill out the second page of their passports, writing down their fathers' names and jobs, and drawing pictures of their respective families. Hiro quickly hit a snag as he couldn't remember his mother's name (I began to worry about whether he had a mother or not), and didn't have a clue what his father did for a job. Then he drew his entire family, two sisters included, with round faces and short military crew cuts. I had glimpsed his family at the school gate, and all three females had shoulder-length hair. When I pointed this out, he started jabbering and hitting himself.

Hiro's bout of anger had alerted me to that fact that classes full of writing practice were going to put the boys to sleep—or even worse, in a pot-banging mood. I needed inspiration to keep things lively and jovial. The shiny magazines and glossy pictures would buy me a few more weeks of attention but I would soon need a new angle, some new games, something novel...

The following Monday was Hiro's birthday and I spent the week planning and preparing a surprise party for him, to take place during Friday's class. Mrs Hotta was consulted and I was given permission to buy small fairy cakes, which apparently contained very little sugar. Candles were banned but small prizes for party games were acquired and lovingly wrapped in newspaper. I borrowed a CD player from the music teacher and scoured my CD collection for a suitable soundtrack.

I went to bed on Thursday evening in an excited mood. I was still bubbling with anticipation the next morning, and deliberately delayed my arrival to class in order to build suspense.

I had no sooner opened the door than the boys spotted the CD player, the *Pin the Tail on the Donkey* game and the four fairy cakes. Within seconds Hiro was on his feet dancing. Jun was giggling, patting himself on the head and hiding his eyes.

Mrs Hotta barked at them to calm down, and they nervously stood to attention and bowed. I bowed back and broke into a rendition of 'Happy birthday'. Mrs Hotta and Jun recognised the tune and sang along in Japanese. Although he'd earlier shown an aversion to singing, Hiro grinned and sang himself 'Happy birthday' in a quiet voice. At the end he blushed profusely and looked at his shoes.

From there we launched straight into the party games. *Pin the Tail on the Donkey* was an overwhelming success. Both Hiro and Jun failed to get anywhere near the donkey—or even the blackboard—but Hiro loved putting on the blindfold and Jun loved the picture of the horse.

I'd rigged things so that whoever lost *Pin the Tail* would get the prize in *Pass the Parcel*. I awarded Hiro the *Pin the Tail* prize as he had managed to get closest to the blackboard.

We played *Pass the Parcel* to the James Bond theme, and once Hiro had stopped dancing the parcel-passing assumed a frantic pace. I managed to keep up with the pause button on the CD player, and eventually Jun was the delighted winner.

I'd gone to great lengths to make the prizes identical—two green pencils with sheep and kiwis drawn on them, and two kiwi-shaped erasers. However, the erasers were in two different colours and this caused a slight problem. Hiro preferred Jun's green eraser to his red one, but Jun was in no mood to trade as green was his favourite colour. There were a few heated words, and a tense stand-off ensued.

In desperation, I brought out the *TV Hits* and flipped it open to the glossy pictures of the scantily clad girls. Hiro and Jun quickly calmed down. They oohed and aahed over the pictures, and when I produced the fairy cakes and my CD collection Jun nearly went crazy. He couldn't believe his eyes. He loved the pictures on the CD jackets, and pointed and clapped in ecstasy. The cream cakes were devoured in seconds and Jun managed to get cream on his nose and eyebrows.

Meanwhile, Hiro sat quietly with a giant grin on his face. Class ended and he shook my hand as I left the room.

For the following weeks and months these two boys would be my staunchest supporters. It was not long before word of the first-period Friday class spread. Other special students asked to attend, and before I knew it student numbers had risen to five.

The first new arrival was Fumio. Fumio was a dyslexic third-grade student, and had been in 'normal' English class for three years. He could read quite well and was able to write long sentences and remember simple vocabulary. Incredibly well-mannered and cheerful, he attended our class only once a fortnight and, although well ahead of Jun and Hiro in ability, was more than happy to join in games of bingo. These three-player games provided hours of laughter and entertainment. Fumio would usually win, but I noticed that he'd often pretend not to have a winning line so the others wouldn't feel sad.

The second newcomer was female, which I feared would disrupt the boys' attention or inhibit their enthusiasm. Yurika Nakamura was the small girl with thick glasses who had escorted me to my first-grade class. She spoke with a slow drawl, but notwithstanding her eyesight—her spectacles looked like two magnifying glasses welded together on top of her nose—she was of above-average intelligence.

A first-grade student, Yurika had been achieving good scores in English tests and exams. However, she had developed a small crush on me and wanted an extra hour a week of my tutelage. As the Japanese education system failed to differentiate between physical and mental handicap, she was eligible for demotion to the young minnows' stream.

Yurika's presence presented a dilemma. In two months Jun and Fumio would graduate, and I was slightly concerned about how the class dynamics would change once they had departed, as Yurika was able to converse normally in English while Hiro was still unable to count to ten without help.

The final addition to the class was Teru-Chan. Teru-Chan came to school only when she felt like it. She was a large, humourless girl who was perfectly round. Despite her comical appearance, though, she scared the hell out of me. She never spoke to me, and rarely uttered any words at all. Instead, she would sit sullenly, staring up at the roof or out the window. Other teachers had warned me to beware of her temper and never force her to do anything.

This newly acquired range of tempers and abilities presented a logistical nightmare. Trying to please everyone was fast becoming impossible, and although the class went moderately smoothly it now lacked the enthusiasm and hilarity of the early days.

I decided to teach the students how to talk about the weather, and started by teaching them to play the 'hot/cold' game. True to form, the boys loved hiding objects around the room but weren't brilliant at giving the 'hot/warm/cold' clues so the others could find them. Jun wandered around checking everywhere. Teru-Chan stood stone-still and alone. Yurika struggled to see the tiny objects that were hidden inside drawers and on top of cabinets.

Slowly, things started to go downhill, and as the weeks went by tempers frayed. Nobody managed to pick up any weather words so I turned my attention to 'shopping', creating a supermarket backdrop and printing large volumes of fake money emblazoned with sketches of the students' faces.

We practised shopping and paying for groceries, and interest levels seemed to flicker back to life. However, shortly after one class a colleague told me that fake money would encourage the students to become counterfeiters; I would have to destroy all the young minnows' currency before I got into big trouble. I grudgingly conceded, but secretly gave Jun a 1000-yen bill that had his face on it. If Jun goes on to mastermind a Yakuza counterfeiting operation, I shall be wholly responsible.

At the same time as the young minnows' class was proving a challenge at school, a mind-boggling mystery was developing at home. I had started to receive a large number of 'hang-ups' on my answerphone. The messages were all recorded during the middle of the school day, when I would obviously be at work. There was never a name or message, just long pauses with a few breathing sounds.

Then one evening while I was at home eating my dinner, the phone rang. Knowing that anyone I wanted to speak to would leave a message, I ignored it. After several rings the answerphone clicked on, and the phone switched to speaker mode. Mrs Oki's nasal voice wafted into my living room and she started having a one-way conversation with the machine.

'Hello? Heymishi? Talk to me. Please speak Japanese.' She then hung up before the beep, in the same fashion she'd been doing for the past fortnight.

She called back thirty minutes later, and it turned out that the reason for my two week's worth of anonymous calls was that she was worried I might be cold. It was currently twenty-three degrees. I tried to tell her that I was fine, and that this temperature was similar to a New Zealand summer. She ignored me and asked again if I was cold. I said no.

In between talking to herself, her cat and the TV, Mrs Oki asked what I had planned for the coming weekend. Would I like to come to her house for dinner? I told her that unfortunately my weekend would be taken up with the Kanan Town Danjiri Festival, but it was unclear whether she was still listening, as she mumbled something about cat food and hung up the phone.

Sure enough, the next Friday evening, just as I was racing out the front door to catch a train to Wij's birthday party, Mrs Oki called again. After a few confused minutes, she asked me what I had planned for Sunday morning. Trying to stay calm while visualising my train pulling out of the station without me, I reminded her that the town festival was scheduled for both Saturday and Sunday.

'Oh!' she said, 'I didn't know your town had a festival.' The phone clicked and she hung up.

## 5

# Fame

*Kanan Town Danjiri Festival had* been etched on my calendar pretty much since my arrival in Japan. My supervisor and the men at the Board of Education had been raving about it for months. Over the summer, Magnum PI had given me long explanations of the festival's history, and Mr Fujimoto had told me about the exhaustive preparations.

The festival always took place on the third weekend of October. A tradition dating back hundreds of years, it had originally been held to celebrate the end of the rice harvest and the beginning of autumn. The citizens of Kanan Town joyfully took to the streets, wearing long white 'hapi' coats emblazoned with slogans unique to the town zones, and spent the weekend drinking, dancing and pushing around the danjiris, huge floats shaped like Buddhist temples, with intricate woodwork panels depicting religious scenes.

The danjiris of Kanan Town were reputed to be among the most intricate and expensive in all of Japan. As they measured up to three metres tall and weighed over a tonne, large teams of strong men were needed to push and roll them through town. A four-person band would sit at the helm playing flutes, clanging cymbals, beating drums, and leading the revellers in rousing anthems about the glory of Kanan Town.

Each town zone had its own danjiri valued at several million dollars, and the crews competed fiercely to be the loudest, fastest and most colourful. This had caused bitter rivalries, and feuds between rival teams stretched back generations. The two loudest teams, Kankoji and Shiraki, now regularly attracted loyal, aggressive youths from around the district. Many of the old hands felt the presence of these yobs had diverted attention from the original intention of the festival. Nevertheless, I was strongly encouraged to attend.

The opening day dawned cold and drizzly. Autumn was definitely taking hold in my small alpine town, and summer was now a thing of the past. Around noon I set off. I was not entirely sure where I should be heading. By now the danjiri crews would have spent the morning parading through their respective town zones and most of the members would already be drunk. I had heard that in the middle of the afternoon they would converge on a recently harvested rice paddy somewhere in the countryside. No one was able to give me precise directions, but I was not expecting significant difficulty in finding several thousand people and ten massive mobile shrines on a bare patch of farmland.

I cycled past the school and into unknown territory. I bounced and daydreamed for several kilometres along a picturesque path through rice paddies until at last I rejoined a main road and saw, far off in the distance, a large dancing procession of people in white coats. Hiding my bicycle under some bushes, I raced across the paddy-field. The instant I reached the procession I was accosted by a group of my first-grade female students, who took my photo, filled me in on where to buy the best candyfloss, and proudly displayed their white coats with the brash red symbol for Kankoji. Several of the group did not, in fact, hail from Kankoji: they had switched allegiance because the danjiri crew apparently contained loads of cute guys.

Suddenly the girls stopped giggling and dispersed as a short sprightly old man wandered over. The man shook my hand and exclaimed in barely audible tones that he was overjoyed that I had made it to the festival. In short order he had bought me two cans of beer and was leading me by the arm around the festival ground. I was torn between confusion at not understanding what was being said, and a haunting misgiving that I knew this old man from somewhere. I tried to make my escape, fearing he was a crackpot who might try and hang out with me for the rest of the afternoon. I certainly didn't want this old codger cramping my style with the ladies.

Repeatedly foiling my attempts and excuses, he prattled on about the danjiris and pointed to various faces in the crowd. I was puzzled to see people bowing respectfully, and then the identity of my mystery companion dawned on me. It was none other than the town mayor, Mr Kitahashi.

I spluttered into my beer and managed to pull off some polite Japanese in the nick of time, commenting on how beautiful the danjiris looked and what a wonderful town we lived in. Mr Kitahashi, who had replaced his normal black business suit with a checked shirt and denim jeans, beamed broadly. I was hoisted on the top of several danjiris and word was sent for the town photographer to come and take photos of Mr Hamish for the town magazine.

By mid afternoon the rice paddy was packed. Locals of all ages mingled happily, while agitated youths strutted around showing off their bleach-blond hairstyles, facial piercings, Terminator sunglasses, groomed goatees and gaudy hapi coats. My students, too, were out in force. The teenagers had been preparing for the festival for months, diligently growing their hair long enough to spike, curl, or puff up into a multi-coloured ball.

Hanging out with the mayor had given my popularity and level of fame an immense boast. Little children raced over and gave me plates of food from unknown benefactors. I was hauled into countless group photographs and introduced to gushing parents. Meanwhile, some of the danjiri crews regarded me suspiciously, unhappy with a lanky white guy stealing the limelight from their spiked pink hair and crayon-yellow afros.

The mayor suddenly reappeared and I was invited to join a group of town officials on their picnic mat. A huge array of food and drink awaited. The mayor sat next to me and kept my sake glass topped up. I overheard him telling several people that I thought the danjiris were beautiful and that Kanan Town was a wonderful place to live. This produced awed gasps and reverent whispers. I would then chip in with a drunken rendition of 'Oha!' and the onlookers would politely fall about laughing. As always, I would be proclaimed an expert on Japanese culture and an inspired linguist.

By the time darkness started to fall I was a wreck. Mr Kitahashi had single-handedly forced me to drink the equivalent of a carton of sake, and I had long since lost track of the number of beers the town officials had poured for me.

Magnum PI and old Mr Fujimoto from the Board of Education joined us on the picnic mat. Both were also red-faced and intoxicated. Magnum was, he declared, pleased with the festival thus far but Sunday would be even better, with more food and drink on offer. Mr Fujimoto agreed, but foolishly suggested that the Hiraishi zone's danjiri team was performing well this year. Magnum, a staunch Kankoji supporter, took deep offence and a heated debate ensued.

I chortled to myself on the mat. In my happy state I had failed to realise that most people were packing up and moving on. Mr Kitahashi bade me farewell, sternly instructing Magnum to take good care of me. Magnum saluted and suggested we go and get a drink. With Mr Fujimoto in tow and the quarrel seemingly forgotten, we staggered off down the road towards the convenience store.

Magnum dared me to chat up a group of young women. I approached stealthily, summoning all the charm I could. A suitable Japanese chat-up line failed to materialise in my head, so I played my one reliable card— the lost foreigner. 'Excuse me,' I slurred, 'could you tell me the way to the convenience store?'

'It's over there,' they replied nervously. They pointed 100 metres down the road to the brightly lit frontage of the only building on the road.

'Hey, Mr Hamish, hurry up and get their phone numbers,' Magnum yelled. The girls fled in terror.

Several beers later, I had lost all track of where I was. Hazy recollections of stowing my bicycle under a bush swam through my head, as did admonitions not to cycle through rice paddies in the dark. Dismissing these random thoughts, I plodded down the road with Magnum. Mr Fujimoto had called his wife to come and find him. He had now disappeared into the darkness and was probably asleep in a ditch.

'Here we are,' Magnum announced as he knocked on the door of a darkened house. A light went on, and it occurred to me that it was one o'clock in the morning.

'Good, they're still open,' he said, and rubbed his hands. It seemed we had arrived at the house of one of Magnum's friends.

From the sign, it appeared that the front room of the house doubled as a small tea shop during the weekday lunch hours. A sleepy couple in pyjamas opened the door hesitantly. Magnum bowled in and ordered a couple of beers. His friend appeared to find this intrusion most amusing. He, too, ordered a beer, and his wife staggered off to the refrigerator.

Somewhere in my head, a small voice suddenly suggested I get myself home. I lurched out into the cold night air and, through some miracle, found my hidden bicycle. I hopped aboard and and started pedalling, taking the long route along well-lit paved roads rather than the pitch-black track through the rice-paddy. After the best part of an hour, I made it home. I congratulated myself with a glass of water and slumped into bed.

Early the next afternoon, not wanting to miss the grand finale, I groggily rejoined the festivities. My drinking buddies seemed in poor health. Magnum was apparently in trouble not only with his wife, but with his friend's wife at the tea shop. Mr Fujimoto had a headache and apologised that he would be unable to stay up for a second night's drinking.

We stood around in the car park eating fried noodles. Old men bought me beers to thank me for educating the town's young folk. Their wives asked me what I thought of Japan, and if I liked the local food. Hiro from the waka-ayu class appeared with a plate of octopus balls, which he had bought especially. He then introduced me to his father and, noticing that I was cold, offered me his jacket. Even when I put on my own jacket to show him I had come prepared, he insisted that I drape his tiny red jacket over my shoulders.

After ten minutes Hiro started shivering violently. I handed him back his jacket and bought us both some piping-hot savoury pancakes. Hiro was delighted and got sauce all over his chin. I did little better, and thanks to a temporary ineptitude with chopsticks ended up with food down the front of my jacket.

Eventually the danjiris started to appear, and their bands struck up loud, clanging anthems. The crowds cheered. Fireworks crackled and exploded, and the festival roared back into life.

The danjiris now lined up neatly in a row: the final showdown was about to begin. Each team had twenty minutes to create as much of a spectacle as they could. This involved the huge floats being pushed and pulled as fast as possible up and down the length of the car park, with frantic drumming, passionate anthems, whistles, cymbals, fireworks, and an acrobatic maniac who danced on the roof secured only by a rope around his ankle.

The crews, who had been practising for months, knew their roles by heart. The older team members were positioned behind to push, while the younger, sumo-like ones were in front to pull the massive yokes. The people with the most extreme hairstyles were placed on the outside to add a theatrical element. The bigger teams had also employed nubile females to dance alluringly in front of their floats.

Within an hour some of the smaller town zones had completed their performance, and the local favourite, Kankoji, was preparing for its big moment. Magnum, as part of the Kankoji Danjiri Council, was allowed to walk behind the danjiri with other middle-aged alumni, flaunting his hapi coat and joining in the singing. Making me promise to applaud loudly, which would apparently help Kankoji become the crowd favourite for yet another year, he strode off to join the throng of supporters.

Once Magnum was out of earshot, Mr Fujimoto tugged my shirtsleeve and whispered in a hushed tone, 'Mr Hamish, I would like you to join the Hiraishi team. People will be very happy to see you push their danjiri.'

I was unsure about this. For starters, I didn't live in Hiraishi. The festival was a surprisingly serious affair and membership in the crews was highly sought after. A gangling foreign ring-in was bound to create jealousy and loathing.

Secondly, I didn't have a hapi coat. The danjiri crews were fastidious about their appearance: they all wore hapi coats, white pyjama pants and rice-paddy slippers. Despite the flash hairstyles and fancy sunglasses, this was still Japan and group uniformity was paramount. I was wearing green track pants and a blue sweater.

Mr Fujimoto, though, had thought of everything. It turned out he was very well connected in Hiraishi circles. He shared a vegetable field with the danjiri's crew captain, and his son was the crazy madman dancing on the roof of the float. I was presented with his old hapi coat, and before I knew it I was being introduced to the team.

Hiraishi was next to perform. Everyone was ushered into position. As I was one of the tallest people in town, I was allocated a highly respected position in the middle at the rear of the float. I was suddenly one of the main pushers and feeling very nervous. The float was enormous and we were expected to get it racing at high speeds.

Firecrackers exploded behind me, signalling the end of Kankoji's performance. It was time for us to take the stage. Without any warm-up, we exploded wildly out of the blocks. I thrust my full weight on to the danjiri and got my legs pumping as fast as I could. As we yelled and whooped, the float seemed to fly across the car park. At the back, the crew jostled and shoved each other boisterously. At each corner the older team members pulled ropes to slow us down, and we turned the danjiri around to begin another run. The dancing girls pranced around us, and Mr Fujimoto's son launched fire crackers into the air.

As we cranked the danjiri up to full speed for its final length of the car park, everything was becoming a mad blur. I puffed and strained as the weight of the danjiri began to catch up with me. The crowd yelled and cheered, the danjiri's lanterns swung crazily, more fireworks exploded, and as the drum beat reached a frenetic climax we crossed the final checkpoint and dug in our heels, fighting to bring the huge float to a standstill.

Ecstasy reigned. The crew danced around me and I was clapped and thumped on the back. We formed a tight huddle and continued the team anthem. Mr Fujimoto's son, who had clambered down from the roof, was hassled for hugs and high fives.

The mayor materialised from the darkness and shook my hand. 'Very good, Mr Hamish, very good,' he enthused. 'So you are a Hiraishi supporter now?'

I like Hiraishi—it's a nice place to live,' I said diplomatically. Mr Kitahasi's smile grew. 'Excellent, excellent. I have a farm in Hiraishi. I'm a Hiraishi supporter too.' Too exhausted to try and correct him, I shook his hand limply and he raced off to congratulate other proud Hiraishi supporters.

All the danjiri teams had now finished their performances. I overheard murmurs that, yet again, Kankoji had been voted the best. I snorted in disgust: maybe my loyalty to Hiraishi was deeper than I imagined.

The danjiris and their tired crews now faced the long trip back to their home zones. For some this would mean several kilometres through dark farm roads and up steep mountain trails. Eschewing any such effort, I walked off to the school and retrieved my bicycle.

Kanan Town was ghostly quiet as I made my discreet exit along empty streets. I turned on to the stretch of road that headed towards the Ishikawa River bridge and stopped dead in my tracks. The road ahead was completely blocked. A huge mob of revellers were dancing and singing. A brightly illuminated danjiri was moving towards me, swaying alarmingly.

I had somehow managed to stumble across the Tondabayashi Danjiri Festival. Although Tondabayashi City was able to boast that it was the bigger, wealthier neighbour, when it came to danjiri festivals Kanan Town left it in the dust. Nevertheless, the large group heading towards me was in fine voice, and their float, although smaller than the giants of Kanan Town, had an enthusiastic band at the helm.

I was enveloped in curious stares and intoxicated hugs. Bowing deeply, the older members of the crew asked if I would care to join their procession. I tried politely to refuse, but there was no way through the crowd and I could not get around the float without falling into the deep roadside gutter.

I locked my bike to a lamppost. I was now part of the Tondabayashi West danjiri crew. I danced along with a group of high-school students, who were keen to teach me their team chant. Judging from their response, I seemed to be doing well. When we passed a convenience store, a drinks break was called and the group swarmed in to buy beers and snacks. I bought some beers for the guys who had invited me on to the team. They were spellbound by my generosity and each bought me two beers in gratitude.

I was then ushered into the middle of the crew. A few minutes later, a panting, red-faced man appeared and presented me with a pristine hapi coat. I was slapped on the back again, and everyone chanted the team song. I was instructed to climb into the helm of the danjiri and lead the crowd in the chant. Once there, I squeezed myself into a nook that could have been designed for Mrs Oki.

I was passed a pair of cymbals, the drinks break came to an end, and the danjiri crew got into position. A young man on my left sang into a microphone and I banged on my cymbals. People in the crowd approached the front of the danjiri, calling out greetings and waving. I smiled and waved back, feeling like royalty. The master of ceremonies draped his arm over me and gave me a bear-hug. 'You are a good man, very cool!' he yelled in broken English into my left ear.

'You sing! You sing!' He thrust the microphone into my hand and pointed to the crowd. 'Sing! Sing!' He yelled the chorus of the team chant, and I haltingly blurted out a few words. 'Yes! Yes!' Another bear-hug. I stammered out a few more words, my voice crackling through the speakers.

'My name is Masashi,' my English-speaking friend shouted. I shouted back that he should call me H, not wanting to get into the rigmarole of explaining how to pronounce my name. 'Hello, Mr Echi,' he smiled. 'Let's sing.'

A small crowd of dancing teenagers was now leading our procession. We developed a routine where Masashi chanted half the chorus and the left half of the dancing crowd echoed it. I then called out the remainder of the chorus, and it was echoed by the right half.

The procession carried on for hours, and I became aware that we were travelling in some sort of loop. In the midst of the singing and clanging and firecrackers and dancing, I noticed that we were again approaching the convenience store. My bicycle was nearby and I decided to make my exit before the procession disappeared into unknown territory. Another drinks break was announced and I said goodbye to my new team-mates.

When I finally slumped on to my futon my clock read 2.37. I had just witnessed the greatest festival in the world.

I had chosen the worst possible week to begin with a hangover. The school's sports day was on Wednesday, and the staff and students were to spend Monday and Tuesday outside practising for the big event.

Formalities commenced with an intense hour-long assembly, in which the students repeatedly practised lining up in perfectly symmetrical ranks. Warm-up stretches were performed to perfection, and the school anthem was sung to death. Once the teachers were convinced that the students were able to line up with military precision, the entire sports day itself was acted out, including mock races, mock high-jump events and mock shot-put displays. The weekend's cool weather had disappeared, and it was again baking hot.

Tuesday was an exact repeat—lining-up practice, warm-up stretching practice, school anthem practice, and practice sports events. I noticed that Hiro from waka-ayu was the anchor runner for his team in the first-graders' relay race. Looking nervous and awkward, he waited for the baton to be passed to him. The stress of the occasion took its toll, and as he dashed out of the blocks he tripped over and fell flat on his face. The other three runners sprinted past, and by the time Hiro picked himself back up he was last.

He had scraped his arm and cut his chin, and was in tears as he bravely struggled across the finish line. Mrs Hotta was ready and waiting for him, and shepherded him away to the sick bay.

Mr Higo approached as I stood idly at the side of the race track. 'Mr Hamish, would you like to make a team with me?' I was a little unsure what he was talking about, but he quickly explained his intention to form a teachers' team to run in the third-grade boys' 1500-metre race.

The idea appealed instantly. A good performance in the teachers' team would be a perfect opportunity to boost my popularity with the students. I would run competitively with the leading pack for most of the race, and then humbly let the leader win in a close sprint-off at the finish. I was already smugly anticipating the awed respect my performance would engender.

Mr Higo was very happy to have me on his team. So far only Mr Urao, the young woodwork teacher, had expressed any interest. Mr Higo confided that all the other teachers were too old and the race would be too hard for them. My smugness increased.

On Wednesday morning I woke up feeling confident. The sun was out and the sky was clear. The 1500-metre race was scheduled as the culmination of the day's events. By the time it arrived, I was feeling even more cocky. I stood at the starting line and surveyed the competition. Apart from Mr Higo, nobody came close to my shoulder height. This was going to be easy.

The runners bent forward to take their starting position. I bent my knee slightly: no need to exert myself too early on. Mr Terada, the physical education teacher, raised the starter's gun. A tingle of nervousness coursed through my body. The race started and everyone sprinted off.

I had expected this. School races back home had always started with everyone sprinting at the start due to nerves. I stayed with the pack, waiting for them all to grow tired and drop off.

By the first corner they were all still sprinting. The second corner flashed by and still nobody had slowed down. If anything, they were now running even faster. We passed the 200-metre mark and then the 400-metre mark. Nobody was slowing down.

By lap three of seven my lungs were burning, but I was still holding my own. I tried sneaking glimpses of the crowd. The parents were on their feet, clapping and cheering. The students had spontaneously invented a 'Mr Hamish!' chant, and a roar went up when I passed the spectators' stand. Mr Tokunaga and the other men from the Board of Education had snuck across the road from the town hall and were also waving proudly.

I passed the special dignitaries' stand. The mayor was on his feet cheering me on. I felt like an Olympic superstar. Then reality cruelly caught up. I had never sprinted for one and half kilometres in my life. The teenage students, meanwhile, were all members of the school track and field team, and practised long-distance running every day of the week. They arrived at school at dawn and ran around the block. After school they ran an arduous cross-country circuit through the rice paddies. They then spent their weekends competing in athletics events.

My workout regime, although admirable, was poor by comparison. I cycled languidly to school. I recovered by drinking Coca-Cola and eating chocolate and steamed buns. I then sat idly writing emails and reading trashy novels. On a good day, I would walk to the convenience store and buy an ice-cream.

Back in my reputation-building race, my body was starting to give way and I felt as though I were ready to die. Slowly, I slipped backwards into last place with Mr Higo. Eventually, we were lapped by everyone except Mr Urao.

As soon as the race was over, I staggered away and collapsed in the shade. Mrs Takaoka came over to congratulate me on a 'brave attempt'. My entire head, she said, had turned purple.

# 6

# Adult entertainment

*It was now autumn,* and I was spending my Wednesday afternoons in the Yamaguchis' lounge, eating potato chips, chatting with Hiroshi, and hoping to catch a glimpse of the lovely Aki. Sadly, Aki had made only fleeting appearances since our initial meeting and I was starting to lose hope of our ever being together.

Another family member who never seemed to be present was Mr Yamaguchi, the head of the household. Being a typical Japanese salaryman, he was forced to devote most of his waking life to his job, and hence had little spare time for himself or his family. Mr Yamaguchi's office, I had learned, was situated in the centre of Osaka, and he worked there until well past eleven o'clock every night, before catching the last train home to Tondabayashi Station, a two-hour journey. I was resigned to never meeting him.

One day, however, I arrived at the normal time and found Mr Yamaguchi standing in the lounge. He was a tall man with a large smile, round glasses and a loud laugh. Mrs Yamaguchi introduced us, proudly pointing out that her husband had once been a national karate champion. I gulped and decided not to publicly declare my intentions regarding his daughter.

Mr Yamaguchi insisted that I conduct my lesson with Hiroshi as usual, and stood quietly in the corner of the room, eavesdropping and trying to repeat the occasional word that he was able to pick up from our conversation. Mrs Yamaguchi had prepared a special meal, and asked if I would like to stay for dinner. I gladly accepted, and we all sat down to the first course, clam chowder. Aki was out for the evening, and I was miffed to have missed this great opportunity to woo her with my charms.

Hiroshi and I chatted about life in New Zealand, and Mrs Yamaguchi eagerly inquired about the price of vegetables and the abundance of fruit. I was in fine form, making up all sorts of facts and figures about farm life, economic development and export commodities. Mr Yamaguchi seemed very impressed and slowly leaned forward to ask a question. I paused in my explanation of current New Zealand exchange rates and waited for Mr Yamaguchi's question.

'Mr Hamish,' he began seriously, looking me straight in the eye, 'what kind of porno do you like?'

My head snapped back, and my jaw melded into a confused triple chin. 'I'm sorry,' I gagged, daintily snorting clam chowder through my nose. 'What did you say?'

Mr Yamaguchi ignored my sudden expulsion of soup and repeated his question, his eyes never leaving mine. 'Mr Hamish, what kind of pornography do you like?'

My brain scrambled to find a less embarrassing translation of the word porno. Surely, I thought, he's talking about some sort of Mexican banking system.

But no, despite having travelled to Mexico with his family the previous year, Mr Yamaguchi held no interest whatsoever in Central American economies or financial systems. 'Mr Hamish,' he repeated, 'what kind of pornography do you like, Japanese or foreign?'

I could feel my scalp turning red. 'Ahhh,' I stammered, 'I don't...ahhh, I'm not...ahhh...hmmmmm...'

Mr Yamaguchi ploughed on. 'Mr Hamish, do you prefer Japanese or foreign pornography? I am a collector of pornography. I like pornography very much. I have a machine that removes the blurred bits. In Japan, pornography movies have naked parts blurred out. My machine can remove the blurriness. What kind of pornography do you like?'

I sat dumbstruck. I looked imploringly at Hiroshi. He smiled up at me. 'It's all right, Mr Hamish, Dad and I watch porn together all the time. I like porn. What kind of porn do you like, Japanese or foreign?'

I blinked in disbelief and looked across to Mrs Yamaguchi. 'Ahhh...I don't ahhh...I'm not ahhh...hmmmm...I don't, ahhh, think I should have this conversation with one of my students.'

Mrs Yamaguchi understood my predicament immediately. She leant forward sternly. 'Hiroshi, whatever Mr Hamish says is secret. Don't tell any of your friends at school.'

My confused blinking was now causing my head to wobble. 'Ahhh...that's not...ahhh...I don't...I'm not...ahhh...'

Mr Yamaguchi perked up. A look of comprehension dawned. He leant forward again, smiling. 'Perhaps you didn't understand my question. Let me repeat it slowly. What kind of porn *do you like*—Japanese *or* foreign?'

It was as if time had come to a standstill. I could feel my mind racing, trying to think up an answer that would maintain my dignity, not embarrass my hosts, and stealthily change the topic of conversation with a witty rejoinder.

'I...ahhh...I don't ahhh...I'm not ahhh...I don't know much about porn.'

'Aha!' Mr Yamaguchi exclaimed. 'I knew it—he likes Japanese porn.'

Hiroshi was ecstatic; the riddle of the century had been solved.

'No...no...' I turned to Mrs Yamaguchi again, giving her an imploring look. 'Mrs Yamaguchi, surely you don't like your husband and son discussing pornography at the dinner table?'

She seemed taken aback. She looked me straight in the eye and said, 'Mr Hamish, we are an open family. I like porn. What kind of porn do you like, Japanese or foreign?'

I slumped back in my chair, completely beaten. There was no way of weaselling out of this conversation. I took a deep breath. 'I don't know much about porn. I'm not a collector.'

A hush descended on the table. The questioning ceased immediately. Mr Yamaguchi rose and silently walked from the room. I hunched forward and sipped my soup, staring at the tablecloth. It seemed that I had deeply offended my host. He was probably now off getting changed into his karate suit, preparing to kick me out the gate for not appreciating the finer aspects of the adult entertainment industry.

The door opened and Mr Yamaguchi stepped back into the room. I breathed a sigh of relief: he was holding a bottle of tequila and smiling from ear to ear. 'Mr Hamish, thank you for teaching my son English. This is a present for you.' He sat down and handed me the bottle. The conversation reverted to the economic state of New Zealand, the strength of the dollar and the cost of flatting.

Main course was served, hearty steak fillets, and dessert followed closely behind. By the end of the meal, most of the redness had drained from my face. My armpits, however, were still very moist and I badly wanted a shower.

Solemnly, the Yamaguchis gathered to farewell me. Mr Yamaguchi shook my hand and thanked me once again for teaching his son. Mrs Yamaguchi presented me with my weekly shopping bag of groceries, and then she and Hiroshi walked me to their car.

Mrs Yamaguchi drove, Hiroshi sat in the passenger seat, and I sat pensively in the back seat, contemplating the bizarre choice of dinner topic. We passed the Junior High School, and Mrs Yamaguchi took an unusual route through some backstreets to avoid traffic.

Suddenly, Hiroshi piped up and pointed at a black shape as it flashed by in the darkness. 'That's a row of porn vending machines. I can buy magazines and videos there, Mr Hamish.'

'Congratulations,' I said, patting him on the shoulder. 'Good stuff.'

'Hiroshi!' Mrs Yamaguchi snapped. 'Don't buy porn there!'

I sighed. At last, some common sense.

She continued, 'No, don't buy porn there! It's too expensive. I buy my porn in town.'

I closed my eyes. Surely an American TV host was about to pop out of the glove box and tell me it had all been a joke. But no, I arrived back at my apartment and the Yamaguchis bade me goodnight. I lugged my bags of groceries up the three flights of stairs, dumped them on the kitchen sink and transferred the lettuce and tomatoes to the fridge, the bread to the bread shelf, and the ice-cream to the freezer.

Strangely, the bags still seemed quite full. I rummaged through the remaining groceries and struck a hard plastic layer. Eight pornographic videotapes stared back at me.

My fear that Hiroshi Yamaguchi would reveal the details of my new video collection to the school fortunately came to nothing, and I was able to continue teaching with an unblemished record. Although I was, technically, working only seventeen hours a week as a teacher—while being paid for forty—there were always school events to be involved with.

I was requested to act as a judge for the third-grade singing competition, in which each class would perform both a traditional Japanese anthem and a contemporary pop song. The town auditorium was booked for the big event, and invitations were sent to parents and grandparents, inviting them to come and witness some spectacular singing. The students had been practising for a month, and I had overheard some fairly terrible performances as I wandered through the hallways.

The singing competition was, in the event, a shambles. All the classes were horribly out of tune, and most of the singing sounded like cats fighting. One class daringly sang an English song, of which I did not understand a single word until Mr Higo pointed out to me that it was a Celine Dion number. Sadly, all the other judges made glowing and encouraging comments, and my negative misgivings were swept under the carpet.

The only bright spot in the whole tedious affair was the third-grade naughty boys. Somehow the three naughtiest ones in E class had convinced their classmates to allow them to be the pianist, conductor and drummer. Nobu, Kazu and Sugitani strutted boldly on to the stage and took up their positions. Nobu sat at the piano and gave the audience a cheeky grin. He seemed full of confidence. His scruffy friend Sugitani, who had his shirt defiantly untucked, started to conduct, at which point it became apparent that Nobu had never touched a piano before in his life. While Sugitani flapped his arms around madly, and bobbed his head up and down as if listening to rock music, Nobu made tentative one-finger jabs at the keyboard.

The red-faced music teacher rushed on stage and escorted Nobu to the wings. Meanwhile, his bewildered classmates started singing, but the initial shock had put them out of time with the backing tape. Simultaneously, Kazu let loose on the drum kit and drowned out the lot. I gave E class my highest score of the day, but sadly this was not enough to save Nobu, Kazu and Sugitani from an afternoon in detention.

When they were not being held back after class to be told off, the three naughty boys also made regular appearances at the touch rugby games that I had started organising during the lunch breaks. These games had proved popular. Hiroshi Yamaguchi, who was always the first on the field, loudly proclaimed he was going to live in New Zealand and play rugby every day.

As word of the lunch-time games spread the team numbers expanded, until we had well over twenty on either side of the field. After several tiresome weeks of repeatedly explaining the rules about passing the ball backwards, and the fact there were at least a hundred penalties for breaching this rule, everyone got the hang of things and the games became very competitive. Several trickier techniques soon followed, such as kicking the ball and some clever little set moves that I made up.

All the boys congratulated me warmly whenever I scored a try, tagged an opposing player, or even managed to pass the ball. They exclaimed that I was a brilliant rugby player, and were adamant that I would one day make it into the All Blacks. I nonchalantly tried to tell them that I didn't want to be in the All Blacks, but they encouraged me to try out anyway. The third-grade students were fast becoming my friends.

I was fast becoming quite fond of the first-graders as well. These little kids were giggly and happy, and responded well no matter what unplanned load of cobblers I took to class as a lesson plan. I generally made a big effort though, and designed fun games and comical routines to get them rolling in the aisles.

When teaching the present tense, I took along a block of chocolate and a carton of strawberry milk. I cheekily ate the entire block of chocolate in front of them and noisily slurped up the strawberry milk, all the while loudly stating that 'I am eating, I am drinking' and rubbing my stomach.

The kids were shocked to the core. To eat in the classroom outside of lunch-hour was strictly forbidden, and would earn an offender a trip to the staffroom for some corporal punishment. They implored me to stop, and one boy looked as though he might cry. I had arranged for the first-grade English teacher, Mrs Takaoka, to storm into the classroom and give me a telling-off. Mrs Takaoka was, however, a kindly soul, and her less than convincing telling-off soon gave the game away.

This simple stunt earned me a huge reputation throughout the school and all around town. Colleagues confidentially whispered to me that I had been teaching radical lesson plans and had all the students talking. I was soon referred to as the teacher who ate chocolate in class, and was even approached in the supermarket by parents congratulating me on my daring lessons.

One class, however, that was never any fun and that I was fast beginning to despise was my Wednesday afternoon 'English Elective'. The elective was the one class of the week that students were allowed to choose for themselves. There was a range of options: woodwork, pottery, art, history, physical education, science, music—and English with Mr Hamish. This class was, therefore, intended to comprise the best and brightest students in the third grade who wanted to and enjoyed studying English.

I had been asked to prepare a blurb which would give students an idea of what they could look forward to if they chose to take my course. I had foolishly given this task only cursory consideration. Surely, I thought lazily, all these brain-boxes will be able to teach themselves? We can laze around, watch some movies, chat in English and enjoy ourselves.

My subsequent, poorly planned blurb read as follows: 'English Class with Mr Hamish. Learn about foreign countries, culture and food. Watch movies and learn about foreign pop culture and music.'

It should have come as no surprise, then, that my English Elective class did not attract the academic élite I had been hoping for. First on the roll were the 'cool girls', Waki, Mayo and Yuki. These three ditzy yet endearing airheads had chosen English with Mr Hamish as they had misinterpreted my blurb and were looking forward to producing their own music video. They gossiped noisily in the front row, fluttering their eyelashes at me, and checking one another's hair.

Next on the list was Jun Fujita. Jun had demanded an extra hour a week with Mr Hamish, and had staunchly refused advice that Elective English might be above his level. Jun sat nervously with Mrs Hotta. He had overheard the cool girls chattering about making music videos, and now hoped that I would be able to help him direct a *Pokémon* cartoon.

Hiroshi Yamaguchi sat in the third row, reliving moments from the day's touch rugby game with three of his team-mates. The team-mates were not thrilled to be part of the English Elective class. They had chosen PE but it was full.

Last but not least were eight quiet and ridiculously shy female English enthusiasts. This timid little academic band sat desperately praying that I would not ask them any questions, or embarrass them by speaking English to them.

English Elective was a nightmare from the very beginning. No one responded to my 'self-introduction' game and the class sat awkwardly when it became apparent that I had absolutely no idea how to cope with such a random assortment of abilities and interests.

Over the weeks, the sessions grew ever more awkward. My suggestion of starting a pen-pal system with students from my old high school in New Zealand was greeted with silence. Hiroshi was the only person to make any effort at all, and I was relieved that he was not losing his enthusiasm for English. Jun tried his best to complete the various exercises, but he was well out of his depth. The cool girls lost their dreams of pop stardom and announced that they had abandoned their music video plans.

By November, I had resorted to showing movies. My first screening was of old *Monty Python* clips. This was, in hindsight, an incredibly bad choice: the British comedy series did not produce a single laugh, and several scenes were greeted with horrified gasps by the nerdy girls.

The following Tuesday night I spent a painful hour at the video store, trying to find an interesting movie that had no swear words, no sex scenes, no violence, wasn't too long (or too short) and catered for the various requests: drama, action, romance, war, and (for Jun) animation. *Awakenings* with Robert De Niro and *Gilbert Grape* with Johnny Depp were close contenders, but I figured the subject matter might upset Jun.

Most of the students had seen *Stand By Me* and *Dead Poets Society*, so I eventually settled for *The War* with Kevin Costner. The story centred on a poor family in the post-Vietnam period in America. The father (played by Kevin Costner) dies in a mining accident and his children have a war with neighbouring kids over a tree house. It was a drama with tame action scenes. There were no swear words, no sex scenes, little violence, and the film was a perfect length. I was overjoyed: I had finally found something the English Elective class would enjoy.

When I screened the first half of the movie the next day, the students did not share my enthusiasm. One of the nerdy girls suggested we do a cooking class the following week instead of watching the rest.

I was not sad when the elective term came to an end a few weeks later. Mr Higo asked if I wanted to take an elective class in the new year. When I politely refused, he nodded understandingly.

I had arranged with the Okis to spend the second Sunday of November riding a cable-car up a mountain in Kobe. They were to pick me up at nine in the morning and then we would drive across Osaka to Kobe port.

When the day arrived I got up early, expecting the Okis to be waiting on the doorstep. They weren't. By nine-thirty they still hadn't shown up. I phoned them and there was a bit of confusion for a few minutes while Mrs Oki consulted the television set and the pet cat. In the end, though, I was sternly reprimanded. Mrs Oki had apparently been waiting since dawn for me to call and say I was ready.

They arrived twenty minutes later and gave me some green oranges. Then we were off to Kobe. Kobe is north of Osaka, so I grew suspicious when we started heading due south. Mrs Oki talked constantly. Did I teach high school or junior high school? What time did I start every day? What did I eat? Was I cold?

I answered these questions for the thousandth time and tried to enjoy the view. After about an hour of travelling south I was starting to worry about where we were going. It turned out that, contrary to plans, we were going up a mountain in Wakayama, the prefecture south of Osaka.

We continued driving for another two hours and the mountain roads grew steeper and windier. Finally we arrived at a lovely place called Kôyasan, a small mountain town full of old temples and cemeteries. Kôyasan was originally a monastic complex, established in 816 AD. Over the centuries it prospered and grew, becoming an important Buddhist centre, and a popular place for commoners to leave the cremated remains of loved ones. In the seventeenth century the town was smashed and pillaged by marauding samurais. Today, only a hundred and ten temples remain and the population is only seven thousand.

Besides its temples and enchanting cemeteries, Koyasan is well-known for its autumn colours. Mr Oki had timed our visit so we would arrive at the height of viewing season. The large maple forests had burst into colour, painting the hillsides with blazing red and gold. Gaggles of Japanese tourists bustled about, gasping as they gazed up at the multi-coloured trees. The trees are able to generate the nutrients needed to maintain these dazzling colours for only a few weeks, and by December the leaves would have slowly turned a deep blood-red, crumpled and drifted to the ground.

We visited several temples, where Mrs Oki pushed me through the crowds of devout worshippers into the front row. We posed for photos beneath large trees and Mrs Oki plucked several gold leaves as a souvenir for me. As we wandered through sprawling cemeteries she questioned me relentlessly about what I wore to work, what I ate in the evenings, and how my mother was.

Mr Oki rambled away as well. During lunch, he asked our effeminate-looking waiter if he were a boy or a girl. When I choked with embarrassment, he concernedly slapped me on the back.

All in all, it was a great day.

The dinner that followed our scenic drive home was equally pleasant. After we had drunk a bottle of red wine sent by my parents and eaten a barbecue meal, I was given a fridge-full of leftover meat to take home. In order that I could recreate the meal at home later, the Okis also presented me with the electric fry-pan it had been cooked in.

# 7

# On being Father Christmas

*The crisp autumn evenings grew colder,* the maple forests shed their dazzling coats, and there was now a distinct chill in the air as Japan moved into the month of December. I had completely forgotten about Christmas until a phone call home reminded me that we were only weeks away from the big day.

'That's it,' I thought, 'a Christmas party for the special team.' And so, for the second time, a party was planned for the young minnows.

The plan was simple: play some Christmas carols on the CD player, hum along with Hiro, and play board games with identical pieces of food as prizes. I had procured Santa hats for the children, and for Mrs Hotta a pair of fluffy reindeer antlers that lit up and played 'Jingle Bells' when squeezed. I had also bought Father Christmas stickers for the students to take home for their families, and a disposable camera with which to capture the happy occasion.

I broke the news of the party to Hiro, Jun, Fumio and Yurika a week before. Teru-Chan was absent as she refused to come to school during winter, claiming that it was too cold for her to get out of bed. This suited me just fine, and I prayed that it would continue to snow until June.

Jun was overjoyed with the news. He clapped himself on the head and gave Mrs Hotta a high five. After a few minutes he settled down and

a secretive look came over his face. Mrs Hotta asked what he was thinking about, but he refused to answer and stated adamantly that it was
confidential.

I set off for the waka-ayu room the next Friday morning wearing a
Santa hat and carrying a bag of treats. As I got near, I could see that the
door was slightly ajar and a curious pair of eyes were peeping out at me.
I peered back and the door suddenly slammed shut. Frantic footsteps
could be heard inside. I could distinguish Yurika's bright giggle, and Hiro
wheezing away about something humorous.

I stepped up to the door just as Mrs Hotta opened it from the inside.
She stepped out into the hallway, obstructing my view into the classroom.
She blushed slightly. 'It's Jun. I didn't know he'd do this. He planned it
all on his own.'

Mrs Hotta seemed nervous, and reluctant to let me into the classroom.
I assured her that whatever Jun had done would not be so bad, and that I
would forgive him. She stepped back and opened the door. Yurika was
giggling again and Hiro was smiling. Jun, however, was nowhere to
be seen.

I entered the room and looked around. No Jun!

Just then, he leapt out from behind the bookshelf and yelled, 'Merry
Christmas!'

I nearly fell over laughing. Jun was dressed from head to toe as a furry
reindeer, complete with tail and ears. He pranced around the room, clapping his hands and jumping up and down to jingle the bells on the end of his
antlers. Everyone laughed and Jun giggled and danced. Hiro joined in and
danced around as well. Fumio grinned quietly. Yurika was beside herself
with joy, and kept tugging on Mrs Hotta's sleeve to make sure that she was
paying attention and not missing any of the fun.

The Christmas party and Jun's antics had put me in a festive mood. However, this was to be severely tested the following Monday.

I had been invited to the local kindergartens to dress up as Santa
and play with the children. The Board of Education had chipped in with a
brand new Santa suit, especially purchased. Sadly, though, no one had

thought to check the size or measurements, and I was presented with a costume five sizes too small. The trouser legs exposed a pasty white expanse of skin for five centimetres above my ankles, and the sleeves on the jacket were as tight as a tourniquet and struggled to stretch past my elbows. When I attempted to fix the fake white beard to my face, the elastic band snapped and the beard fell on the floor.

To make matters worse, I had no suitable footwear to complement the Santa suit. The gaping exposure of my lower legs meant I needed tall boots just to reach my trousers. Mr Smiles happily produced his own pair of black gumboots, but alas I could not even begin to squeeze my size 12 feet into them. The kindergarten teachers hummed and haahed, and eventually came up with the idea of wrapping black rubbish bags around my feet and legs. My level of ridiculousness increased tenfold.

Despite all this, the happy frivolity of the young minnows' Christmas party had given me a deluded self-assurance. I felt confident that no Japanese toddler would see through my disguise, and that my white skin and blond hair would yet again earn me a warm reception and a legion of fans.

The first kindergarten on Santa's itinerary had only eight children. I turned up on time and was rushed around by the head teacher while she gave me hurried instructions. I was to sit in a box, decorated to look like a big parcel, and wait for my cue to leap out the top and greet the excited children. I willingly obliged, and while she rounded up the children I wedged myself into the small box, where my legs immediately fell asleep.

'After you've greeted the children, just tell them stories about your trip here from the North Pole,' another teacher called encouragingly from outside my gift-wrapped cell. I started to get a tad nervous: my Japanese language skills had not yet reached the level of storyteller or stand-up comedian.

I could hear eight tiny nervous little people whispering among themselves. The kindergarten teacher knocked loudly on the top of the box. Somehow I managed to reactivate my numb legs, burst out of the roof and bellow, 'Merry Christmas!'

One of the boys started crying and I knew I was in trouble. I tore my way free of the rest of the box, which caused all the other children to start crying, and tried a friendly 'Oha!' to get things back on track. The kids kept crying and everyone was terrified. The room had been deliberately darkened. Black curtains blanketed the windows and the only light came from flickering candles, which made me look like an enormous ogre with seven hideous shadows.

I was ushered to my chair and told to tell the children a story. In my stilted Japanese, I told a rousing tale of my trip by super jet over Europe, helicopter over China, and sled from Hiroshima. From there it was on to question-and-answer time, and when one of the girls asked where I had come from, I nearly started crying too.

I repeated my story, and then another child asked the same question again. Just when I thought things couldn't get any worse, one of the boys asked what my real name was. All the children then stood up and performed an orchestral rendition of 'Jingle Bells', with the small boy on the end still sobbing and weeping and squeaking as he gasped into his recorder.

Once the eight terrified little people had shakily completed their Christmas carol, they rattled off a shambles of a puppet show and we all ate cake. I finally managed to break the ice by talking about *Pokémon* and video games. The kids stopped crying and became my best friends in the blink of an eye. Finally, they waved me off and I was driven back to the Junior High School to recover from my traumatic experience.

My festive visit to the town's other kindergarten took place the following day. I turned up in an anxious, sweaty state, expecting the worst. This time, however, things went a lot more smoothly and there were no tears or traumatised toddlers. The 'leaping out of a gift-wrapped shoebox' idea had been scrapped, and instead I danced on to a brightly lit stage in a conga line of kindergarten teachers dressed as reindeers.

The thirty children screamed, this time in joy, and rushed on to the stage to slap and kick Santa's shins. I tried to calm them with a few Ohas and Merry Christmases, but alas a game of stamping on Santa's comical rubbish-bag shoes had captured everyone's attention. Groups of small boys were performing devious tag-team routines of racing up to me, kicking my shins, slapping my bottom, stamping on my feet, and then trying to pull my pants down. Someone had stolen my fake beard, and I clung to my trousers and Santa hat as wave upon wave of Japanese preschoolers assaulted me.

The kindergarten teachers eventually managed to drag the hyperactive audience back to their seats, and someone kindly retrieved my facial hair. I launched straight into my now carefully rehearsed 'rocket sled from the North Pole' story and waited for an enthusiastic response.

'What's your real name?' yelled a small girl.

'Your beard fell off! You're not Santa!' shouted a boy.

Everyone laughed, even me.

The school term finally came to an end on December 21, and I packed my bags for a winter vacation in Tokyo. I had arranged to spend Christmas with the Hanaki family and New Year's Eve with the Tanaka family. I had met both these families through exchange programmes during my university days, and they had invited me to spend the festive season with them. The Hanakis had also inivited Natalie and Ben, two of my friends from New Zealand.

Despite the occasional Christmas-themed neon display in the Tokyo city centre and colossal sales in major department stores, I was not expecting any traditional celebrations. Accordingly, I decided to treat myself to a Christmas feast the evening before I departed. Two New Zealand-made meat pies had been frozen and stealthily transported to me by a visiting family member, and I had stored them in my freezer for such an occasion. I splashed out and bought a creamy chocolate cake at Daiei, a can of Coca-Cola from the school vending machine and a bag of popcorn, and rented the last remaining copy of *Gladiator* from the local video store.

I ate my hearty Christmas repast wearing a Santa hat, and took a photo of myself to commemorate my first Christmas in Japan. No amount of sushi and okonomiayaki could match the nostalgia of a good old New Zealand steak pie. I ate slowly, relishing every mouthful. The can of Coke complemented the pies wonderfully, with the gooey blob from Daiei making a slightly peculiar end to an otherwise scrumptious Christmas feast.

I then settled in for my movie, stuffed myself full of sickly caramel popcorn, wrapped my small selection of gifts for my Tokyo families, and lovingly decorated my small wooden Christmas tree.

米

Christmas Day at the Hanakis was untraditional to say the least. Mr Hanaki and his son-in-law left for work shortly after dawn. I sprang out of bed at a healthier hour and greeted Mrs Hanaki in the kitchen with a cheerful 'Merry Christmas!' Looking baffled, she shooed me out of the kitchen and sat me down at the dining-room table, where Natalie, Ben and I ate breakfast of fried rice and pickled plums.

Next, we spent a merry morning at Mrs Hanaki's pottery class creating chopstick holders, turtles, cats' heads, and in my case a scale model of my left hand. Later, we wandered around the nearby village of Kamakura, seeking out a Christmassy lunch. The best we could manage was greasy cheeseburgers at a Burger King near the train station.

The following day, I took a train north to spend New Year with the Tanaka family in Kawasaki. My time here began with an almost disastrous *faux pas*. Before leaving for Tokyo I had been insanely busy, with many people to visit and farewell and numerous Christmas cards and presents to buy. Despite my well-laid plans, I had been horrified to discover on the day of my departure that I had forgotten to buy anything for the Tanakas. With only minutes to spare before my train left Tondabayashi, I had raced around in a blind panic, searching my apartment for a possible gift.

I had suddenly spotted a box of rice crackers and assorted snack food that my principal, Mr Kazama, had given me for Christmas. I am not a fan of salty Japanese rice crackers, but I knew Mr Tanaka was. I quickly decided that he would enjoy the box of crackers a lot more than I ever would. I daintily removed the decorative sticker emblazoned with 'Merry Christmas, Mr Hamish' from the front of the unopened, gift-wrapped box and raced out the door.

By the time I arrived at the Tanaka household several days later, I had completely forgotten about the crisis, and had even managed to convince myself that I had purchased the box of crackers. The Tanakas welcomed me into their home and we sat down for dinner. Our meal of soup and noodles was quickly followed by a presentation of gifts. Mr Tanaka had bought me a computer printer, and Mrs Tanaka a lurid orange and red striped woollen sweater.

I shyly produced my second-hand box of crackers. Mr Tanaka thanked me profusely. He tore the wrapping and opened the box. My heart sank. Inside, a slim white envelope sat unopened. The school principal's tidy handwriting clearly indicated that the envelope and accompanying box of crackers had been destined for 'Mr Hamish'.

I gulped. Mr Tanaka seemed confused. He reached forward and opened the envelope. 'Dear Mr Hamish,' he read aloud, 'I hope you have a merry Christmas and a Happy New Year. Take care in Tokyo. Best wishes, Ryouichi Kazama.'

I blushed. My mind raced. 'Aha,' I proclaimed, suddenly sensing a way out of my predicament. 'These crackers are from me. However, I did not know what a good brand of crackers was. I told Mr Kazama that you all like rice crackers very much, and asked him to help me choose a good selection. So we went shopping together, and he chose these crackers for you. He must have accidentally put that letter inside the box by mistake.'

I held my breath. I prayed that Mr Tanaka would not ask how the envelope had managed to get into the box before the box was gift-wrapped.

He sat perfectly still for a moment, carefully considering my story. 'Hmm,' he mused, rubbing his chin, 'Mr Kazama is a good man. I must thank him.' And with that, he rose and left the table. An hour later, while the rest of the family and I were watching television, he returned and presented me with a slim envelope. 'I have written a letter to Mr Kazama,' he announced. 'Please thank him for the rice crackers.'

I am ashamed to admit that Mr Tanaka's letter did not quite make it to its intended recipient.

As New Year approached I received emails from friends in New Zealand talking of happy days at the beach, great camping trips and sun-drenched cricket matches. Meanwhile, snow was covering the Tanaka home and it was too freezing to go outside.

While the Christmas period had been a riot of shopping, New Year would be the complete opposite. In Japan, most shops shut from January 1 to January 4, with families staying home by the heater and venturing out only to pay homage at a local shrine or temple. The days leading up to New

Year are, therefore, spent preparing for this hermit-like existence. Four days of meals need to be prepared before midnight on December 31, and the entire household needs to be immaculately clean to welcome in the new year. We hunkered down and polished the Tanaka's family shrine, as well as their collection of silver cutlery and rice bowls, and helped Mrs Tanaka make copious batches of rice balls and slice vegetables for the New Year stew.

New Year's Eve finally rolled around, the family assembled in the living room and the television set was switched on. A team of male celebrities was trying to beat a team of female celebrities in a singing competition. Poppy teen idols were singing soppy songs about asking someone on a date and being happy, and elderly celebrities were crooning folk songs about the countryside. Although almost everyone seemed to be out of tune, plastic smiles and obsequious praise abounded.

While I struggled to stay awake, the Tanaka family talked excitedly about which celebrities had undergone plastic surgery and who was dating whom. After six hours the competition finally ended, there was a cheesy countdown to midnight, and the family bowed and clapped. I heartily joined in, thrilled the evening was at an end.

Mr Tanaka leapt to his feet and put on his coat. 'Right!' he announced. 'It's time to go.' Mrs Tanaka informed me that we were going to a shrine. Trussed up in my thick red puffer jacket, I followed the Tanakas down an icy road to the local temple, where a giant bronze bell was chiming one hundred and eight times to cleanse visitors of sin.

The reverent queue stretched 200 metres down the road. As we shuffled forward, Mr Tanaka explained that people came to the temple to pray for good luck and protection for the coming year. Japanese people were not particularly religious, but this was a national tradition.

After an hour we reached the temple steps. I was given an incense stick to burn and bowed my head in prayer. 'Dear Lord,' I began, 'please do not let me spend another Christmas and New Year in Japan. Don't get me wrong, everyone's been super-friendly, but I want to play cricket, have a barbecue at the beach and lie in the sun. Fried rice, pickled plums and Burger King are not my idea of Christmas fare, and I may well lose my sanity if I have to sit through another celebrity singing competition.'

# 8

# Season of change

*The bitter winter eventually ended* and spring arrived. The large cherry blossom tree at the entrance to Kanan Junior High School burst into flower, coating the locker bay and sports ground with a frosting of pink.

Lunch breaks became riotous affairs as five hundred students emerged from winter hibernation, eager to make up for lost games of tag and soccer. The school pool was cleaned and the students began arriving at class with damp hair and red eyes after their daily swimming practice.

The young minnows were also in the mood. I arrived at my Friday morning lesson to discover that Jun, prancing about like a newborn lamb, had managed to lock himself in the classroom. Mrs Hotta banged on the frosted-glass window and yelled, but Jun was unable to unlock the door. Other teachers were called to see if the door could be dismantled by unscrewing the hinges. More banging and yelling at Jun ensued; he became visibly alarmed and distressed.

At last, Mr Ii, a maths teacher, instructed Jun to turn the door knob counter-clockwise instead of clockwise, and the door opened. Three teachers burst into the room, seized a startled Jun Fujita and rushed him to the staffroom, where Mrs Hotta set about giving him a telling-off for being naughty and disobedient.

This staffroom visit would not be his last. The following week I was eating my lunch when the door opened, and Jun was marched in by Mr Omura and led to Mrs Hotta's desk. Mrs Hotta followed, looking slightly alarmed. Jun seemed bewildered. His mouth hung open, and he looked at his shoes and shifted his weight nervously.

I sensed something was amiss, and listened in for any potential gossip or scandal. Mrs Hotta seemed unsure where to begin. Mr Omura looked on uncertainly, and put his hand on Jun's shoulder.

'What on earth were you thinking?' Mrs Hotta asked.

Jun continued to look at his feet. His cheeks were flushed and he wrung his hands. At last he looked up. His brow was locked in a frown and his eyes seemed moist. He opened his mouth and in his slow, husky drawl began to tell his story.

Seven weeks earlier he had developed a crush on a female student. Alas, this was not just any female student but Asuka Kitamura, the prettiest girl in school. Much like me, Jun was afflicted with the soul-destroying compulsion of falling for girls well outside his league and with whom he had little chance of romance. The weeks had gone by with Jun admiring Asuka from a distance and secretly daydreaming about her.

'I think she's very pretty,' Jun said. He blushed and looked at his feet again, 'so I wanted to make her a present.'

A week earlier the young minnows had gone to visit the local kindergarten. Part of the visit had involved making greeting cards for the kindergarten students. Jun, Hiro and Yurika had spent hours colouring in, and sticking pieces of crêpe paper on to pieces of cardboard. The end result had been a mess of glue, tattered crêpe paper, scruffy felt-pen doodles and indecipherable pictures. However, this had not mattered at all to the three-year-old recipients and the visit had been a great success.

This artistic breakthrough had inspired Jun to express his feelings to Asuka via a homemade greeting card. He had acquired leftover scraps of pink crêpe paper and drawn Asuka the prettiest, least scribbly bunch of flowers his love-struck hands could muster. He had then smuggled his creation into his home room, and waited for an opportune moment to present it to the unwitting Asuka.

This moment had arisen at lunch break, when Jun had shyly given the card to Asuka and then fled to the safety of the young minnows' room.

To her credit, Asuka had not laughed at Jun, or embarrassed him in front of the other students. She had quickly gone to find her homeroom teacher. She explained that she had never spoken with Jun, and didn't know why he'd made her a card. She did not share Jun's feelings, but certainly did not want to hurt him.

Mrs Hotta relayed all this to Jun, and I quietly shared his feeling of shame and unhappiness as the bottom dropped out of his stomach, and the small glimmer of hope was snuffed out. 'I'm sorry,' he said quietly. Mr Omura patted Jun on the back and Mrs Hotta smiled.

Asuka's homeroom teacher had now entered the classroom, and she stood smiling awkwardly at Jun.

'Is Nobu still angry with me?' Jun looked up, a worried look on his face Mr Omura's smile instantly vanished. 'Nobu won't bother you again.'

Keisuke Nobunaga was Asuka's boyfriend. He was the coolest boy in school, and rode a motor bike on the weekends. This gave him a Fonzie-style rebel-without-a-cause reputation, and the girls loved him. I shared their admiration. Nobu's clownish pranks made my classes more entertaining. He always had a joke to tell when we met in the hallways, and kept me up to date with who the prettiest girls on TV were.

Unfortunately, though, Nobu had not reacted well to Jun's affection for his girlfriend. Despite Asuka's best efforts, word of the home-made greeting card had quickly reached Nobu's ears. He had stormed off to the young minnows' room and yelled something threatening at Jun through the frosted window.

Jun and Hiro had cleverly locked the door, and remained fortified behind some desks. Nobu's threats had, therefore, fallen on deaf ears, and he had been quickly apprehended by the school counsellor, Mr Kobayashi, and taken away for a 'conversation'.

Jun was still blushing, but a smile had returned to his face. He leant forward to whisper in Mrs Hotta's ear—and, as always, I was able to hear him from across the room. 'I think she's pretty.' His red complexion turned a shade of puce, and he clapped his hand across his mouth.

Mrs Hotta and Mr Omura looked startled. 'Jun!' they exclaimed at once. 'You mustn't do this again.' Jun looked up innocently. 'Of course not. No, I won't do it again.'

As he plodded slowly out of the staffroom, he glanced in my direction. He blushed again and smiled. For some bizarre reason, Jun Fujita seemed happy.

During his remaining fortnight at Kanan Junior High School, Jun never repeated his amorous advances towards Asuka. Asuka was polite to Jun, and would always greet him in the hallways. Jun apologised to Nobu, and in turn Nobu took Jun under his wing and started playing table tennis with him during break times. Jun did not seem upset that his feelings were unrequited, and I never heard the issue mentioned again.

The Japanese school year ends at the end of March, and Jun and his third-grade classmates were set to graduate on March 13. I had known these students for only eight months, but I had grown close to many of them and was not looking forward to their leaving.

Sadly, my final class with Jun and Fumio was cancelled because of exams. I had not foreseen this, and had hoped to have a send-off party in the form of a 'super game day', on which we would play all the favourite board games one last time, and the boys would make a last attempt at pinning the tail on the donkey. Instead, the last remaining day on which Jun would be my student would be the day he graduated.

Japanese school graduations are sombre, formal affairs. The passage from one academic institution to another is deemed to be a highly signifi-cant stage of life—so much so that even kindergartens and primary schools hold graduation ceremonies. The students attend with their uniforms cleaned, shoes polished, and hair cut especially for the occasion. Male teachers and proud fathers dust off their best suits, or even tuxedos, while mothers and female teachers wear formal kimonos and intricate hairdos.

The Kanan Junior High School ceremony, at which 150 fifteen-year-olds would graduate, would be attended by the mayor, the town elders and government officials. The mayor would, as usual, wear a three-piece suit and white satin gloves.

The second-grade students had spent the week decorating the school gymnasium, the venue for the occasion, with black and white ribbons and large bouquets of flowers, and plastering coloured cellophane on to the windows to create the impression of cathedral stained glass. The gym floor had been painstakingly measured and mapped so that all the benches were the exact distance apart and at the same angle to the stage. Mr Kobayashi had spent the week instructing students on how to line up, sit down, bow and stand on command.

Apart from the strictness and pomp of the ceremony, the most striking feature was the intense and morbid mood. Whereas Western graduation ceremonies focus on the students' accomplishments and bright hopes for the future, Japanese ceremonies dwell on the past, and serve to remind students that they are about to step outside their comfort zones and potentially lose all their friends.

The ceremony started with the typical Japanese formalities. The national anthem was played over the loudspeakers and everyone stood to attention. The school hymn was sung with gusto, and then everyone sat down at the exact same microsecond. The principal welcomed the mayor. The mayor welcomed the parents, and gave a speech about the students having done well, but now being on the scary unpredictable path called life. He then thanked the principal for having had the opportunity to speak, and the principal thanked the parents for feeding and clothing the students for so many years.

Growing restless, I looked at my programme. Alas, the next hour and a half promised to be even more tedious, with endless certificate presentations. This would be very drawn-out. The third-grade dean would present the principal with a scroll, which contained the class roll for the entire third grade. The principal would carefully unfurl the scroll and read out each name. Upon hearing his or her name, the respective student would stand swiftly to attention, yell 'Hai!' in a loud voice, and walk up on to the stage to receive their certificate. Once the student had returned to his or her seat, the next name would be called, until all 150 students had received their certificates and the audience had lapsed into a coma.

I leant back in my chair and started looking for patterns in the cellophane stained glass. The third-grade dean stepped on to the stage and presented the scroll to the principal. The principal turned and walked slowly back to the podium. He carefully unfurled the scroll and cleared his throat.

At that precise moment the school music teacher started playing the piano. It was a slow, sad tune that I had heard her rehearsing for weeks. I looked to my left and found that Mr Higo had burst into tears. Somewhat surprised, I tried to ignore his weeping and and resumed my cellophane stained-glass viewing. I heard sniffling to my right and noticed that Mrs Hotta was crying. I looked around in confusion. Most of the teachers in my row were sniffling, and the first student had only just received his certificate.

As the students walked up to receive their certificates, most were in tears. I surveyed the rows of third-grade students in front of me. All had their heads bowed and many were sobbing.

The piano teacher reached the end of the song and launched straight into another. I recognised the tune immediately: it had been played on the school's loudspeakers every lunch break for a fortnight. 'Sayonara, daisuki na hito' is a love ballad; the title translates as 'Goodbye, my favourite person'. This song produced a new wave of tears from my colleagues, and I pinched my wrists to keep myself in check.

The sad music continued, song after slow, sad, tear-jerking song: the music teacher seemed to know every morbid piano piece ever written. All the teachers were crying now, and the students were loudly whimpering and sobbing. My own lips were quivering and I was inflicting painful nail marks on the webbing of my hands to keep my tears in check.

Fumio had graduated.

Hiroshi Yamaguchi had graduated.

Asuka had graduated.

The naughty boys, Nobu, Kazu and Sugitani, had graduated.

The airheads from English Elective class, Waki, Mayo and Yuki, had graduated.

The student lists of four of the five homeroom classes had been read out, and the respective certificates presented. Suddenly, Jun Fujita's name was announced. I looked up, and felt a stinging sensation in the bridge of my nose.

Jun leapt to his feet and stood as stiff as a rod, his chest puffed up and eyes fixed proudly ahead. I saw his chest rise as he took a deep breath. He paused. Something flashed in his eyes, a sudden realisation perhaps, and his face collapsed in panic. His frightened eyes darted about. His deep breath was trapped in his tense shoulders. His arms hung stiffly by his sides, but his fingers twitched wildly.

The music was still playing, but I could no longer hear it. Jun Fujita was not moving.

People looked around. I saw Mrs Hotta's knuckles whiten as she realised Jun was on the verge of crying. The principal paused, and read out Jun's name again. 'Move, Jun, move!' I heard myself yelling inside my head. 'Go and get your damn certificate!' My eyes were now wells of moisture. The bridge of my nose felt as though it were on fire.

Jun stood stone still. His eyes shone with terror and confusion. It had just dawned on him that his life was about to change dramatically. He had spent the last three years in happy, familiar surroundings. He had made friends. He had spent his lunch-times playing table tennis. He had decorated the waka-ayu classroom with pictures of Pikachu and other *Pokémon* creatures. He knew all his teachers by name and they were always kind to him. He felt at home at Kanan Junior High School, yet he was now being forced to leave.

Jun would not continue on to a normal high school with his classmates. Instead, he had been enrolled in the local special-needs school. His lunch-time table tennis friends would not be joining him. He would no longer have the freedom to decorate the walls of his classroom with pictures of cartoon animals. His exposure to normal schooling was at an end.

His chest rose and fell as he took another deep breath. He stood rocking on his feet for a few seconds and I wondered if he was going to sit down, or perhaps turn and run away. The shy boy with curious eyes, who had hidden behind a pot plant when he met me, now had eight hundred people looking at him.

The principal called Jun's name a third time. Somewhere in the deep recesses of Jun's mind these two words struck a chord. His face relaxed, and his eyes again focused on the stage. He rocked back on his heels, and with a look of great pride he called out 'Hai!' in the loudest, clearest voice I had ever heard him utter. This single word reverberated around the school gymnasium, and I burst into tears.

Jun walked to the front of the assembly hall and steadily climbed the steps to the stage. He smiled as he accepted his certificate and bowed politely. His face, which only moments earlier had seemed lost and bewildered, was now lit up by his wide grin. Jun turned and waved at the crowd. A small murmur went up.

Jun walked proudly back to his seat and flashed a smile at the teachers as he passed our bench. A lone tear had rolled down his face.

A few minutes later the ceremony was at an end. I filed out of the gymnasium feeling dazed and emotionally spent. Groups of students were standing with their parents in the bright sunshine, taking photos and talking excitedly. Several approached me, and before I knew it I was part of family pictures. Nobu and the cool boys gathered me up for a series of hip-hop photos. Asuka and pretty girls lined me up for 'V for Victory' shots.

Suddenly, I felt a timid tap on my shoulder. Jun was standing next to me, looking up shyly. 'Mr Hamish, this is my mother.' He beamed.

I smiled and shook her hand. 'Thank you for teaching my son,' she said. 'He always enjoys your classes and tells me all about them.'

Jun blushed and giggled. I laughed as well and gave Jun a clap on the shoulder. We shook hands and Mrs Fujita took our photos.

'He's one of the best students in the school,' I said, and added in a confidential whisper, 'The waka-ayu is my favourite class.' Mrs Fujita smiled and Jun's chest puffed up with pride.

I saw Jun only one more time. Nearly a year after he graduated, he dropped into the Junior High School on his way home from special school. He had grown considerably taller and was slightly fatter. He still had his hair clipped short and his shy, curious eyes were still as bright and cheerful as I remembered them.

He had brought me a present. He had won a table tennis tournament at his school and had been awarded a T-shirt as a prize. Alas, the person who had chosen the T-shirt must have done so under the influence of a mind-altering substance: the T-shirt was at least five sizes too big. Jun had decided it was best suited to the biggest person he knew, namely me. I was deeply moved and gave him one of my Japanese Spice Girls' collector cards in return.

Jun thanked me for all the happy memories from his young minnows' class and shook my hand. I escorted him back to the locker bay where we had first met, and tried not to chuckle as he hopped around on one foot putting on his shoes.

He bowed politely and walked out of the school.

I had not seen Mr Tokunaga and my friends from the Board of Education for some time and decided to give them a call. Sadly, it was midday and everyone was either at a meeting or out on business. The office ladies promised they would let Mr Tokunaga know that I had phoned.

The Japanese do not often indulge in pointless social chats over the telephone, so I should not have been surprised by Mr Tokunaga's frantic call twenty minutes later, desperately wondering what was wrong. When I said I was simply wondering how he and the rest of the Board of Education were, and if they were keen to go out for a pint of beer and an octopus tentacle, he hummed and coughed. At length, however, he agreed that a catch-up drink was overdue, and agreed to talk to the others.

I returned home early from work, and began setting up a computer desk I had just purchased. The phone rang. It was Mrs Oki; she wanted to know if I could go to her house for dinner the next Saturday. When I said I had other plans, the phone call was cut off mid-sentence in typical Oki fashion.

I had just managed to correctly install the sliding drawers into the desk, when the phone rang again. This time it was Mr Tokunaga. He asked if he could come round and see me at once. 'Sure,' I said, secretly worried as to what could be so important.

He turned up fifteen minutes later, carrying two huge shopping bags full of food. Fresh vegetables, steak and an assortment of expensive condiments that I could never afford for myself were hastily unpacked on to my kitchen bench. Mr Tokunaga then asked if it would be all right for him to eat dinner with me. He apologised profusely for not having paid me enough attention lately: the cold winter months must have been a lonely and difficult time for me.

I tried to assure him that nothing could be further from the truth. Undeterred, he shrugged and apologised again. He assured me that he would take better care of me this year, bowed, and proceeded to wash and prepare the vegetables.

Mr Tokunaga had spent an obscene amount of money: there was enough food for five meals. While he whipped up a gigantic stir-fry of chicken, carrots, onions, green peppers, cabbage, rice, and large, expensive shiitake mushrooms, I was in charge of frying two massive steaks. Our vast meal was accompanied by beer and orange juice. Meanwhile, I tried to make a point of talking about all the adventures I had been having and the numbers of friends I had made in an attempt to assure Mr Tokunaga that I was not lonely or suicidal.

At the end of the evening, Mr Tokunaga apologised again, sadly informing me that all the other members of the Board of Education had plans for the coming weekend. He wondered, however, if I would be interested in a camping trip in his recently repaired campervan. I accepted and he coughed happily. The date was set for the coming Saturday, the first day of the spring. I was not to worry about a thing: he would plan and prepare everything.

Saturday morning dawned and Mr Tokunaga arrived at my apartment fifteen minutes early. He had decided to take me camping in the mountainous back country of Okayama Prefecture, five hours' drive northwest of Osaka. As chance would have it I had come across a tourism brochure for Okayama the previous week, been captivated by the picturesque valleys and crisp mountain rivers, and had put the place on my 'must visit' list.

Mr Tokunaga had also decided to invite a woman to come with us. Kimi Kuriyama worked in the town publications section at the town hall. She spoke good English, and had helped me translate tax statements, medical receipts, insurance forms and other baffling documents.

I had also worked closely with her on my monthly article for the town magazine. These articles, usually only half a page in length, were accompanied by a photo of me out and about in Kanan Town. They got my name and face into the home of every person in Kanan Town, and I would often receive a wave in the street, a handshake in the supermarket, or a friendly comment from an elderly passer-by. Kimi's assistance in translating the articles into correct, colloquial and humorous Japanese had contributed greatly to my acceptance in Kanan Town.

Kimi was, however, yet to venture into the great outdoors and try her hand at camping. Mr Tokunaga had been aghast when he heard this, and had demanded that Kimi accompany us so she could experience the true meaning of life by spending a night in a tent.

Kimi was sitting excitedly in the passenger seat of Mr Tokunaga's campervan, scouring maps and camping brochures, and planning the day's schedule in meticulous detail. I sat in the back seat, and as Mr Tokunaga navigated the rats' nest of Osakan streets I soon dozed off. I woke up as we entered Okayama Prefecture, and was amazed at the change in scenery. On my right, an emerald river flowed slowly. An old man sat patiently fishing in a wooden canoe, his head shielded from the sun by a rice-paddy hat. On the left, a steep mountain towered over us, clad in dense bush. Everything seemed magically untouched, unlike the manmade forests that clung to the hillsides of south Osaka in perfectly straight lines, or the ubiquitous concrete-lined rivers.

We continued driving for another hour, before stopping at an all-you-can-eat barbecue lamb restaurant for lunch. Mr Tokunaga had read about this restaurant, and had a made a detour to get there so I could eat food that would remind me of home. Touched by this, I decided to take full advantage of Mr Tokunaga's kindness and ate several large helpings of lamb chops.

I was feeling on top of the world. The next stop of the day was a refreshing dip in a hot spring. I was fast becoming a fan of Japanese communal baths and hot springs. My own bathtub was pitifully small and I had long ago given up trying to use it. Unfortunately, though, my shower had also been designed for someone half my height, and I needed to bend in half in order to wash my hair. During the midst of the evil winter, I had often ventured out to the local bathhouse in search of a piping hot tub in which I could simmer and unwind without needing to chop my legs off.

A Japanese public bath is, for most Westerners, initially an embarrassing ordeal. Men and women are segregated into separate bath areas.

The bather then strips completely naked, and using the showers provided scours and washes their body until it is red, raw and sparkling clean. This ritual is painstakingly observed, and to enter a public bath without bathing first is an unpardonable crime, as no chlorine or other chemicals are added to kill germs.

I would often observe rows of men sitting on the small plastic stools, furiously soaping and scrubbing their bodies, lathering their heads in shampoo, shaving and clipping their toenails in preparation for their bath. Some men even bathed in pairs, helping to scrub each other's backs.

I would sit by myself on a stool in the corner and shower timidly, while trying to hide my private parts from any onlookers. I would then march briskly to the nearest bath, nonchalantly covering these same private parts with a face cloth, and slither in. With no bubble-jets to disguise nakedness, shyness and self-consciousness needed to be rapidly overcome.

My inaugural trip to a Japanese bathhouse took place shortly after I arrived in Japan. My English assistant, Mrs Isoi, had suggested that I visit a public bath with her and her family. After we arrived, she and her daughter had disappeared off to the women's area, leaving me with Mr Isoi and their eight-year-old son, Ryohei.

The three of us had shuffled off to the men's changing area, where I had reluctantly shed my clothes. Young Ryohei had been introduced to me for the first time earlier that day; before this, he had never encountered a Western male. I did my best to hide in the corner and cover myself up with a handkerchief-sized face cloth, but Ryohei stared at me fixedly.

I could feel my face burning with embarrassment, and tried hiding further away in another part of the changing area, praying that my face was the only part of my anatomy that had turned beetroot red. Meanwhile, Ryohei continued to stare, and even craned his neck to get a better view.

Mr Isoi was taking an eternity getting undressed, and I was beginning to lose patience with his voyeuristic son. Finally though, Mr Isoi slowly removed his last sock, folded it carefully into thirds, and placed it tidily inside his shoe. His perfectly stacked pile of clothes was then delicately placed in a locker, and a rogue sock that had fallen on to the floor during the process was slowly and carefully refolded.

Mr Isoi pointed to a closed door ahead of me. 'The bath is through there. Please, go first.' I raced to the door, keen to get away from Ryohei and his inquiring gaze. I flung open the door and froze in shock. A young woman of about my age stood fully clothed in front of me.

My face cloth was clasped tightly in the hand that was clutching the door knob. I was completely exposed. 'Where the hell am I?' I cried inwardly, terrified that I had inadvertently wandered into the women's changing area.

The young woman did not even blink. 'Welcome to the Sakai bath-house,' she trilled. 'Would you like a face cloth?' I had just met the bath attendant.

I spent an uncomfortable half-hour in the bath. Ryohei continued to stare at me, and I was completely unable to understand the reason for a fully clothed twenty-one-year-old female to be present.

This incident did not put me off public bathing forever, and as it turned this was the one and only time I ever encountered a woman inside the men's area of a bathhouse. After several trips to the local Tondabayashi bathhouse during winter, I started to become used to being naked in a pool full of equally naked men, and discovered that a warm hot bath in the middle of the icy winter months was extremely therapeutic.

And so Mr Tokunaga's suggestion that we spend the afternoon in the Okayama mountain spa was very welcome. Once we had soaked in the bath, dressed again, and Kimi had finished drying her hair, we proceeded to the camp ground. It was beautiful, and much more spacious than I had imagined. There were no vending machines, no power lines and not a hint of concrete. For a few moments, I forgot that I was in Japan.

It was already late in the afternoon, and Mr Tokunaga was eager for us to start preparing for dinner. He proudly produced his gas barbecue from the back of the campervan, but within minutes we discovered that the gas bottle was empty. We quickly took stock of the situation. An array of food needed to be cooked: Mr Tokunaga had spent up large on beef steaks, lamp chops, sausages, potatoes and an assortment of green vege-tables. The nearest shop that might sell a gas bottle was at least an hour's drive away.

'I'll build a fire!' I announced heroically, and raced off into the undergrowth. Kimi was terrified. 'Mr Hamish,' she called after me, 'be careful! You might get lost! Don't fall and hurt yourself!'

I emerged unscathed, carrying a heavy log. 'There's lot of good wood in there,' I declared. Mr Tokunaga smiled, but Kimi was still worried. 'Oh, that wood looks sharp! Don't cut your hands!'

I spent the next twenty minutes scouting out suitable-looking wood. Mr Tokunaga stacked the logs, and triumphantly returned from the campervan with a tube of lighter fluid. This terrified Kimi even further: she seemed convinced that Mr Tokunaga and I would ignite a large forest fire.

Mr Tokunaga distracted her by handing her the bag of potatoes and requesting that they be washed, peeled and sliced finely. She set to at once. Meanwhile, Mr Tokunaga and I erected the two tents and got the fire going.

Kimi surveyed her tent nervously, unsure if it would protect her from the elements, or marauding farm animals. She then swept both tent floors and scrubbed down all the foam mattresses in case they were covered in dust. The camp fire was now roaring happily and Kimi insisted she also cook the entire evening meal. After enjoying our second hearty barbecue of the day, we sat back and enjoyed the warmth from the fire, before turning in.

It was pitch-black, and the sudden lack of light was disorienting. I slept little, but Mr Tokunaga dozed off almost instantly and snored like a bulldozer until dawn. The next morning Kimi was up early. By the time Mr Tokunaga and I had put the tents down, she had served breakfast, swept the camp site, packed all her belongings into the campervan, and washed and polished Mr Tokunaga's frying pans and cooking pots until they gleamed.

Mr Tokunaga was a great boss. As well as showing me around town, escorting me to festivals, arranging pub outings and taking me camping, he turned a blind eye when, for the next three weeks, I disappeared without explanation. It was the spring holidays and I travelled round

Thailand, Cambodia and the Philippines with my foreign English teacher friends without using up any of my precious annual leave. But my luck was about to change.

I returned home in mid April from my secret holiday with the cunningly formulated cover story that I had been at the public library for three weeks diligently studying Japanese. Hopefully nobody would notice my newly acquired sun tan, or test me on my 'vastly improved' knowledge of Japanese.

On the first day of the new school year, I cycled off to work early, intending to drop in and say hello to my friends at the Board of Education on the way. At the town hall I bounded up the stairs to the third floor and strode towards Mr Tokunaga's desk.

It seemed remarkably different. A chubby, nervous-looking man was sitting in the chair. What was going on?

'Ah, there you are,' Magnum chimed. 'We've been looking for you everywhere. Where've you been?'

'At the library,' I replied timidly.

'Ah, really? Hmm. There is some big news. Have you heard?'

I shook my head, suddenly feeling worried.

Magnum frowned, and his moustache drooped. 'Aah, you have a new boss. Mr Tokunaga is gone. We had a farewell party last night. We tried to call you, but you weren't there. You have a new boss.'

He pointed at the chubby man. 'This is Mr Horrii.'

Every year during the spring holidays, the Japanese government decides to stick its oar into things by transferring civil servants to new postings, sometimes in completely different institutions. I felt guilty. While I had been trekking around Angkor Wat and swimming in tropical seas, Mr Tokunaga had been packing up his belongings and moving to a new position as vice principal of an elementary school in Tondabayashi.

Just like that, my life in Japan had changed. I did not realise it yet, but more unpleasant changes were in store.

# 9

# Magnificent Mr Doi

*I arrived at the school fashionably late* as always, locked my bike in the rack and hurried into assembly. The students seemed to have shrunk. The lanky third-graders from the previous year were nowhere to be found. Jun Fujita was now across town in his special-needs school. Hiroshi Yamaguchi was in Dunedin. I imagined him sitting in a drafty house, eating pies and feeling far from home as he was now unable to watch porn with his father.

One hundred and fifty-three new students had entered the first grade. They were short, scrawny and oily-faced. Oversized school blazers hung limply on their skinny bodies, and sleeves and trousers legs seemed three sizes too long.

Stern teachers patrolled the grounds, barking orders and yelling at any student not standing perfectly in line. After a formal welcome from the principal, the assembly came to a close, and I sauntered slowly to the staff-room, where a meeting had been called to welcome newly transferred staff. The meeting was short and to the point. The new teachers stood and introduced themselves. They then bowed, and promised they would do their best to be good teachers and hoped that we would all think fondly of them. The lukewarm reception I had received on my first day was recreated. The new teachers received blank stares, a few frowns and a couple of scowls.

There was a new English teacher. Ms Domae, the nervous young woman who had helped me prepare my welcome speech at last year's summer assembly, was gone. Her desk was now being occupied by Mr Hioki. Mr Hioki was in his early forties. He wore a grey tracksuit and had a bowl-shaped haircut.

There was a new minder in the young minnows' class. Mrs Hotta was gone; her role was to be filled by one of the former PE teachers.

There was a new PE teacher, Mr Tanaka, who looked like a fairly cool dude. He had a fashionable haircut and trendy horn-rimmed glasses.

There was a new maths teacher, Mr Shimizu. He had a crew cut, and eyebrows like Bert from *Sesame Street*.

And lastly there was a new woodwork teacher. Mr Doi was middle-aged, and wore a checked flannel shirt with the collar turned up, and enough buttons undone to display the neckline of his crisp white T-shirt. The cellphone in his shirt pocket was ingeniously secured by a bright orange, stretchy plastic cord.

Mr Doi exuded self-confidence. He strutted about the staffroom, keenly talking about himself and promoting his own magnificence. The other teachers tolerated his booming voice, hoarse laugh and loud cellphone jingles. They did not, however, appear to enjoy talking to him, and whenever he appeared they would leave the room or suddenly need to make an urgent phone call.

Less skillful at these avoidance tactics, I soon became easy prey for Mr Doi. 'Excuse me,' he boomed, towering over my desk. 'I speak English. I think I will speak English with you.'

'Ah, hello,' I replied. 'My name is Hamish.'

'Hem? Heim?' he stammered. Arms tightly folded, he eyed me suspiciously. 'I do not know that name.'

'My nickname here is Hame.'

'Hame? Where did you come from?'

'New Zealand.'

His eyes narrowed further. 'So you are not American?'

'No.'

'Hmm.' A frown creased his forehead. 'You are not from England?'

'No.'

'Hmm. I do not know New Zealand. Do you speak good English there?'

'Yes, we speak the Queen's English.'

Mr Doi's frown deepened: he did not appear to understand that particular term.

'So, not American?'

'No, I am from New Zealand.'

Mr Doi seemed disappointed. 'Can you speak Japanese? I think you find it difficult to live here.'

'I can speak Japanese a little,' I replied curtly. I was not keen to make conversation time with Mr Doi a regular event.

'Hmm. I think I speak English better than your Japanese. Ha ha. I live in Wakayama. Have you been there?'

I nodded and Mr Doi rattled on. 'I am new at this school. I would like to learn English. I think you can teach me. I think you are a great man. But I think you find it difficult to live here. Do you have a car?'

I shook my head. 'No, I don't need a car. I can take the–'

Mr Doi was not listening. 'Why don't you have a car? Can't you drive?'

His arms were even more tightly folded now. My reputation as a great man was suddenly in jeopardy.

'Yes, I can drive but I don't need a car in Japan. I have a bicycle.'

Mr Doi laughed. 'Bicycle. Ha ha ha. Do you know that I was once a racing-car driver? I can drive very fast.'

I shook my head and looked for an escape route.

Mr Doi's phone beeped and his chest vibrated. The conversation was thankfully at an end.

I was now on my own with the waka-ayu team. The absence of Jun, Fumio and Mrs Hotta was a real loss. Hiro seemed sad and lonely. There were no more random outbursts of laughter or croaky sniggers. Instead he sat quietly, his head down.

Yurika, meanwhile, had spent the holidays studying, and had been promoted back into the mainstream English class. She was, however, skipping one science period a week in order to continue to attend special English with Mr Hamish. She sat eagerly to attention next to Hiro, and had her hand up and all questions answered well before I could finish asking them.

Then there was Teru-Chan. Teru-Chan had started the new year vowing to attend school each day and take part in class. Sadly, though, this amounted to nothing more than lolling in her seat, looking scared, homicidal and confused—all at the same time.

Mrs Hotta had been replaced by Mr Omura, one of the PE teachers, but unfortunately he was busy during first period on Fridays and unable to attend my class. He did, however, seem to have a good rapport with Teru-Chan, and I often saw him joking with her in the corridors and even making her smile. I prayed his comedic routines would continue to find favour, as they were possibly all that was keeping Teru-Chan from killing someone with the paper scissors.

Apart from Yurika, the young minnows seemed to have forgotten everything we had done in the previous year. Hiro, for example, had forgotten all the English numbers and couldn't even count to ten. He had started learning them two years earlier.

I was both annoyed and happy about the collective amnesia—annoyed because I had wasted my time, but happy because I would be able to re-use the class plans from the previous year without anyone noticing.

I spent no time preparing for the following Friday's class. Hiro's lack of enthusiasm, Teru-Chan's scariness and Yurika's irritating chirpiness had knocked my fondness for the team. *Snakes and Ladders* sat in my top drawer, ready to be taken out and played for the umpteenth time. The bell for first period chimed and I mentally prepared myself for a mind-numbing hour.

'Mr Hame, I think you have young minnows' class now.' Mr Doi was standing next to my desk, arms folded. 'I will come to class with you. I want to see your lesson. I think we should make English club. We can have English conversation for one hour.'

I shuddered inwardly. 'Sure, Mr Doi. What would you like to talk about?'

'Hmm, what do you usually talk to the students about—current affairs maybe?'

I struggled not to laugh out loud. 'That might be a little difficult, but let's try.' I gave Mr Doi a jolly thumbs-up and the cheesiest grin I could manage. I ferreted through my drawers and pulled out page one of the previous year's ambitious English passport project. 'Let's go,' I announced cheerfully.

Without Jun's spirit and Mrs Hotta's calm influence, the class fell flat within seconds. Hiro struggled to remember the alphabet and needed assistance writing the letter Z. Teru-Chan struggled to say her own name, and left her passport page untouched. I won three games of *Snakes and Ladders* in a row.

Mr Doi sat sullenly at the back of the class, conversation about the Japanese economy and New Zealand weather patterns temporarily on hold. His attempt at getting English lessons on the sly was not going to wash with me.

The following week's class was even worse. Mr Doi's attendance forced me to attempt to teach something in order not to appear lazy, so I took along worksheets that involved colouring in cartoon faces and learning the words for ear, mouth, nose, hair, head and face.

Jun and Hiro had ripped through these the previous year, with Jun clapping and giggling and covering his eyes in glee. This merry atmosphere was, sadly, not to be recreated. Before we even started, Teru-Chan refused to pay any attention, and stared at the ceiling. This made Yurika upset; she tugged on Teru-Chan's arm. Teru-Chan picked up a handful of felt-tip pens and spent several minutes colouring in her pencil case. Yurika started crying. Hiro, meanwhile, sat quietly, head bowed, unsure what to make of his female classmates.

I gave up on the worksheet and pulled out the *Snakes and Ladders* board. Hiro, Yurika and I played a subdued game for forty minutes until the bell rang. Teru-Chan stared at the ceiling and refused to take part.

As I was leaving the class, Mr Doi strutted over coolly. 'I think the students' level is very low,' he observed wisely.

'They're a little quiet at the moment,' I admitted. 'Last year they were a lot more energetic.'

'You have a different accent to American people. I am not sure if your English is as good as American people.' And with that Mr Doi strode off to the staffroom, leaving me fuming and grinding my teeth with rage.

The young minnows' class may have been exasperating, but it was nothing compared to what lay in store for me with the new English teacher and the first-grade students. Mr Hioki got our professional relationship off to a flying start by making me sing the ABC song to the class, solo, forty-eight times in four days.

Not content with inflicting this ritual humiliation, he insisted that I make a tape recording of myself singing the song so he could play it to the students when I wasn't around. The students therefore spent their first fortnight of English education doing nothing but singing the ABC song. Mr Hioki scolded them when they didn't sing loud enough, and gave several boys detention for not getting into the spirit of things.

The following fortnight was even more tedious. Mr Hioki decided the children now needed to have the greeting 'How are you? I'm fine' drilled into them if they were to succeed in life.

His lesson plan went as follows:

I stood at the front and asked myself, 'How are you?'

I paused, and then answered my own question by saying, 'I'm fine.'

The students were then instructed to repeat these two sentences three times.

This monologue, which made me look like an insane person, was repeated at least twenty times during the hour-long class.

Mr Hioki seemed oblivious to any suggestions for changes or additions to his lesson plan. At one stage, however, a small miracle occurred: he agreed that I could play a word game with the students during the final ten minutes of class. This window of freedom closed when, only moments into the game, a boy spoke out of turn and we were all forced to sing the ABC song as punishment until the bell rang.

After a fortnight Mr Hioki decided to take the novel approach of involving his students in the lesson plan. 'I will choose one of you at random,' he announced, 'and ask you an English question, to which I expect a response.'

'This,' he declared, 'is what it would be like if you lived in a foreign country.'

Mr Hioki surveyed the pale faces and pointed at a sleepy-looking boy. 'How are you?' he demanded.

The boy looked confused.

'HOW ARE YOU?' Mr Hioki thundered.

The boy sat completely still and looked straight ahead.

'HOW... ARE ... YOU?' Mr Hioki's face was now an angry red.

The boy looked at his desk and bit his tongue.

An awkward silence descended. The boy burst into tears. He continued to cry for the ensuing thirty minutes until the bell rang.

I took refuge from my increasingly soul-destroying job by packing my weeknights and weekends with activities. Mr Tokunaga and I caught up regularly for drinks and dinner at the local Korean barbecue restaurant. He was finding his new job difficult and stressful, and was spending more and more time at the office.

I visited the Okis at least once a month, and we would usually dine at fancy sushi restaurants. Mrs Oki remarked on my choice of clothing and wondered if I was hot, what classes I taught, and how my mother was.

Hiroshi Yamaguchi's departure to New Zealand had brought an end to my Wednesday visits to the porn family home, and I never saw Aki again. I did, however, make contact with several other families in Kanan Town and was occasionally invited around for midweek dinners or cups of tea.

I chatted with my neighbours on the way home from work each day. Fu-Chan had started school and was keen to show me the books she was reading. Old Mrs Okuda continued to ask if I were living alone, and was overjoyed and impressed to find out I was. Young Mrs Okuda continued to provide me with seasonal vegetables and fruit and to remark on the contents of my grocery bags.

I spent a lot of time on my bicycle as well. The warm spring days were perfect for long bike rides, and I would often meet up with my friend Justin and go cycling in the rice paddies and mountains. In the weekends my friends and I visited numerous inner-city bars where we had become regulars, even having our photos on the wall. I had become accustomed to Japanese alcohol and had developed an appreciation and love of warm sake. However, I was still unable to touch chuhai.

米

Mrs Terauchi was the spokeswoman for a group of elderly Japanese women who called themselves my Japanese mothers. She had appeared at my desk in the staffroom one day in late April, sweeping past Mr Kazama, who was attempting to greet her politely, and jabbered at me in quick-fire Japanese.

'Oh sensei,' she exclaimed, referring to me as 'teacher' in Japanese, 'I'm so glad to finally meet you.'

I blinked in surprise. I had absolutely no idea who this crazy-looking woman might be. I suspected she might be the representative of a religious cult.

'My name is Hiroko Terauchi,' she continued. 'I represent a group of local ladies. We have read about you in the Kanan Town magazine. We enjoy your articles very much. We wish to learn English, and would like to invite you to one of our homes for dinner. Would you be kind enough to visit us this Thursday afternoon, sensei? I will pick you up.'

Dumbfounded, I simply nodded.

Mrs Terauchi laughed. 'Oh, thank you, sensei, thank you. We are most happy. Oh, thank you so much.' She clapped her hands together and smiled at me. 'I will meet you after your school finishes on Thursday.'

The following Thursday at 4.15 sharp Mrs Terauchi materialised at my desk and insisted we depart immediately. 'My group of ladies will be waiting. Please, sensei, we must go.'

A few moments of confusion followed. I tried to get Mrs Terauchi to wait while I shifted my bicycle out of the bike racks, as these were locked at six o'clock each night. I tried to explain that I would need to cycle home after dinner.

Mrs Terauchi beamed and chuckled and thanked me for agreeing to have dinner with her friends. 'We must leave now, sensei, they are waiting.'

'But what about my bike?' I repeated. 'I need to bring it.'

'You can ride your bike to Mrs Kiguchi's house. That is where we will have dinner. It is not far. I will drive my car. You follow me, sensei.'

With that she hopped in her car and sped off. I was hard-pressed to keep up with her. She drove badly, speeding up during up-hill stretches—which constituted most of the journey—causing numerous near misses at intersections, and getting tooted at by pretty much everyone. Each time I caught up with her, she slammed on the brakes so I nearly crashed into the back of her car.

Eventually we started to go downhill and Mrs Terauchi now chose to drive like a snail. My brakes screeched constantly as I tried to avoid her rear bumper. It wasn't until we arrived at our destination twenty-five minutes later that I realised she had taken me in a complete circle. We were now only four minutes away from the school.

We had arrived at a large beautiful wooden Japanese home, set within a stunning traditional garden. Big flat stones formed an enchanting path through an emerald-green carpet of moss. Tall stone lanterns stood among carefully tended bonsai trees, and flowers in dazzling colours grew in clumps next to rows of tomato plants. Beyond the house were fields of newly planted rice paddies, and in the distance towered the misty Kanan mountain range.

It was the most picturesque Japanese house I had ever seen.

Mrs Terauchi's friends were waiting eagerly inside. I could hear them chattering behind a thinly veiled window, and as I walked up to the door there was a patter of racing feet. The vast front door opened, and four smiling faces greeted me.

'My friends, sensei is here. Let's give him some dinner.' Mrs Terauchi clapped her hands and the four faces erupted in high-pitched laughter.

'Welcome sensei, welcome,' they chorused. 'Please enter.'

I removed my shoes and stepped into the magnificent home. As I tried to take in the interior, I was bustled through to the dining room by Mrs Terauchi.

The women had taken their places at the dinner table. 'Time for introductions,' announced Mrs Terauchi. 'This is our host, Mrs Kiguchi. She has a lovely home, don't you think?' I agreed enthusiastically and everyone clapped and laughed.

Mrs Kiguchi stood and shook my hand. She had a noble way of carrying herself, and a friendly twinkle in her eye. 'I cannot speak English. I am so sorry,' she said in Japanese, bowing her head. I smiled, and said that I was so happy to visit such a lovely home.

Mrs Kiguchi laughed loudly and quickly covered her mouth. 'My home is not so nice,' she said modestly. 'Thank you for coming.'

Mrs Tanaka, Mrs Tsubota and Mrs Matsui all spoke English with varying levels of ability. No one, however, was as outspoken as Mrs Terauchi, and it was no wonder that she had become the group's spokesperson.

Mrs Kiguchi quietly whispered to Mrs Terauchi, who nodded along happily. 'Yes, yes, I think so too,' she said.

'Sensei, you look hungry,' she said, turning to me. 'It is time for us to have dinner. I hope you like Japanese food. We have prepared you a welcome feast.'

Dishes started arriving from the kitchen. A large plate of steamed vegetables. Another piled high with okonomiayaki pancakes. A bowl of beef stew. A bowl of garden salad. A bowl of potato salad. A plate of tempura vegetables. A platter of sushi and an assortment of raw fish.

My eyes bulged, my stomach rumbled.

Mrs Kiguchi sat on my right, eager to serve me beer, orange juice or sake. Mrs Tanaka and Mrs Matsui filled my plate with food, and everyone sat back and waited for me to take the first bite.

I thanked them all again for having gone to such trouble, and bit into a large piece of tempura pumpkin. It was delicious, and I indicated as much to my host. Everyone clapped and Mrs Kiguchi laughed. I noticed she had a habit of nodding her head and covering her mouth when she laughed.

This first dinner with the group was a tremendously happy occasion. I managed to polish off three large okonomiayaki pancakes, and several platefuls of beef stew, sushi, vegetables and salad. We chattered until late in the evening, and I did not even notice that it had grown dark outside.

Mrs Terauchi, meanwhile, had become slightly tipsy. She had, she informed me, lived in England for seven years after graduating from college. She then announced to the women that Christchurch was the capital of New Zealand and also the biggest city, the country had a population of six million people and the inhabitants were all Scottish.

At the end of the dinner, Mrs Kiguchi shyly approached me and asked in Japanese if I would agree to return to her home every second Monday afternoon for English conversation with her and her friends. I keenly accepted.

Everyone clapped and Mrs Tsubota shook my hand. 'We are your Japanese mothers,' she said. 'We want to cook you nice food, and help you in your life in Japan. We will take care of you if you ever have any problems. We are happy to have met you.'

And so my fortnightly meetings with my Japanese mothers began. Filled with laughter, gossip and food, they soon became one of my highlights. The mothers would complain about their husbands and their in-laws, wonder what New Zealand women were like, and continually ask if I had any plans for marriage. At the end of the evening, Mrs Kiguchi would pass me an envelope filled with 10,000 yen. The mothers would then refuse to accept my polite attempt to turn down the money. On one occasion when I had steadfastly refused to take their envelope, Mrs Terauchi quietly slipped it into my backpack when I wasn't looking.

As I was leaving, Mrs Kiguchi would race off to the kitchen and return with a bag of chocolate or fruit, insisting I take them home for a snack. The elderly women would then kneel delicately on the front porch and wave goodbye as I wheeled my bike down Mrs Kiguchi's carefully manicured driveway.

In time Mrs Terauchi started to become a bit of a handful. It seemed she was attempting to upstage me to protect her role as group leader. At random moments she would pipe up and inform us all of her knowledge of the outside world.

'New Zealanders love to eat entire pigs, including their brains, and do so quite regularly,' she once told us.

I assured everyone that I had never eaten a pig's brain.

'Well, Koreans eat dogs,' she countered. 'You can buy dead dogs in Korean marketplaces.'

I admitted that this was possibly true in some areas of Korea. Mrs Terauchi smiled. Her point had been made.

During my next visit she announced that most of Europe had sunk to third-world levels because all the buildings were old, the pipes were dirty, and everyone was drinking grubby water. Also, Westerners didn't use sugar when cooking, and had a dark and heavy culture.

She frequently brought up hardships that she had experienced during World War II, and once told us that, because of a complete lack of food throughout the entire country, she had been forced to eat grass for several months.

Mrs Kiguchi raised her eyebrows. She herself had been able to eat very well during the war, she said sternly, looking at Mrs Terauchi. 'Did you live in a cave?'

Everyone laughed. Mrs Terauchi was, for once, lost for words.

# 10

# Under the weather

*Japanese doctors are renowned* for two things, prescribing swags of antibiotics for even the most mild sniffly nose and skirting around some of the more difficult illnesses, such as cancer, by deciding it would not be in the patient's best interest for them to be informed of their true condition. Thus it was novel that when the school principal, Mr Kazama, was diagnosed with cancer at the start of the year, his doctors had informed him of this and prescribed life-saving treatment.

Mr Kazama had fortunately bounced back very quickly, and as soon as he arrived back at school in April he sent a newsletter to the entire school community, saying how thankful he was that his doctor had decided to tell him he had cancer as this had allowed him to seek the necessary treatment and get better. He prayed that the Japanese medical system would move towards a more enlightened era, in which all cancer patients would be informed of their illness, instead of it being swept under the carpet as was common practice.

Mr Kazama was interested in how New Zealand doctors would deal with patients suffering from illnesses such as cancer or HIV/AIDS. I assured him they would inform the patient immediately. He nodded sadly. Japanese doctors, he explained, believed it was not in their patients' best interest to fret about serious illnesses, and a patient would make a speedier recovery if they thought they had a simple flu or head cold. The real reason, he confided, was that the doctors did not have the courage to be the bearers of bad news and inform someone they were going to die.

Needless to say, all this instilled in me a severe mistrust of the Japanese medical system. I prayed I would not fall ill, and had a recurrent nightmare of breaking a limb that would then be left to heal incorrectly with the support of a couple of Hello Kitty Band-Aids. I drank miso soup every day, ate fruit and vegetables regularly, and had extra helpings at meals if I started to feel run down.

In July, as I approached my one-year anniversary in Japan, my luck finally ran out and I came down with a head cold that sucked every ounce of energy from my body. After I had spent all weekend in bed, Monday dawned and I summoned all my strength to get to school. Normally, I would have taken the day off and watched sumo wrestling on television, but my illness coincided with the one week of the year that required my attendance. My new supervisor, Mr Horrii, and I were to spend Monday and Tuesday touring Kanan Town's five elementary schools attempting to promote English-language learning with the town's tiniest students. The visits had been painstakingly scheduled by the Board of Education, and a last-minute cancellation would cause Mr Horrii to lose an incredible amount of face with the school principals.

After a few dizzy spells in various classrooms, I noticed that my head cold had shifted to my throat. My glands were swelling up like golf balls, and eating, drinking and even swallowing were causing my whole body to convulse in pain. Doing my best to ignore my deteriorating condition, I threw my flagging energy into introductory lessons and games of 'fruit basket'. I met some 'super-handicapped' children who, Mr Horrii informed me, would be too handicapped to graduate to junior high school and would instead proceed to a special-needs school across town. One girl with a bushy monobrow started sniffing my jeans and then barked at me. I jumped in surprise, but no one else batted an eyelid. Another girl foamed at the mouth during class and then began to crow. Again, she was studiously ignored.

On Wednesday, the day after the elementary school visits, I woke up blind: during the night my eyes had oozed and crusted over. My entire body ached and I felt faint. Stupidly, I cycled off to school, and spent a dire day full of first-grade classes in rooms with no air-conditioning.

On Thursday, I again displayed idiotic disregard for my wellbeing. It was the day of the school swimming sports, and I had promised Mr Higo that I would participate in the students v. teachers relay race. In my fluey state I forgot to pack sunscreen, sun hat or sunglasses and spent the morning by the pool, sweating, convulsing and slowly turning pink. However, my lunch of potato salad, noodles and ice-cream seemed to soothe my throat and I began to feel a little better—so much so that I assessed myself as fit and ready to compete in the swimming race.

Mr Higo, the first-grade PE teacher Mr Nakata, the second-grade PE teacher Mrs Nonaka and I were to take on the third-grade boys' relay team. When my team-mates voted unanimously that I should be the starting member, I grew suddenly nervous. As well as not having performed a racing dive in years, it was possible that during a throat convulsion I would swallow a lungful of water and sink to the bottom of the pool.

The start of race was called. Loud cheers went up when my name was announced and then when our team took our starting positions. My self-doubt vanished as quickly as it had arisen. Most of our opponents were tiny; the tallest came up only to my chest. However, I had been advised that one of them was the fastest swimmer in the school. The previous year's athletics race had taught me never to underestimate any of the students, and I didn't intend to go easy on them.

I waved to the crowd one last time and bent forward to take my mark. Mr Terada raised the starter's gun and pulled the trigger.

Bang! I did a perfect dive into the pool and took off. I hadn't been in a pool in over a year and hadn't participated in a swimming race for several years, but none of this seemed to matter. I cut through the water like a torpedo and made it to the other end without needing to take a breath. I tagged off to Mr Nakata and looked around hastily. The students were still half a pool length behind, and flailing around feebly. I hoisted myself out of the pool and watched as the teachers' team sailed to an easy victory.

On Friday night I went to the local medical clinic, where the resident doctor announced that I had a fever, a cold and a bad throat. I was given a bag of pills and sent home to bed. By Sunday my bag of magic pills was beginning to run out. The next night my nose bled like a fire hose and I had a pounding headache. For the tenth day straight I went to bed early. I woke the next day with a burning throat and one eye swollen shut. When I sneezed the pain was about the worst I'd ever experienced.

Over the next three days my state of health fluctuated alarmingly. There were times when I was feverish and considered getting medical help. These were followed by times when I felt fine and decided I could recover without putting myself through the ordeal of trying to get admitted to a Japanese-speaking hospital. Then at night I would become woozy again, and wake up the next morning aching and gummed up.

I was approaching my third weekend of feeling like hell. A local family, the Tsubois, had kindly invited me to dinner at their home and I did not want to cancel at the last minute. My body, though, had decided to apply the brakes. By the time I got to Tsubois' I could hardly eat, and after managing a few small mouthfuls I excused myself, went home and fell asleep.

I awoke in agony. I called the school and said I would be taking the morning off. I arrived at the medical clinic when it opened at nine and waited in line for an hour. The doctor I had seen only a few days earlier took one look at my throat and announced that I had tonsillitis. I would be transferred to a specialist clinic, where the most likely treatment would be sticking a syringe into my mouth, down my throat and injecting my inflamed tonsils.

The nurses in the specialist clinic did little to alleviate my panic. After they had delivered a few painful pokes and prods and mashed my poor swollen glands with an ice block stick, they hooked me up to an intravenous drip and left me to lie on a hard bed that was too short for me.

After an hour, I was wheeled on my short little bed to a respiratory device and told to inhale a purple gas for several minutes. I had absolutely no idea what this was all about, but after a few puffs I no longer cared. The magic gas eliminated the pain in my throat, and my fevered brow became light and fluffy. I was given a big bag of medicine—twice as big as the one I'd received the previous week—and told to return for another drip session the next day. Within a couple of days, I was on the mend. The swelling in my throat subsided and I was finally able to cope with eating solid food again. My medicinal ice-cream lunch break, however, was strictly maintained for the next few weeks.

Baseball, baseball, baseball—the entire nation of Japan seemed be going loopy over the sport. It was mid July and the national baseball season was in full swing. As well as this, the national high school league was about to kick off, thereby plunging Japan into baseball overload. Baseball was on television, in the newspapers, and was the constant topic of conversation in the staffroom.

I was trying my best to avoid the sport completely, much as I had tried to avoid getting sick for the past year. I kept my head down and attempted to focus on my fast approaching second summer holiday in Japan. Health-wise, I was on the mend and looking forward to making full use of the six-week break.

With only one week of the school term left, my resistance to the baseball bug finally broke down. I decided to go and watch a game with my friends Blake and Justin. None of us had ever been interested in baseball, but rumours of the Hanshin Tigers' rowdy supporters had tweaked our interest, and we were keen to see what fun could be had.

Hanshin, at this time far and away the worst baseball team in Japan, was currently enjoying a seven-match losing streak. The Osaka supporters, however, readily forgave their beloved team's poor performance, and their cheering and loud chants were the pride of the prefecture.

Justin, Blake and I sneakily took the afternoon off work and snuck out of our respective schools in time to beat rush-hour traffic and get to the game for the opening pitch. When we arrived, Hanshin Stadium was nearly full. Most of the spectators were decked from head to foot in the Tigers' grey and yellow team colours, and carrying trumpets, clackers and giant plastic drumsticks, which they banged together to produce a clanging sound.

The crowd was divided into sections. The front of each section was patrolled by stern-faced chant leaders wearing oversized bandanas and proudly flashing the badge of a Japanese official—white satin gloves.

The leaders were taking their roles extremely seriously, shrilly blowing their whistles and conducting the pre-match chants with the precision of police officers directing traffic.

The first ball of the game was pitched to a fanfare of hooting trumpets and clacking drumsticks. The innings then settled into the sluggish, boring pace of any other baseball game on Earth, and we eagerly held our breath for some drunken revelry from the crowd. Perhaps some witty insults or sledging would be fired at the outfield players? Maybe a large inflatable object would be thrown on to the field. Perhaps even a streaker?

We waited...

The first player struck out and walked back to the dugout.

A few trumpets blasted.

We waited...

The next player managed to make a quick dash to first base.

A few plastic clackers sounded.

We waited...

The innings wore on, and we continued to wait expectantly for some drunken silliness to spice up the action.

Nothing.

The innings ended and the fielding team raced off to the dugout. At this point the chant leaders leapt to their feet and blew their whistles. The crowd responded immediately, and thus began one of the most bizarre displays of cheering I have ever seen.

The entire crowd stood and began singing the Hanshin Tiger's team anthem at the top of their lungs, complete with weird hand gestures, vigorous salutes and pretend swings of the bat. They rocked and swayed in perfect unison. At the exact moment the players took the field for the second innings, the singing came to an end.

Each innings was much like the first: tediously slow baseball, punctuated with an occasional trumpet blast or plastic clack. The supporters seemed content to limit their cheering to the breaks, and it was the break at the end of the seventh inning that produced the most comical moment of the night. Throughout the innings, stadium officials had been circulating and handing out balloons. I had come close to throwing mine away, but a man sitting next to me had assured me I should hold on to it.

The innings came to an end, and everyone stood up. A voice from the loudspeakers instructed us to prepare our balloons and wait for the countdown. I inflated my balloon and looked around; a stadium full of grey- and yellow-clad baseball fans stood clutching inflated balloons. A countdown sounded, and on zero everyone released their balloons. The balloons spiralled and zipped through the air. Universal applause.

The voice from the loudspeakers resumed, politely asking us to take a few moments to bend down and pick up any balloons near our feet. The baseball game halted for five minutes while the stadium full of spectators did their civic duty and picked up slobbery second-hand balloons to dispose of in the rubbish.

The chorus of whistling balloons had had a magical effect on the Hanshin Tigers. Their batsmen were suddenly able to hit the ball, and at the end of the ninth innings the final batter hit the ball out of the stadium to win the game with a dramatic home run. The seven-game losing streak was broken and the ecstatic fans politely filed out of the stadium and made their way home.

The following day, the Isoi family invited me to go to a baseball batting centre with them. I readily accepted, although I was still not comfortable around eight-year-old Ryohei and his inquisitive gaze.

The invitation had come at a fortuitous time: Mr Higo, who doubled as the coach of the school baseball team, had scheduled a staff v. students' baseball game for the final day of term. With my cricketing ability, I had pictured myself effortlessly belting the ball out of the park and reducing the lead pitcher to tears. The truth was, though, that I had never swung a baseball bat. What's more, after I had secured my place in the team I had learned that the students' star pitcher was one of the best in his age group for South Osaka, and could pitch the ball at speeds of up to 130 kilometres per hour.

The trip to the batting centre started out well. Despite the temperature being 37 degrees and Ryohei constantly hugging my leg, I was in fine form, and with the ball machine set at 80 kilometres per hour sent numerous balls zipping into the 'home run' target plate.

Mr Isoi then cranked the ball machine up to 90 kph and I missed every single shot. There was no way I'd be able to hit a ball travelling at 130 kph. It seemed my only options were to visit a local temple and pray for the opposition pitcher to hurt his arm, or lie a little and say that it was my first time holding a bat, in the desperate hope that the pitcher would take pity on me and toss a slow ball.

The day of the game rolled around. It was scheduled for one o'clock, the hottest part of the day. The temperature was in the mid thirties. We were playing on a dry dusty field and there was not a hint of a breeze nor a glimmer of shade.

The teachers' team batted first. Mr Higo managed to get to second base with a brilliant shot into the outfield. Mr Terada followed up with a cheeky bunt and managed to steal first base.

I was amazed at my new-found knowledge of baseball lingo and inwardly commentated the game to myself. Sadly, though, this was not enough to help me hit the ball. I was struck out most embarrassingly by the substitute pitcher, and Mr Terada yelled insults at me from first base for having swung and missed three balls that had been well outside my strike zone.

I spent the fielding innings out on the boundary ropes with Mr Doi, who ranted about his glory days playing high-school baseball, and how he was able to pitch the ball at over 140 kilometres per hour.

Overhearing this, Mr Higo asked him to pitch for a while. Delighted, Mr Doi strode to the pitcher's mound. Unfortunately, his glory days were well and truly at an end, and he struggled to throw the ball more than a metre. He was dispatched for two home runs in quick succession, and Mr Higo sent him back to join me on the outfield.

I played little better than Mr Doi, and was struck out a further three times at bat. As a team, however, we managed a 9–3 victory, although this could have been attributable to the students giving their weaker players a turn. My only achievement was to turn slightly brown in the heat. In reality, though, my newly acquired tan consisted largely of dust and dirt from the baseball diamond. Within days it had faded and disappeared.

Thus ended the school term. The summer vacation rolled around once more, and I was free from teaching English and associating with the magnificent Mr Doi for a blissful six weeks.

# 11

# Foreign devil

*The newspapers may have been* trumpeting doom and gloom about Japan's economic health, but in Kanan Town the education business was booming. The mayor and the education superintendent had put their heads together and decided the town needed another foreign English teacher.

The town's junior high school was being well catered for by Mr Hamish from New Zealand, but what of the five elementary schools? The town's young people needed to start learning English younger, so they would have a headstart at junior high school, and later be able to leap-frog into prestigious universities. Another foreign teacher was required, and so Rachel Brown from Northumbria, England was hired.

Mr Horrii, my supervisor at the Board of Education, requested that I accompany him to Shin Osaka station to meet the new teacher. I was happy to do so. I was looking forward to having a single female living just around the corner, and anticipating delightful summer afternoons out and about in Tondabayashi, and bike rides for two in the paddy-fields of Kanan Town.

Mr Horrii and I spent an awkward hour on the train ride to Shin Osaka Station. I had never really clicked with Mr Horrii as I had with Mr Tokunaga. He seemingly had no interests outside work and appeared oddly jealous of my exciting social life. 'I have to work long hours,' he would complain. 'You are lucky. I am not lucky. I have no time to enjoy with my friends.' I decided that this was because Mr Horrii had no friends.

We waited awkwardly at the station for Rachel to arrive. Mr Horrii stared at his cellphone and constantly checked his watch. I whiled away the time at a newspaper kiosk, flicking through comic books I didn't understand.

Finally the train arrived. Rachel's pale brown hair and wan face stood out in the crowd. She looked tired.

Mr Horrii greeted her. 'Hello, Rachel. I am Mr Horrii, your new boss. Ha ha.' He laughed nervously.

Rachel laughed and frowned at the same time.

'And I'm Hamish,' I chipped in. 'I live round the corner from your new apartment.'

'Hi.' Rachel had a strange, slightly whiney accent. 'It's so hot,' she said. ' I can't stand it.'

'Yep.' I laughed.

Mr Horrii shuffled away to buy our tickets to Tondabayashi.

'It's like this every day,' I continued. 'Over thirty degrees. It gets cool in the evenings though—maybe twenty-eight, twenty-nine degrees.' I smiled.

Rachel's shoulders slumped. 'It sucks.'

I laughed again, trying to keep the mood cheery. 'Don't worry, it should start to cool down some time round October.'

Rachel's frown deepened and her mouth pursed into a pout.

During the train ride, Rachel and Mr Horrii started to make conversation. It turned out that Rachel had neither spoken nor studied a word of Japanese in her life.

Back in Tondabayashi, Mr Horrii and I showed her around her new apartment. Mr Horrii had decided that Rachel, being female, would be too delicate to withstand the first-day treatment to which I had been subjected. Her only duty would be to stroll a hundred metres down the road to the local restaurant for a 'Welcome to Japan' dinner hosted by the board and attended by the staff.

When I informed her of this, Rachel shrugged her shoulders haughtily. 'They better not expect me to eat anything strange. I'm a vegetarian. I don't eat fish.'

I assured her that the restaurant had a huge assortment of different foods on the menu, but suggested it would be in her interest to try one or two local dishes.

'Humph, I'm not eating anything raw. That's gross.'

'Have you eaten raw fish?'

'No way. It's disgusting. I'm never gonna eat sushi. And why don't I have an oven? I need an oven to bake things with.'

There was a huge turnout for the welcome party. By the time we arrived, the special room at Wasshoi pub was packed. The Board of Education and Social Education Department were in attendance, and even the office ladies had turned up. A few other dignitaries had also been invited.

Everyone bowed reverently when Rachel entered the room, and the education superintendent stood and said a few formal words of welcome. Rachel's eyes widened in alarm: she had noticed the food. The tables were laden with fried noodles, fried chicken, fried rice, salad and assorted vegetables.

I had sent word that Rachel was a vegetarian and unable to eat anything that contained meat or seafood. Vegetarianism is a foreign concept in Japan. Restaurants never have a vegetarian selection, and most soups or sauces have some form of seafood stock or flavouring. Even the most harmless-looking salad will be complemented with fish flakes or seafood dressing. I had therefore lied a little and said that Rachel was *allergic* to meat and fish. She could, however, eat chicken.

It soon became apparent, however, that Rachel would not eat chicken, or very much else. 'I'm not eating any of this!' she hissed at me.

The party was in full swing, and people were mingling and talking loudly.

'Why not?' I replied, concerned at the potential damage she was about to do to her reputation.

'I dunno. It just doesn't look very nice.'

'Are you joking?' I asked in surprise. 'This place serves great food. It's really tasty. I eat here all the time.'

'It looks gross. I don't know what any of this is.'

'Rachel, Rachel, please try some.' Mr Smiles interrupted us. He was red-faced, had his necktie around his forehead and was already very drunk. He had prepared Rachel a plate of fried noodles.

'No thanks, I don't like noodles.' Rachel did not bother to smile.

I translated.

Mr Smiles blinked in surprise. 'No noodles? Hmmm, fried chicken perhaps?'

I translated.

'No. I only like roast chicken.'

I translated.

'Oh.' Mr Smiles seemed shocked. I suddenly realised that he had ordered all the food.

'Hmmm, maybe fried rice?' Mr Smiles mimed a happy person enjoying a big feast and getting a fat stomach.

I translated.

Rachel's pout grew an inch bigger. 'No, it looks greasy.'

I translated.

Mr Smiles snapped his fingers and called for the menu. 'Mr Hamish, please help translate the menu. We must find some food for Rachel.'

I set about painstakingly translating the menu dish by dish. There were over sixty dishes.

'Rachel, Rachel, would you like a drink? Would you like beer? Wine? Sake? Orange juice?' Kindly old Mr Fujimoto had joined us. He was carrying a pot of sake and a pint of beer.

'No. I don't like alcohol. Just water for me,' Rachel bleated.

I translated this for Mr Fujimoto. He seemed sad and shuffled off to get a glass of water. I quietly relieved him of the pint of beer.

Finally we reached the bottom of the menu. Rachel had turned her nose up at fifty-nine of the sixty dishes. Most of them were apparently either gross or yuck.

'Baked potato!' Rachel pointed stubbornly. 'Is that like baked potatoes back home?'

I was tired and irritable. 'Yes.'

'I'll have that then.'

I looked up and noticed my drinking mentor Magnum PI in the corner. He was eyeing Rachel suspiciously. Our eyes met and he nodded supportively.

Mr Fujimoto returned with Rachel's glass of water.

'Humph,' she pouted.

I translated. 'Rachel says thanks.'

Mr Fujimoto smiled. 'Mr Hamish,' he began, 'could you recognise Rachel easily at the train station? Was the passport photo I showed you enough?'

'Yes. Her hair is a little different now. She had straight hair in her photo, but now it's a little curly.'

'Ah yes, so it is.' Mr Fujimoto smiled and looked at Rachel.

Rachel's ears pricked up. 'What's he saying about me? I heard my name!'

Mr Fujimoto smiled, unable to understand a thing. 'He asked if I could recognise you,' I explained. 'I told him that your hair is curly now, but that it was straight in the passport photo attached to your application letter.'

'Are you saying I've got frizzy hair!' Rachel glared at me.

'Ah no, I was saying your hair is different to that in your passport photo.'

'I can't believe you think I've got frizzy hair.' Rachel's voice was loud and whiney.

Mr Fujimoto took a step back. Mr Smiles stopped smiling.

'That's not what I said.' I suddenly disliked Rachel Brown immensely.

'Is there a problem?' Mr Fujimoto seemed worried.

'No, no, she's just asking what I think of her hair,' I said in Japanese.

'Oh.' Mr Fujimoto seemed confused. 'Would she like another glass of water?'

I translated.

Rachel pouted and shook her head petulantly. 'Rachel says no thank you,' I replied in Japanese.

I had had enough of babysitting Rachel and mediating her rude responses, and decided to leave her to her own devices. She stood in the corner, sullenly eating her baked potato with the office ladies.

I spent a sleepless night, guiltily worrying about Rachel. Her apartment's air-conditioning unit was not scheduled for installation until the following week, and Mr Horrii had not managed to arrange for her to have an electric fan in the meantime. I, on the other hand, had a fully functional air-conditioning unit and two large electric fans, one of which I rarely used.

Early the next morning I rose, showered and began carrying the two-metre-tall electric fan four hundred metres down the road to Rachel's apartment. The sun had already risen, and heat was shimmering above the concrete surface of the footpath. The fan was surprisingly heavy, and its height and bulky ends made it awkward to carry. Sweat gathered on my forehead and I could feel my shirt sticking to my back.

I staggered awkwardly up the stairs of Rachel's apartment building. The fan was too long to fit around the tight corners, and I constantly had to readjust my grip and carrying angle. By the time I arrived at her apartment door I was exhausted.

I rang the bell. Rachel blearily answered the door. She frowned at me suspiciously. 'You're early. We still have ten minutes until the bus leaves.'

'Yeah, hi, good morning. Hope you slept all right.'

'No, it's bloody hot. It sucks.'

'Yes, I thought you could borrow my electric fan for a while. It'll keep the place cooler.'

'Oh yeah?' Rachel pouted. She paused, as if unsure what to say. 'You know, I'm still mad about what you said about my hair last night. It was so unfair.'

I stared at her in disbelief. I felt like an idiot for having lugged the fan all that way. 'Are you ready to leave?' I said. 'If you hurry we might manage to catch an earlier bus.'

We rode the bus in silence. I turned up the volume on my MD player and looked out the window. Simon and Garfunkel's greatest hits were a pleasant soundtrack to the wavy rice paddies.

At the town hall, Rachel was greeted warmly. Mr Smiles asked if she had slept all right. I translated. Rachel shrugged. 'Her apartment is a little hot,' I replied in Japanese.

'Did you enjoy your baked potato?' Mr Smiles asked keenly.

Rachel shrugged, frowned and grunted.

Mr Smiles looked at me expectantly. 'Yep, she enjoyed it,' I said in Japanese.

'Good, good. Do you eat many potatoes in England?' Mr Smiles was overjoyed: conversation was finally flowing.

I translated. Rachel shot me an acidic glare. 'I dunno. I guess so. Why does he care?'

'Rachel is not sure,' I told Mr Smiles.

'Oh.' He seemed a little hurt. Rachel's body language spoke volumes.

I was sick of Rachel Brown. I excused myself and went and spoke with Magnum and Mr Fujimoto. Mr Smiles also excused himself and went back to reading his newspaper.

A few minutes later I noticed Mr Horrii attempting to inform Rachel that she was to meet the mayor in twenty minutes.

Rachel stared up at him blankly.

'Yes, twenty minute after,' Mr Horrii repeated himself.

'What?' Rachel's voice echoed in the quiet office.

'Ah.' Mr Horrii cleared his throat and looked nervous. 'Ah...twenty minute after, you meeting with mayor—town boss. Ha ha.' Mr Horrii laughed his nervous laugh and blushed.

'What? What do you mean—twenty minute after? I don't understand you.' Rachel's pitch increased.

'You have a meeting with the mayor in twenty minutes,' I interpreted from across the room.

'What! You didn't tell me that! Shit! I have a present for him, but it's at home. I have to go home. Now!' Rachel stood up. She looked about to stamp her feet and throw a tantrum.

Mr Horrii stepped back, his face drained of colour. 'Ah...but go home now no time. Meeting is twenty minute after. Go to Rachel's house and come back, thirty minutes.' He looked close to panic. Keeping the mayor waiting would earn him a severe telling-off from the education superintendent.

'No,' said Rachel. 'I want to go home. *I want to get the present.*'

Mr Horrii's white face turned green. He bowed his head and raced across to Mr Smiles' desk. Some frantic whispering ensued and Mr Smiles nodded sagely.

Mr Horrii started striding towards the door. 'Come. We go now.'

After they had left Magnum eyed me thoughtfully. 'So,' he began, 'will you and Ms Rachel become married? Do you think you could be a good couple?'

I shook my head.

He laughed heartily and his eyes twinkled. 'I don't think so either.'

Minutes later the education superintendent appeared from his office. 'Where is Rachel?' he demanded angrily.

I hid behind my newspaper.

'She has gone to fetch her presents for the mayor,' Mr Smiles said quickly. Mr Smiles' senior rank in the office made him less likely to receive a public telling-off.

'Mr Horrii is driving her,' he added.

'WHAT!' the superintendent thundered. 'Why did he do that? They'll be late now. This is unthinkable. Why is he doing this? I want to speak to him the second he returns.'

The phone rang two minutes later. Mr Smiles answered and nodded gravely. 'They are stuck in traffic,' he announced as he hung up the phone. 'They will be twenty more minutes.'

Everyone gasped—Mr Horrii was doomed. I pictured him sitting in the traffic jam sweltering as Rachel pouted and frowned in the seat beside him. For the first time ever, I started to feel a little sorry for Mr Horrii.

Mr Horrii and his frosty passenger finally returned, bedraggled and sweaty. Mr Horrii's face was white: he knew he was in trouble.

The superintendent stormed out of his office, yelled several angry words at Mr Horrii, and strode off to the mayor's office. Rachel and Mr Horrii followed slowly behind.

'Ah, Mr Hamish, can you help please?' Mr Horrii looked frantic. 'Can you help translate during the meeting?'

'Sure,' I smiled.

Mr Kitahashi, the mayor, was in typically cheerful mood. He smiled at me and announced what a success the previous year's danjiri festival had been. 'Mr Hamish is a Shiraki fan,' he said gleefully.

The superintendent frowned. Rachel pouted. Mr Horrii sweated.

I smiled and thanked Mr Kitahashi again for showing me around during the festival. He smiled and turned to Rachel. 'And how are you? Do you enjoy Japan? How is your first impression of our town?'

We were seated in the dark leather armchairs in his formal reception room. Rachel shrugged. Her lips protruded into her trademark pout. 'I dunno. It's all right. It's too hot.'

Mr Kitahashi's smile turned to confusion. He did not understand Rachel's comment, but her attitude spoke volumes. He turned to me expectantly.

'Rachel likes Kanan Town,' I lied. 'She is finding the heat a little difficult.'

Mr Kitahashi's smile returned. 'Ah yes, Mr Hamish, you found the heat difficult too, didn't you?'

After we had chatted for several minutes, he attempted to engage Rachel in conversation again. 'So Ms Rachel, are you looking forward to teaching at the elementary schools?'

'I guess. Will they have air-conditioning?'

I translated as best I could. Mr Kitahashi nodded understandingly. 'Sadly, the elementary schools do not have air-conditioning yet.'

Rachel's pout vanished. She now looked angry.

'So,' Mr Kitahashi began hesitantly, 'tell me about your country, Ms Rachel. Do you have hot summers like this?'

Rachel murmured something under her breath. I translated. 'England is not as hot as this.'

'How about food—what food do you like?'

'Humph.' Rachel stared blankly at the mayor.

'Rachel is a vegetarian,' I answered on her behalf.

'Tell me about your family then,' Mr Kitahashi asked politely.

Rachel looked cranky: this relentless interrogation was upsetting her fragile patience. 'Father, mother, sister,' she mumbled.

The normally chatty Mr Kitahashi seemed to run out of conversation topics. The meeting was over.

Rachel's day had just started: she still had the rest of the Board of Education to impress. I snuck off to lunch and returned from a peaceful stroll to the convenience store to find Rachel and Mr Smiles in deep concentration at the office internet terminal. Rachel was pouting more than usual, and Mr Smiles was looking intently at the screen.

'Oi!' she yelled at me the second I entered the room. 'I've been looking for you.'

Her voice sounded ominous. 'What's up?' I asked.

'I've been trying to download a tax form, but this stupid computer won't work.'

Mr Smiles tried calming her with a comedy routine. 'Computer is no good,' he said happily, as he mimed a blind man trying to use a computer.

I laughed.

Magnum laughed.

Mr Smiles repeated his routine a second time, and pretended to strangle himself in frustration.

Rachel exploded. 'It's not funny!' she thundered. She leapt to her feet, thumped her fists on the computer desk and stormed out of the office.

Mr Smiles stopped smiling. His face turned red and he went and sat down at his desk. A silent tension descended on the office. Rachel had just managed to offend the happiest man in Japan.

Displaying anger or strong emotions is social suicide in Japan, and Rachel had just put herself irreversibly offside with her employers. I knew she would never be truly welcomed and accepted by staff within the town hall.

Unfortunately, distancing myself from Rachel Brown was now going to be very difficult. The Board of Education staff regarded her as a ticking time bomb, and were unsure how to deal with her temper and belligerent attitude. I was therefore called upon to act as a go-between and to assist Rachel adjust to her new surroundings.

As well as helping her learn how to shop at the local supermarket, I was asked by Mr Horrii to take her to the Kanan Town summer festival the following Saturday evening. Stalls selling savoury pancakes and octopus balls would be set up along the banks of the fishing pond next to the town hall, and most of the town's teenage inhabitants would turn out to mix, mingle and watch a large fireworks display above the pond. It was a good chance to meet and socialise with students.

I invited Rachel to accompany me and she grudgingly accepted. At six o'clock she arrived at my apartment as planned, expecting to catch a bus to the festival. 'No, no. Buses don't run on Saturday night,' I lied. 'We're going to cycle. Don't worry, I have three bicycles and it's a lovely warm evening—perfect cycling weather.'

'I can't ride a bike,' she shrieked. 'I've never ridden a bike in my life.'

I was dumbfounded. Rachel's sheltered upbringing was becoming more and more tiresome. I refused to accept her excuses; it would do her good to try something new. She sheepishly mounted a bicycle, teetered and wobbled around on the footpath, and eventually announced she was ready to go.

I had chosen an easy backstreet route that involved no traffic or steep slopes. Rachel rode slowly and unsurely, and several times we had to stop when she became too scared to continue. Eventually, though, we arrived at the festival ground to a swarm of greetings. Rachel seemed unsure how to respond. A smile usually helps, but sadly she seemed unable to master even this simple universal greeting.

The next day, Sunday, I was woken at eight by Mrs Oki. She had accidentally dialled my number and had no reason for calling. I stumbled back to bed and was just getting back to sleep when the phone rang a second time. It was Rachel.

'I need help buying a tank for my fish,' she demanded. She had won a goldfish at the festival.

I told her I was sleeping.

'I need a fish tank,' she repeated.

I told her I would meet her at the supermarket in an hour and went back to bed.

The purchase of the fish tank took an hour and a half. By the time she made her decision I was bored and irritable. I carried the tank back to her apartment, announced I was busy for the rest of the weekend, and returned home.

I called my English friend Blake and complained at great length about Rachel and her petulant behaviour.

'She's from Northumbria, eh?' he said thoughtfully.

'Yes,' I replied.

'Well, that explains it. She's a hillbilly. Northumbria is England's hill-billy land. She's probably never left her village in her life. Her parents are probably cousins. Bad luck, my friend, you've got yourself a hillbilly for a neighbour.'

I thanked Blake for his wise words and hung up.

I was determined to find a way to rid myself of Rachel's company. I had not spent eight years of my life studying Japanese and then travelling to Japan only to spend my days babysitting a rude spoilt English brat. I was damned if I was going to carry any more goldfish for her, or hold her hand while she looked for baked potatoes at the supermarket.

Unfortunately, though, Mr Horii had insisted that Rachel and I spend the remainder of the summer holidays working at the town hall, preparing Rachel's teaching curriculum. Two weeks of summer holidays remained before I could escape to the solace of Junior High.

I grimaced. Mr Doi and Mr Hioki would be waiting for me there.

I racked my brain for ways I could avoid going into the Board of Educa-tion every day with Rachel, while not using up any of my precious paid leave. As luck would have it, Kimi from the town magazine office called later that night. Kimi was very worried because a typhoon was coming and was forecast to strike Osaka the next morning. She recommended that I stay away from work the following day as it was much too dangerous to go outdoors.

The next morning I called the office and said I was too scared to leave my apartment. I invited Justin around and we spent the morning playing darts on my balcony. I had spent the previous few weeks adorning the balcony with pot plants and decorating it with fairy lights. It was now a green oasis where I could lounge eating ice-cream and admiring the view of Jinaimachi.

The typhoon was very feeble. I'd seen worse wind on a normal day in Christchurch. However, I had managed to get out of work and enjoy a day away from Rachel.

That night I was in bed, trying to nod off to sleep, when the phone rang. I checked my clock: 10.45. I stumbled out of bed. A whiney female English accent was on the other end.

'Hamish—there's something in my bathroom.'

I prayed it was a tiger or a lion.

'It's some sort of insect. It's long and thin and looks like a stick. What should I do?'

I told her that it was late and I was trying to sleep.

She didn't apologise. Would I come round and remove the insect at once. I noticed her complete inability to use the word 'please'.

I told her to get a magazine, roll it up and squash the creature. Then I hung up the phone and turned it off at the wall.

The next day I decided to push my luck a little further by not going into the Board of Education office for the second day in a row. I called Mr Horrii and suggested that I be given the morning off to fill out an application form for a Japanese examination in December. He accepted this dubiously; I could hear the suspicion in his voice.

At noon my cellphone rang. Mr Horrii sheepishly asked if I had finished my exam application. I hummed and haahed guiltily. 'I need another hour or so.'

'Ahhh...we need you to come into the office as soon as you can.'

When I arrived at the office less than an hour later, Mr Horrii looked shifty. 'Rachel wanted to see you.' He looked at his shoes.

Rachel was sitting sullenly in the corner. She pouted as I approached. 'I need you to help colour in these activity posters,' she demanded.

Rachel was having her revenge for my refusal to help slay her stick insect. I was now forced to spend the afternoon colouring in pictures of cartoon animals. Rachel's pout curled into a sly smile.

I seethed with anger as I cycled home at the end of the day. I would need to come up with an ingenious plan to get myself away from the office for the next two weeks.

I refused to use up my entire year's allowance of paid leave, and was convinced I could create some sort of scenario that would fob off the ever-sceptical Mr Horrii. I would need to think carefully, though, and my story would have to be suitably crafty. I would need to make myself completely uncontactable.

I took a long route home through the paddy-fields to clear my head.

I passed an old temple, and a cemetery on a hill.

I paused for a moment and stopped in my tracks.

I looked back at the temple.

A thought flashed in my mind.

My lips curled into a smile.

Eureka! I had just devised a winning plan.

Early the next morning I cycled furiously to the Board of Education office. Rachel would still be twenty minutes away on her bus. The staff were already at their desks. I sighed with relief: so far my plan was on track.

The men had started to gather on the balcony for their morning cigarette. They welcomed me happily. Mr Smiles mimed a sleepy person and rubbed his eyes. Mr Fujimoto smiled. Magnum asked me if I wanted a cigarette.

Mr Horrii eyed me suspiciously. Why was I at work so early?

I tried to appear as sincere and truthful as I could. 'Mr Horrii,' I began, in a voice loud enough for all to hear, 'it was such lovely weather last night that I went for a bike ride in the countryside. I was using one of the town's tourist pamphlets as a map so I could visit some of the local temples and archaeological sites.'

Mr Smiles clapped his hands. 'Oh, excellent, excellent. Where did you go?'

Everyone was listening. My plan was working.

'Yes, but I got lost in the rice paddies. I couldn't understand some of the Japanese characters on the map.'

Mr Smiles was horrified. 'Oh, my. Are you okay?'

I smiled weakly. 'Yes, yes, I found my way home eventually.'

Mr Smiles and Mr Fujimoto breathed audible sighs of relief.

Mr Horrii eyed me suspiciously.

I paused for dramatic effect. 'And so I had an idea. What this town needs is English maps. Not just English maps, but also English tourism pamphlets—explanations in English about all the great tourist attractions.'

Everyone gasped. I was a genius.

'So,' I looked at Mr Horrii carefully, 'I was hoping to spend the next two weeks visiting all the temples and prehistoric tomb sites around Kanan Town, drawing an easy-to-follow map in English and writing up English pamphlets.'

Mr Smiles cheered. Mr Fujimoto cheered.

Mr Horrii looked sceptical. It was up to him, as my supervisor, to authorise my proposal.

I looked at him pleadingly. I was well aware he could be jealous and resent my time away from the office, so I had chosen my audience carefully. Mr Smiles and Mr Fujimoto both outranked Mr Horrii, and to disagree with them would cause him a severe loss of face.

'That's a brilliant idea.' A man with fluffy hair piped up enthusiastically. I smiled.

'Yes, that's a brilliant idea,' the fluffy-haired man continued. 'That's just what the local prehistoric tombs need. I've wanted to produce English pamphlets about them for ages.'

Mr Akai was the curator of Kanan Town's kofun, or prehistoric tombs. He was also a member of the Social Education Department. His enthusiasm and backing was just what I had been hoping for.

Everyone looked at Mr Horrii. He shuffled his feet. 'Yes, it sounds like a good idea,' he said at length. 'So you will spend the rest of the summer holidays doing this?'

'I think so,' I said cautiously. 'I'm not sure how long it will take. I will need to visit each of the sites so that I can appreciate them properly. Then I will need to write up the pamphlets. This will take much time.'

'So you will not come to the office every day?' He looked slightly peeved.

'No, but I will visit when I can.'

Mr Akai interrupted us, conveniently ending my conversation with Mr Horrii. 'Here,' he said, thrusting a handful of pamphlets towards me, 'these are the current Japanese pamphlets about the tombs and temples of Kanan Town. Maybe these will help.'

I thanked him profusely. 'Well, I best get started,' I said. 'I'm going to visit the local temple first.'

The staff smiled and clapped me on the shoulder. I was a hero.

'Do you want to wait for a while?' Mr Horrii asked hopefully. 'Rachel will be here soon. You can see if she wants to help.'

'No, I think I need to get started as soon as I can,' I said adamantly. 'I want to get my cycling done before the midday heat. Plus, Rachel can't ride a bike or speak Japanese. I don't think she can be of any assistance.

'I'm afraid that I will be out of cellphone range while I'm cycling in the rice paddies, so don't be concerned if you can't contact me.'

Mr Smiles, Mr Fujimoto and Mr Akai nodded understandingly. 'Yes, you must take care in the midday heat,' they urged. 'Do not push yourself too hard.'

I floated out of the office and started cycling home. I noticed Rachel's bus stopping in the distance and could see her sweltering in the heat as she started to walk down the busy main road. Keeping my head down, I zipped away along my secret rice-paddy track.

I decided to take heed of the advice about avoiding the midday heat, and met up with Justin and Matt in downtown Osaka. That evening I translated the Japanese pamphlets and maps into correct and informative English. My two-week project had been completed in two hours, and I was now free as a bird.

The following day I went swimming with Justin, and the two of us spent the afternoon playing darts on my balcony and eating ice-cream before attending a local fireworks display.

The day after, I watched baseball on television until four o'clock, when the temperature finally dropped below the mid thirties. I decided I should honour my promise to the Board of Education and do some cycling around town. I hopped on my bike and rode straight to the Junior High School to have a swim in the pool.

I had the pool to myself. I completed a few leisurely laps and then attempted to beat my own under-water swimming record. I managed a length of the pool and rose to the surface for a breath.

I gasped. Mr Horrii, Magnum, George and Mr Fujimoto were all standing at the pool entrance. In a stroke of incredibly bad luck, the Board of Education had decided to conduct an inspection of the pool's plumbing and filtration system.

I panicked. I was about to be busted. There was nowhere to hide, and despite having broken my own underwater swimming record I would be unable to hold my breath for the duration of their inspection.

'Hey, Mr Hamish, what are you doing here?' Magnum had spotted me.

I climbed out of the pool, unsure how I was going to get out of this one. Everyone seemed happy to see me—except Mr Horrii. He eyed me suspiciously.

'Hi guys,' I stammered. 'I was cycling in the mountains, but I got so hot I needed a swim to cool down.'

I paused.

'Excellent, excellent!' Magnum was happy. 'So you are using my son's old mountain bike? How is it?'

'It's great,' I said. 'It's so nice to have a bike with gears.' I wasn't lying: Magnum's son's bike had been a godsend.

'So, where did you go today?' Mr Horrii asked, his eyes narrowing.

'Ummm...I cycled to that temple in the mountains. What's its name?'

'Kofukuji,' Mr Fujimoto answered on my behalf. 'Very nice temple. I like it very much.'

I nodded enthusiastically. I had visited the temple several months earlier and enjoyed the peaceful grounds and garden.

Everyone was smiling, except Mr Horrii.

'You must be thirsty.' Magnum smiled, his moustache bristling. 'Let's go to the pub. My treat.'

During the remaining ten days of my summer holiday I did make several adventurous cycle rides around Kanan Town, to places I had never been before, down roads I had never known existed, and to all the tourist attractions that my English-language pamphlet would promote. On one particularly hot afternoon, I stopped and asked directions from an old man on the side of the road. I had been trying to find a large keyhole-shaped tomb and had become hopelessly lost.

The old man shone a toothless grin and said he recognised me as the town's English teacher. 'Thank you for helping this town,' he said.

I blushed.

He looked at me carefully. 'Sensei, you look hot. You must take care in this heat.' He looked concerned. 'Here, please take my towel. Please take it with you and use it to mop your forehead.'

He pressed a fresh towel into my hand. I bowed respectfully, thanked him profusely and mopped my face.

He paused and looked at me thoughtfully. 'Sensei, you look thirsty. Are you thirsty?'

I tried to assure him that I was fine, but he shook his head. He rummaged around in his overall pockets and produced a shiny 100 yen coin. 'Sensei, please wait here.' He crossed the road to a vending machine and purchased a can of Coca-Cola. His toothless grin now larger than ever, he returned and pressed the can into my hand. 'Here, please enjoy this cool drink. You look so hot.'

I stammered out the most polite form of 'thank you' that I knew.

'The tomb is very close, sensei, just around the corner and down the street. I am happy that you are interested in the history of this town.' He bowed and shuffled away.

This simple gesture of kindness had put me in a very positive mood. I stared happily at the lush green rice paddies. Rachel Brown and Mr Doi were now distant memories.

# 12

# In search of love

*I had been in Japan for over a year* and I was still single. I had had no problem befriending and enchanting the elderly female population. My Japanese mothers loved to cook and fuss over me. Mrs Oki called religiously, inquiring what I was wearing to school and how my mother was. Old Mrs Okuda was regularly entranced by the fact that I lived by myself, and old women approached me in the supermarket to thank me for coming to Japan and teaching the town's young people.

Likewise, I was a hit with my female students. Fourteen-year-old admirers would linger around my desk in the hope of being able to glimpse what I was eating for lunch, or which chocolate bar I preferred. They seemed to be compiling some sort of spreadsheet that listed my horoscope, all my likes and dislikes, my favourite singers and actors, and what cartoon characters I liked.

But while my life was filled with females aged under fifteen and over sixty, there were few in between. In truth, though, I had not been completely alone for the year. In May an acquaintance had introduced me to a twenty-one-year-old solo mother named Tama Chan. Tama Chan had bleached blond hair, a round face with pretty eyes, and a nine-month-old baby girl named Sayaka.

Tama Chan, Sayaka and I embarked on a peculiar romance. Before meeting Tama Chan I had never held a baby, let alone taken care of one. Suddenly I was thrust into an unfamiliar world of nappies, mashed food and chubby little limbs. Our outings required meticulous planning. Train travel was full of problems; long distances would make Sayaka cranky and she would start screaming or wailing, which would bother fellow commuters. Most train stations lacked elevators or wheelchair ramps, so we were forced to lug her massive pram up and down steep flights of stairs. Dining out was an even bigger challenge, as were most normal everyday activities.

Our inaugural outing was a picnic in Nara Park, about an hour by train from Osaka. This was how I learned that Sayaka did not like long train journeys. After only a few stops she was crying and wailing, and had managed to throw her toys and pacifier all around the carriage.

By the time we arrived at the park I was a nervous wreck. We laid out a picnic rug, Sayaka fell asleep, and soon afterwards Tama Chan excused herself to go and find a bathroom. At this point Sayaka awoke, and noticing that her mother had been replaced by a stranger, started to scream her head off.

I performed my very best rendition of 'Oha!', but alas Sayaka was not up to speed with Japan's latest comedic trends. The screaming continued, and passers-by eyed me suspiciously.

I hesitantly tried to pick up Sayaka to give her a calming hug. However, the second I leant forward her screaming crescendoed, and I beat a hasty retreat to my side of the picnic blanket.

I was on the verge of panic. Someone had no doubt called the police. I was probably about to be arrested, Sayaka would be put into foster care, and Tama Chan would not want a second date.

Suddenly I had an idea. I started singing—nothing in particular, just a nonsensical song about waiting for mum to come back from the toilet so we could eat cake and go back to sleep. I borrowed the tune and melody from the early 90s' hit 'Don't cry' by Guns and Roses. The lyrics got better as I went along, and I even managed to make a few of them rhyme.

Sayaka stopped screaming. I continued singing. Mum was in the toilet, but she was coming back soon and we would have some orange juice.

Sayaka was listening. Her little face crinkled into a frown, and she looked at me as if I were mentally unstable. I was being glared at by a nine-month-old baby.

I added clapping actions and wobbled my head. The wrinkly frown deepened, and the beady eyes followed my every move. At last, Tama Chan returned from her expedition to the toilet, and remarked how peaceful Sayaka appeared to be.

By the end of the picnic I had developed a game with Sayaka that I named 'rocket ship'. I would hold her in a standing position and count down from five to zero in English. I would then whoosh her upwards into the air and let her go for a split second before catching her again. Sayaka seemed to love the game and soon picked up the rhythm of the five-second count-down, flapping her chubby legs in expectation of lift-off. Her wrinkly frown was replaced by a wide, toothless smile.

Tama Chan looked on thoughtfully.

A fortnight later, Tama Chan, Sayaka and I met up for another picnic, this time in a local park. Sayaka seemed to remember who I was, and games of 'rocket ship' and 'peek-a-boo' were a huge success.

Our next outing was to a park in central Osaka. More baby games ensued, and Sayaka began crawling across the picnic rug to be by my side. I was starting to enjoy my novel exposure to babies, but slowly I began to realise that I was more interested in spending time with baby Sayaka than with her mother. Tama Chan was becoming demanding. I was faced with a heart-wrenching decision: break up with Tama Chan and never play 'rocket ship' with Sayaka again, or stick around to play with Sayaka and be shackled to Tama Chan and her uncertain temper.

In the end, the decision was not difficult. Tama Chan had also been experiencing misgivings and so, after seven weeks of playing mothers and fathers, we parted company.

I was now again single and fancy-free in Tondabayashi—and, as I was soon to discover, destined to stay that way. My chances of romantic success with Hiroshi Yamaguchi's sister, Aki, had long since faded. I had barely seen her since our initial meeting, and her appearances during my English lessons with Hiroshi had decreased dramatically since the porn-themed dinner party.

Another local family were more forthcoming in promoting the idea that I date their eldest daughter. Mr and Mrs Hayashi were the donors of one of my three bicycles. (The Board of Education had provided the first, and Magnum the second.) The Hayashis' generous gift did not, however, come without several strings attached.

Mrs Hayashi's first request, in exchange for the bicycle, was that I visit her home once a week and conduct cheerful English conversations with her. She had majored in English at university many years earlier, but had never found an opportunity to use her English skills, and had never before met an English-speaking foreigner with whom to converse.

Her second request, after several weeks of cheerful English conversations, was that I spend some time socialising with her wayward daughter, Sachiko. She explained that Sachiko had recently fallen in with a bad crowd, and needed a well-mannered young man in her life to help her get through this rebellious phase.

During my visits to the Hayashi home I had never met Sachiko as she was, presumably, out misbehaving and gallivanting around town with rogues and scoundrels. The following Tuesday evening I arrived ready to sweep her off her feet with some gentlemanly charm.

Mrs Hayashi was waiting eagerly. 'Come in, come in,' she enthused. 'Wait here. I will call my daughter.' She scuttled out of the entrance hall and I took a seat in the dining-room.

A frowning female appeared at the door. Sachiko regarded me suspiciously. Despite her surly demeanour, she was quite attractive—tall, with a slim elegant face and streaked brown hair. Her ears, however, spoke volumes: they were full of silver studs and rings. She wore torn black jeans and a black 'Ramones' T-shirt.

'This is Mr Hamish.' Mrs Hayashi beamed joyfully. 'He's from New Zealand. He works at the Junior High School. He is the same age as you.' Mrs Hayashi nodded at Sachiko knowingly.

'Mr Hamish, this is my daughter Sachiko. At the moment she has a part-time job. She is a truck driver's assistant.'

Sachiko managed a smile and bowed. I bowed back and said hello in Japanese. Sachiko blushed. My dapper charm was beginning to work.

'Yes,' Mrs Hayashi trumpeted quickly, noticing her daughter's reaction, 'you two should spend some time together.'

It was my turn to blush. Mrs Hayashi was being a tad forward.

Sachiko smiled. 'What sort of music do you like?' she asked. I opened my mouth to reply. I had been a heavy-metal fan during my high-school days, and was about to sweep Sachiko off her feet by reciting an extensive list of alternative music bands and singers.

'Mr Hamish likes Japanese folk music,' Mrs Hayashi exclaimed, before I could say a word. 'We listened to one of my favourite CDs the other week. Mr Hamish is a *nice* guy. I think he looks like Harrison Ford.'

Sachiko's smile transmuted into a grimace. I flinched. Mrs Hayashi had just murdered any potential relationship between her daughter and me. The last thing rebellious Sachiko wanted was a nice-guy boyfriend who listened to crappy Japanese folk songs with her mother. I suddenly felt self-conscious. I had come straight from school and was wearing neatly ironed chino trousers and a tidy blue shirt. Sachiko probably thought I was gay.

That was the last time I ever saw Sachiko, and my English lessons with Mrs Hayashi slowly became less frequent, until several months later they ceased altogether.

I would need to take my love life in hand. Waiting for suitable introductions from friends and acquaintances was obviously going to be a long and tiresome road. It was midsummer, the start of the festival season. This, I decided, would be where I would meet some attractive young women.

My good friend Justin delighted in my lovelorn tales of bad luck and missed opportunities. He announced that he would be more than happy to act as my wing man and accompany me to the local festivals.

First on our list was Perfect Liberty's annual fireworks display. It was a warm summer's evening as Justin and I squeezed our way into the crowds wedged in the streets surrounding the cult's headquarters and the neighbouring public golf course, and waited for the sky to darken and the fireworks to begin.

In no time we were talking to two young women. Momo Chan and Rie were university students, majoring in English. The four of us chatted easily. Momo Chan seemed to be laughing at all my corny jokes, and claimed I looked like Tom Cruise. Rie chipped in and said I looked more like Arnold Schwarzenegger. Justin started choking with laughter. Rie said Justin's long bushy hair made him look like Ludwig van Beethoven. It was my turn to laugh.

The fireworks started and we oohed and aahed at the dazzling explosions and bright colours. When they were over, we escorted Momo Chan and Rie to the local train station. The laughter and happy conversation continued, and Momo Chan shyly inquired as to whether we could all meet up again. She and I swapped cellphone numbers and we made tentative arrangements to go out for a meal.

As Justin and I left our new friends at the train station, Justin slapped me on the back and assured me that Momo Chan had been giving me the glad eye as she left. 'She's keen on you, mate!' he crowed. 'You're in with a real chance.'

I, too, was pretty confident of my chances and spent the following week exchanging flirtatious text messages with Momo Chan. I arranged to meet her for a meal in downtown Osaka, but as the big day approached I noticed a slight decline in the regularity and enthusiasm of her communications. I assumed she was busy and brushed off my niggling concerns.

Two nights before our first date, however, Momo Chan sent me a text with the most bizarre fob-off I have ever received: 'I'm sorry, I can't meet you on Saturday. My neighbour's house burned down. Bye.'

I called immediately to check how she was. 'I'm okay,' she assured me, 'but my neighbours are not so good. I can't meet you on Saturday.'

'Oh, that's a shame,' I said sadly. 'Are you good friends with your neighbours?'

'Hmmm...kind of. But I can't see you anymore. So I better go.'

'Huh?' I began. 'I don't understand. What do you mean?'

'My neighbour's house burned down. I can't see you anymore. Goodbye.' The phone went dead.

Justin burst out laughing when I told him. 'That's the lamest excuse I've ever heard,' he chuckled. 'Well, the danjiri festival is coming up again. We'll see what crappy excuses you can pick up there. Or maybe you can find yourself another stalker.'

I smiled. The previous year's danjiri festival had provided me with a slightly scary admirer. In the weeks following the festival, an odd-looking woman in her mid thirties had started waiting for me outside her house on one of the streets along which I biked to school every morning. She had waved me down one day and gushingly told me how much she had enjoyed chatting with me at the town festival. I had no recollection of this at all but nodded along politely; she seemed slightly unstable and I was keen to make an exit.

Sadly, though, the odd-looking woman continued to wait for me on the street every morning for the following week and waved lovingly as I sped past. I made every effort to avoid her, and deliberately sped up as I approached her house. I was therefore horrified when, several days later, she appeared at the gates of the school as I was arriving.

'Excuse me,' she lisped in a slow drawl, 'would you like to come for dinner at my house? My parents would like to meet you.'

'I think I'm busy that day,' I stammered.

'Oh.' She seemed confused. 'But my parents would like to meet you. I've told them all about you. You are a nice man. I enjoyed meeting you at the town festival.'

'That's very nice, but I'm very busy at the moment,' I lied. 'Goodbye.' I hurried away.

Unfortunately, several of my female students had overheard our exchange, and word quickly spread through the school that Mr Hamish had an odd-looking girlfriend in her mid thirties. I was most unimpressed. I varied my cycle route to school, and took particular care whom I spoke to on the street.

'Don't worry,' Justin assured me. 'We'll find you a nice girl at the danjiri festival.'

Sadly, though, the festival turned out to be less boisterous than the previous year. On the first day rain cast a veil, and by the afternoon the rice paddies were muddy. My friends from the Board of Education made only cursory appearances. Mr Fujimoto had caught a cold, and sneezed and coughed violently. Magnum arrived late in the afternoon and then apologised profusely, saying he was very busy with his family for the weekend.

Justin and I were, nonetheless, welcomed by the town officials and dignitaries with whom I had revelled the previous year, and provided with sake, fried noodles and hapi coats. In the evening we took to the streets and followed the Kankoji float, waving large banners and proudly displaying our new coats.

Towards the end of all this revelry it suddenly became apparent that we had made scant progress in finding me a girlfriend. Justin was keen to return to our original plan. We spied a group of young women dressed in Italian designer clothes—Gucci jackets, Prada shoes and Louis Vuitton handbags—and immediately struck up a conversation. After they had giggled at our jokes and applauded my Japanese, they fiercely debated which Hollywood stars we resembled, until consensus was reached that I looked like Matt Damon and Justin looked like Leonardo DiCaprio.

As we paraded behind the Kankoji float, I got ready to ask for some phone numbers. 'We're very busy these days,' one of the women confessed shyly. 'Maybe we can meet up after our exams are finished.'

'Oh, you're university students?' I asked, surprised to learn they were so young. 'What are you studying?'

The women covered their mouths with their beautifully manicured hands. 'We're not in university—we're still in high school. Year two.'

Justin exploded with laughter. 'So you're all seventeen?' he chuckled. The girls nodded, and we bade them farewell. My love life was not looking up.

On day two, rain bucketed down and Justin and I stayed at home nursing our hangovers. The festival season was not producing the plethora of romantic prospects for which I had been hoping. It was time to venture into the big city to look for a girlfriend who did not drive trucks, set fire to houses, and was not still in high school. Osaka, I assured myself, was teeming with such young women.

After more than a year, my friends and I knew Osaka City like the back of our hands. We had visited most of the beer gardens, dined at numerous pubs and bars, and danced the night away at every nightclub.

We had spent many lazy Saturday afternoons trailing around the web of streets and arcades that surrounded central Namba Station. Usually we met on the middle of Dotombori Bridge, a local icon where tourists gathered to take photos of the enormous neon displays reflected in the river, and local youths came to meet, flirt and be seen.

On Friday nights we had often ended up at Shinsaibashia, a district crammed with trendy clothes shops, and backstreet bars selling drinks at ridiculously cheap prices.

And then there was Amerika Mura—America Town—where hip-hop- and skateboard-obsessed teens pretended to be living on the rough streets of New York. The district was full of American-style urban clothes stores and, unlike the rest of Japan, respondent with graffiti to create the illusion of actually being in New York. Large American billboards and businesses such as Domino's Pizza dominated.

This sheen of coolness attracted not just crowds of rebellious Japanese teenagers, but also a criminal element from West Africa. Large thuggish goons dressed as gangster rappers in oversized clothes lurked on street corners. 'Hey beby,' they would yell at passing women. 'I em fram Ameriika! Beby, you like Ameriika? You want Ameriika boyfriend, beby?'

These chat-up lines seldom met with success; it was reassuring that the young women of Osaka appeared uninterested in falling in love with West African bovver boys. However, finding a young woman who was willing to fall in love with Hamish Beaton from Christchurch, New Zealand was proving to be a bit of a challenge. My friends assured me that I would one day meet someone at a bar or nightclub. Matt had met his girlfriend, Naoko, at a bar. A new member of our drinking circle, Andy from Leeds, had met his girlfriend, Megumi, at a bar. Wij had also met a girl at a bar, and had even convinced her to go back to his apartment with him. He had then drunkenly fallen asleep during the train ride home, and woken up the next morning alone at Osaka International Airport.

I began to think that my Japanese language ability was more of a hindrance than a blessing. My spoken Japanese was certainly sufficient for talking about groceries with Mrs Okuda, describing the content of my mother's wardrobe to Mrs Oki, and discussing the weather with my Japanese mothers. And I was able to entertain my teenage students with silly jokes and humorous nicknames. But after a year of living and working in rural Japan I had picked up a bizarre linguistic hodgepodge, consisting of old-fashioned expressions used by rural pensioners and classroom slang used by thirteen-year-old-girls. I certainly did not sound like a hip Japanese Fonzie, and even my best rendition of 'Oha!' was an uncool chat-up line.

It seemed I would have more luck at impressing women by not speaking Japanese at all. As soon as young women learned I could speak their language, they would enlist me as an interpreter to help them befriend my more 'mysterious' and 'cool' friends who were still unable to count to ten in Japanese.

I grew tired of translating questions about Matt's favourite food or Blake's favourite pet animal. I fumed in frustration when females gasped in wonder at Wij's stammering attempts to introduce himself in Japanese, and boiled with rage when they asked me to tell Wij that he spoke beautiful Japanese and was very handsome.

It was time, I decided, to stop speaking Japanese in bars. This soon led, however, to equally frustrating conversations conducted in broken English.

'Hello, my name is Hamish,' I would say with a smile.

'Hem? Hem? Name?' would come the refused reply.

'My name is Hamish,' I would repeat even more slowly. 'What is your name?'

If successful, I would follow this up with, 'What is your job?'

'Huh? Job? I don't know job. What is job?' Blank confused stare.

'Ummm...job. What do you do? What work do you do?'

I refused to say the word 'job' in Japanese. I was damned if I was going to give in, speak Japanese, and be written off as a nerdy foreigner. No, by the end of this conversation the woman would consider me mysterious and cool, and no doubt very handsome as well.

'Huh, walk? What walk do I do? I don't understand. I stay here. Not walk.' A frown of non-comprehension.

'No, no, I mean *work*. What *work* do you do? Do you have a job? I am a teacher. What is your job?'

'Teacher? I don't understand. Are you American?'

'No!' I explode with frustration. 'No, I am from New Zealand. I am a teacher. What is your job? Job. You know, shigoto. What is your *shigoto*?'

'Oh, job! Aha! I am an office lady. You speak good Japanese. Umm…'

The English conversation ends, and the young woman switches to Japanese. 'Do you know that man over there?' She points at Wij. 'I want to talk to him. Can you translate for me?'

My patience with the Osaka bar scene was nearing breaking point when Justin and I finally met a pair of young women who not only made coherent conversation but wanted to spend time with us. Rina and her older sister, Haruko, danced happily with us for an entire evening. Rina had long dark hair and an alluring smile.

I quickly told Justin that I was interested in Rina and that he would therefore have to make do with her slightly less attractive sister. Justin was miffed: the dimly lit nightclub made it difficult to tell whether Haruko had two separate eyebrows, or a disturbingly long, caterpillar-like mono-brow. I reminded him of his promise to act as my wing man, and pointed out that, in any event, I had seen Rina first and she was nearer my age than his. He reluctantly agreed.

The four of us danced and drank until dawn, and then ate a big greasy breakfast at a family restaurant. We arranged to meet again the following Friday, and Rina gave me a kiss on the cheek as she left.

I was ecstatic. I spent the next week at school grinning and smiling and looking forward to my Friday night date with Rina. There were no last-minute cancellations due to neighbours' houses burning down, and the four of us duly met at a downtown Indian restaurant. Rina was looking ravishing. She was wearing tight crocodile-skin trousers and an expensive black Italian jacket. I caught Justin sneaking a few admiring glances.

Dinner was a happy affair, full of laughter and easy conversation. It soon became apparent, however, that the real reason the girls had accepted the invitation to dinner was that Haruko had a crush on Justin and was eager to spend more time with him. At one point during our entrée of samosas and chicken curry, Rina leaned across the table and whispered in

my ear that Haruko thought Justin was very handsome and looked like
Johnny Depp.

I burst out laughing and she scolded me for not taking the situation
seriously. 'Does your friend like my sister?' she asked earnestly.

I looked at Haruko. She seemed very serious and very determined. I
suddenly realised that if Justin did not like Haruko, Rina might not see
any point in the four of us meeting up again.

'Yes, I think he likes her,' I lied. 'Maybe we should go out again next
week to give them more time together.'

Rina frowned. 'Hmmm...I'm busy next week. I have bought a bar in
downtown Osaka. It is the bar's grand opening on Friday.' She paused,
looking thoughtful. 'Would you and Justin like to come to my bar
opening? It will be a good chance for Justin and Haruko to talk some
more.'

'Yes, yes, Justin would like that.' I chuckled to myself. A second date
with Rina had just been arranged.

When the women went to freshen their make-up in the bathroom,
I informed Justin of my devious conduct. He was less than impressed.
'You little bugger,' he ranted. 'You owe me for this. This is the last double
date I'm coming on with these two. Haruko keeps smiling at me and
fluttering her eyelashes—it's really creepy. Next time you can get Wij or
Matt to fill in for me.'

I assured Justin that there would be no need for a third double date, as
I would ask Rina out properly at the bar opening. 'You better,' he said.
'And don't give Haruko any funny ideas.'

Rina's brand new bar turned out to be situated in the heart of Osaka's
red-light district. Justin and I apprehensively made our way through a
dense neighbourhood of strip bars and hostess clubs.

'What sort of place did she say she was opening?' Justin asked. 'Do
you even know what this new girlfriend of yours does for a job?'

I was suddenly a little concerned. 'Actually no,' I replied. 'I thought
she worked in an office.'

Justin grinned. We had arrived at Rina's bar. 'You have some terrible
luck with girls,' he smirked. The bar was on the fifth floor of an eight-
storey building. Outside the hostess club on the ground floor, leggy

women were strutting up and down the street handing out fliers and drinks coupons.

We made our way past the hostess bar and up the elevator. Rina's dimly lit bar was almost empty. Rina stood behind the counter. Haruko sat in a booth in the corner. Some mean-looking Japanese men sat at the bar drinking.

Rina ushered us over to Haruko's table. We noticed a few other patrons, but both Justin and I were transfixed by a well-dressed old man who was sitting at the bar, flanked on both sides by the mean-looking men.

Haruko was drunk. She smiled at Justin longingly. Justin went pale and made me sit between them.

Rina returned to the bar to serve the old man and his entourage. 'Wow, this place is great!' Justin lied. 'How'd your sister manage to buy it?'

Haruko giggled drunkenly. 'She borrowed the money from her'—she paused, searching for the words—'from her friend.' She gestured towards the old man at the bar.

'That's her friend?' I asked stupidly. 'But he's kind of old. Where did she meet him?'

Haruko blushed. She looked around cautiously and lowered her voice. 'He is a gangster. Rina used to work at one of his hostess clubs. He was her best customer. So he agreed to lend her some money to buy this bar.'

Haruko paused. She seemed a little worried. 'I hope my sister's bar will be successful. It will be very bad if she has a debt to that man.'

Justin slapped me on the back. 'Man, you really know how to pick them. Your girlfriend is in debt to the Yakuza.'

The bottom dropped out of my stomach. How on earth had this aspect of Rina's life managed to go unnoticed until now?

I looked at my hands—my eight perfect fingers and two healthy thumbs. Becoming romantically involved with Rina and her mobster pals could lead to my losing some of my digits. I liked my hands the way they were. It was time for Justin and I to distance ourselves from debt-ridden Rina and monobrowed Haruko.

I tapped Justin on the shoulder. 'Let's get out of here,' I hissed. Justin nodded.

'Where are the toilets?' I asked Haruko.

'Down the hall,' she pointed, smiling drunkenly at Justin.

'We'll be right back.' We sprinted out the door.

I now added the occupations of hostess-club worker, strip-club owner and Yakuza debtor to my existing list of truck driver's assistant, pornography collector's daughter, potential arsonist and stalker as unsuitable girlfriends. I crossed inner-city bars off my list of potential places to meet lovely women. I was resigned to waiting for fate to intervene, and for the perfect girlfriend to fall from heaven into my waiting arms.

The next day, with girlfriend-hunting now off the agenda, I set off to north Osaka City to do some shopping. I soon found myself in a large bookstore that stocked English novels and magazines. I had visited the store many times before and knew my way around. I was busy scanning the English magazine rack, when I suddenly looked to my right. A beautiful angel was standing on tiptoe, trying to reach a magazine on the top shelf. She was dressed in a simple summer dress, and her dark brown hair was tied in an elegant twist.

She retrieved the magazine and looked around. Our eyes met and the angel smiled.

I stepped forward in a daze. 'Excuse me,' I asked in English. 'Could you tell me where the English books are?'

The angel's smile widened. 'Ah, yes, I am looking for an English novel too. Do you know *Pride and Prejudice*?'

I blinked in surprise. The angel spoke perfect English. 'This way,' she beckoned, and led me to the English fiction section, where I had been standing only minutes earlier. We chattered happily as I helped her locate Jane Austen's classic novel. I then pretended to be looking for a Charles Dickens' novel to prolong the conversation.

The angel's name was Yumi and she was in her final year studying English at a university in Kyoto. She had come to Osaka for a day's shopping and was trying to find *Pride and Prejudice* for a coming reading assignment. I quickly explained that I had studied *Pride and Prejudice* at high school and was very familiar with Jane Austen's work. I neglected to mention that I had completely detested the book and never actually read the ending.

'Would you like to go and have a drink?' I asked impulsively.

To my surprise Yumi nodded and suggested we go to a nearby café. For the next three hours we talked non-stop. Yumi laughed at my stories of life in Kanan Town, and I was smitten with her stories of her rural Kyushu childhood and her life at university.

Conversation soon turned to our respective interests in music and movies, and Yumi suggested that we move to a nearby CD store so she could show me her favourite Japanese artists. We laughed our way around the CD store, joking about each other's taste in music. In a lovesick haze, I splashed out and bought a CD I had never listened to before (and, after listening to it at home later that night, decided never to listen to again).

It was starting to grow dark outside, and I daringly asked Yumi if she would like to have dinner. Again to my surprise she agreed, and we ate at a pasta restaurant on the top floor of a department store with an amazing view of the city. The sun set and the lights of Osaka came to life. The meal was delicious. I did not want the evening to end.

'I know it's getting late,' I said at length, 'but would you like to go for a ride on the Ferris wheel on the top of the building? I've always wanted to ride it, but have never had a chance before.'

Yumi nodded enthusiastically. She too, she explained, had wanted to ride the Ferris wheel for some time. 'I hear it's got the best night-time view in all of Osaka.'

The Ferris wheel certainly gave an unobstructed view of greater Osaka. I was sure I could even see Tondabayashi's awful PL Tower. I pointed. Yumi peered into the darkness. 'I don't see anything,' she teased. 'You're making it up.'

The lights of the city twinkled merrily beneath us. It was a truly breathtaking view. I was still dazzled by the day's unexpected events and convinced it was all a dream, and that Yumi would soon announce her romantic allegiance to a mafia overlord.

The ride came to an end. 'I'd really like to see you again,' I gushed. 'Would you like to go to the movies next week?'

Yumi smiled. 'I'd really like to see you again too, but my university trip to America leaves this Thursday. I'll be back in three weeks and we can meet up then.'

I blushed. 'Oh yes, sorry—I know you told me that.' I remembered now that Yumi had mentioned her trip to America at least twice. 'Well, I'd really like to go to the movies with you after you get back.'

She agreed enthusiastically and we exchanged phone numbers. I walked her to the station, and stood on the platform waving as her train slowly pulled away.

I raced home and was on the phone to Justin within seconds of arriving at my apartment. 'You'll never guess what happened to me today,' I began breathlessly.

Justin listened patiently as I recounted the day in intimate detail. 'So, she doesn't own a strip club?' he asked sarcastically when I finished my story.

I laughed. 'No.'

'Her neighbours haven't had their house burned down recently?'

'No!'

'And she's not on drugs, escaped from prison, or secretly a man wearing a summer dress? Then good luck. It sounds like fate is finally on your side.'

I was still grinning as I hung up the phone. For the next three weeks I counted the days until Yumi's return. I had already planned a romantic evening in downtown Osaka. Finally, my cell-phone beeped and I jumped with joy. There was a text message from Yumi.

'Hi,' it read, 'I'm back from America. I had such a great time. It is a wonderful place. I want to go back some day. How have you been?'

The message ended with a smiley face. I usually detested emails or text messages decorated with smiley faces, but in Yumi's case I was prepared to make an exception.

'I'm very well,' I replied. 'I'm glad you enjoyed America. I'm looking forward to hearing all your stories. If you want, we can catch up sometime this weekend.'

I pressed 'send' and waited breathlessly. Five minutes passed. I checked my list of sent messages. Maybe I hadn't sent it properly? I frowned. The message had been sent.

Ten minutes passed. I checked the reception level on my phone. Maybe I was out of range?

I wasn't.

Twenty minutes passed. Still no reply. A hundred reasons for Yumi's lack of reply raced through my mind. Maybe her phone battery had died. Maybe she was out of range. Maybe she was in the bath. Maybe she was busy unpacking her suitcase. Maybe she was tired from her flight and already fast asleep in bed.

Yumi's deafening silence lasted the rest of the evening. A complete lack of classes to teach at school the next day did little to distract me from my concern about Yumi's silence. Finally, at lunchtime I could bear the waiting no longer, and nervously composed a nonchalant text message. I didn't want to appear desperate, but I didn't want to wait forever either.

'Hey, how's things?' I began. 'Hope you've recovered from your long flight. My friends and I are going out to a bar this weekend, and I wondered if you'd like to come along. Let me know.'

I waited. Five minutes passed. My phone beeped. Something about the beep told me that I was not going to enjoy Yumi's reply.

'Hi there. Sorry, but when I was in America I met a very nice boy. He really loves me, and he wants to come to Japan to be with me. So I can't see you ever again. Goodbye.'

Justin, to his credit, was initially quite upset. 'Oh, that's a real shame,' he said. 'She sounded nice, too.' I thought I could hear him start chuckling to himself. 'I think you need to write a book about all this. Each girl could have an entire chapter devoted to her. I'd gladly pay money to read it.'

Mariko Kitamura was the loveliest person I had met thus far in Japan. She entered my life on a warm night at a rooftop bar in downtown Osaka. Mariko was good friends with Matt's girlfriend Naoko, and had recently returned to Japan after four years living in a small town in the South Island of New Zealand. She was intelligent, worldly, fluent in English and incredibly beautiful.

Heads turned when Mariko entered the bar, and my chest puffed up with pride when she took the seat next to me at our table. Naoko had invited her to join us, and I soon got the distinct impression that Naoko was dabbling in a little matchmaking.

The conversation turned to Mariko's four years in New Zealand, and she and I soon fell into deep conversation. She was missing New Zealand tremendously, and we reminisced about Marmite on toast, Wattie's baked beans and mince pies. I was mesmerised by her smile and laugh. Her eyes twinkled when she spoke, her cheeks flushed when she giggled, and her nose crinkled when her giggle developed into laughter.

She had returned to university and was studying criminal psychology. She was well-read and had started studying French a few months earlier.

The conversation switched to Mariko's dislike of urban Japan and her contempt for sexually perverse Japanese males. I recounted the story of my porn-themed dinner party with the Yamaguchi family, and her nose crinkled.

All too soon it was time for Mariko to make her exit and catch her train home. She made Naoko promise to invite her along to our next evening out and waved to us all as she left.

Within seconds Justin and Blake were at my side, slapping me on the back and nodding knowingly. 'Man, it's so obvious you like her,' Justin said. 'I think she likes him too,' Blake said.

My ailing love life had become a regular topic of conversation among my friends. It was only a matter of time before bets started being placed on whether or not I would eventually find a girlfriend.

Justin and Blake continued to debate my performance, eventually concluding that I had conducted myself well, and that Mariko was indeed lovely. 'Top class,' Blake chirped. 'Hamo, you have my full endorsement.'

We quickly arranged to go drinking again the following Saturday night, and Naoko was given specific instructions to invite Mariko and to discreetly inquire about her first impressions of me.

I met Mariko for the second time the following weekend. My friends and I were drinking at one of our regular Irish bars, and had arrived early to garner a cozy table in the corner. Chairs and seating order had been strategically arranged. The one empty chair was placed next to me. Blake arrived late and tried to take the chair. Justin and Wij politely told him to sod off.

Mariko arrived shortly afterwards. Heads turned. I felt my cheeks flush. She was looking even more beautiful than I remembered. Light blue jeans complemented her sleeveless white top, which revealed porcelain-smooth arms. Her bright eyes twinkled, and as she sat down next to me she beamed her mesmerising smile.

I suddenly felt under enormous pressure. I stammered away trying to make polite conversation, and was horrified to hear myself start talking about *Star Wars* movies. Blake cringed. Wij frowned. Justin chuckled. Mariko's smile widened. 'I love *Star Wars*,' she enthused. 'Oh, that new movie's coming out next month. We should go and see it together.'

I gasped. Mariko had just asked me out. What's more, she had asked me out because I had foolishly jabbered on about *Star Wars*. Surely she was the perfect woman for me.

I could feel my friends smiling as they sipped their beers and continued their pretend conversations with each other. The rest of the night was a happy blur of mesmerising smiles and delicate, bird-like laughter. Mariko and I exchanged phone numbers and the future of my love life seemed bright.

We arranged to meet for coffee the following Friday evening, even though the release of the eagerly anticipated *Star Wars* movie was still several weeks away. We spent a charming evening drinking hot choco-late and ploughing gaily through pronunciation exercises in Mariko's French textbook. I had not spoken French since university, but my Jacques Cousteau accent, flowery hand gestures, exaggerated facial expressions and rolling 'r's made her laugh.

The following Wednesday we met for a midweek meal at a Mexican restaurant. A three-piece band was playing in the corner, and I dedicated a song to Mariko. On Saturday evening we wandered through neon-lit streets, poking around novelty stores and trying on fake plastic noses and oversized glasses. We browsed through designer fashion stores, com-peting for who could find the most ridiculously overpriced item. We took our photos in purikura booths and tried to figure out why anyone would play pachinko.

The following week we met twice, and on the days when we did not meet we called and sent copious text messages. Mariko learned of my tendency to fall apart during sad movies, so the following Friday she suggested we go and watch a newly released tear-jerker so she could see me cry. I managed only a single manly tear. Mariko, meanwhile, wept like a baby, and punched me in the arm when I pointed out that her plan had backfired.

Nearly a month of happy encounters with Mariko had passed, but I was yet to express my true feelings for her. My friends were becoming concerned.

'You're going to have to hurry up and tell her,' Justin warned.

'Yeah, she'll start to think of you as a "nice guy" friend,' Blake added.

'You have to make some sort of move soon,' Justin continued. 'When are you guys going to see that *Star Wars* movie? You should tell her then.'

'No, don't tell her,' Matt cautioned. 'You need to kiss her. You'll never get anywhere just by telling her how you feel. You need to *show* her.'

My head spun. This was becoming scary.

'I think he's right,' Justin agreed. 'You can't be a nice guy. Nice guys ask girls out and get told that their neighbour's house has burned down. Nice guys hesitate and don't do anything and then the girl disappears. You're going to have to kiss her.'

I knew they were right, but I was petrified. Kissing Mariko Kitamura sounded like the most difficult thing in the world.

We met the following Thursday evening to watch *Star Wars: Episode II* at the Namba cinema. I was nervous and sweaty, and barely able to concentrate on the movie. Mariko, on the other hand, was her usual self and did not seem to notice my clammy behaviour.

The two-and-a-half-hour-long movie felt like an eternity while I agonisingly rehearsed my attempt to kiss Mariko a hundred times in my head. Thousands of unpleasant and embarrassing reactions to my kiss replayed themselves over and over in my mind.

The end credits started to roll. 'Shall we go and get a drink?' Mariko asked. 'I want to talk to you about something.'

'Huh?' I was a million miles away. 'Okay, yes, a drink would be good. Where do you want to go?'

I was suddenly very worried. I had neglected to choose a suitable location for my award-winning kiss. I had imagined it would take place somewhere romantic, on top of a tall building surrounded by twinkling lights, or perhaps on top of a mountain while a symphony orchestra played in the background. Now I was suddenly faced with the possibility of having to kiss Mariko in a brightly lit café, or in front of a train-load of Japanese commuters.

'I know a good café near Amerika Mura,' Mariko smiled. 'C'mon, let's go. I'm thirsty.'

As we strolled to the café I managed to make polite conversation about the movie. Mariko had enjoyed it and eagerly recounted her favourite scenes.

We sat down in the café. My stomach was full of butterflies and my palms were sweaty. We ordered apple juice and I sat back in my seat, mentally preparing myself for my big moment.

'There's something I want to talk to you about,' Mariko said suddenly.

I looked up. She was blushing.

'I've met a guy I quite like.'

My mind raced, and my heart skipped a beat.

Mariko paused, her cheeks burning.

I smiled. Mariko was about to tell me she liked me.

'Yes,' she continued, looking up. 'I've met this guy in my French class. He's from France. He's really nice, and I was wanting to ask him out for a meal. What do you think I should do? Should I ask him out?'

I felt myself leave my body and spin dizzily around the café. I slurped my apple juice in a frantic effort to compose myself.

Shit, shit, shit! What on earth was going on?

Mariko was looking at me hopefully. I was to give her advice for her romance with this French tosser. I hated the Frenchman. I hated him for being in Japan. I hated him for being from France. I hated his country.

I slurped my apple juice some more. My glass was empty. I needed another.

I paused. It was now or never. I either tell Mariko how I feel about her and hope she will suddenly realise she feels the same way about me, or I watch as she rides off into the sunset with a French tosser.

'Mariko,' I said slowly, 'you do realise how I feel about you, don't you?'
Mariko looked at me blankly.

'I mean, you do know that I really, really like you, don't you?'
Mariko looked confused.

I took a deep breath and continued. 'I've liked you since the moment
we met. I love spending time with you, laughing with you, talking with
you. I had hoped things might develop further between us.'

My cheeks were burning. I felt foolish, but I had said my piece. There
would be no 'what ifs' in my mind after tonight.

Mariko sat silently for a few moments. Her mesmerising smile had
vanished and she seemed very sad. She opened her mouth to speak, and
the evening switched to autopilot.

I had received the 'just good friends' speech around thirteen times and
in two different languages. Mariko's rendition was no different to any of
the others.

It went something like this:

'Oh, wow! I never knew you liked me.' Silence while the speaker looks
at the ground or table. 'Well, I guess I sort of knew you liked me, but I
wasn't really sure.'

More silence.

'Yeah, well, I've only ever thought of you as a friend. I think you're a
*really, really nice guy* and a *really special friend*. So yeah, I've only ever
thought of you as a friend. I always thought you wanted to be my friend
too. I really think we should stay as just good friends. Sorry.'

Both the speaker and the spoken-to blush and look down. The activity
—usually dinner, drinks, or a conversation in a private corner of a school
sports field—comes to an abrupt end, and the two parties depart, never
to speak again.

Mariko finished her sterling recital of the 'just good friends' speech and
we both blushed and looked at the table. I paid for the two apple juices and
we walked silently to the train station.

'I still want to be friends,' she said quietly as she stepped on to her
train.

I smiled wanly. 'We'll see.'

Justin was even more upset by my story than I was. Blake was outraged and Matt was furious. 'Forget all about her,' they lectured me. 'There are more fish in the ocean.'

Mariko's 'just good friends' speech had been a bitter pill to swallow. I decided it needed to be washed down with therapeutic sake and copious amounts of beer. I was in luck, as the following weekend provided more than ample opportunity. I was scheduled to attend the school staff party from six until nine on Saturday evening, and Justin's thirtieth birthday drinks from nine until dawn.

I had decided well in advance that Justin's birthday was the more important of the two celebrations, and I intended to take things easy at the staff party so that I could still be at my coherent and witty best for the rest of the evening. These good intentions were, however, short-lived.

The Kanan Junior High School staff social committee had spared no expense organising the party. A lavish ballroom had been booked at a swanky inner-city hotel, and everyone except me arrived in formal attire. Expensive sushi and sashimi platters adorned the tables and tuxedo-clad waiters stood to attention, ready to top up beer glasses and replace empty sake jugs. As with all staff parties, the school principal, Mr Kazama, had kindly paid the bill and we were invited to eat and drink as much as we possibly could.

I was seated at a table with Mr Higo and the other young male teachers. Everyone was determined that I should sample the delights and flavours of Japanese beer, and my six red-faced colleagues made sure my glass was constantly topped up. When I carelessly announced that I enjoyed warm sake, Mr Higo quickly dispatched one of the waiters to fetch several jugs of the hotel's finest rice wine. The PE teachers, Mr Omura and Mr Terada, switched seats and joined our table, bringing Mr Omura's favourite bottle of whisky. Mr Kazama, who had been sitting at the other side of the ballroom, noticed our whisky consumption and joined us.

After a while I lost track of what I was drinking and how many glasses I had downed. Mr Higo cranked up a karaoke machine in the corner of the ballroom, and he and I slurred out a hideous rendition of a Deep Purple rock anthem. Mr Terada cheered loudly. Someone had recently taught him the English term 'dark horse', and he enthusiastically applied it to me for the rest of the evening.

By the time the party ended, I was dizzy and light-headed, could not walk straight, and was cackling to myself demonically. As luck would have it, Justin's party was taking place at a bar only three blocks away. Mr Kazama was reluctant to let me wander off into the darkness by myself, but Mr Terada assured him that I was a 'dark horse' and obviously well used to the streets and drinking holes of downtown Osaka.

I staggered off and joined my friends. They had eaten a large dinner at a Korean barbecue restaurant and, having lined their stomachs sufficiently to see them through to dawn, were alarmingly sober. I bought Justin a drink to wish him happy birthday, and then we all ordered vodka shots. The bartender turned out to be a fellow Cantabrian and we reminisced about life in New Zealand. After I purported to be a huge fan of the Canterbury rugby team, the Crusaders, he patted me on the shoulder and announced I could drink whatever I wanted for the remainder of the evening free of charge.

I promptly ordered two sambucas, another vodka and a rum and Coke. Justin, Wij and Blake were now on the dance floor, so I tried to make intelligent conversation with our American friends, Jocelyn and Elise. Jocelyn had been having boy problems and had broken up with her boyfriend. I nodded supportively as she told me her tale of woe, and cocked my head to one side so my eyes could focus on her properly.

'That's no good,' I volunteered. 'You shouldn't put up with that short of nonshensh. What you need to do is—'

My wise words of advice sadly went unfinished. My head lolled to one side, I toppled backwards off my bar stool and landed heavily on my back.

I picked myself up. Where was I? I had to get out into some fresh air. A burly bouncer stood in front of the door. I staggered up to him, swayed for a few moments, vomited at his feet and passed out.

I awoke several hours later. I was sitting on the bar's balcony. My jacket was draped over a chair and my shirt and trousers were covered in vomit. My head pounded. I checked my jacket. It was covered in vomit as well.

'Ha, you're alive.' Wij was laughing at me. 'That was quite a party trick. Boy, you sure made a mess of the entranceway. You managed to stink out the whole bar. People were coming in off the street, gagging and walking straight back out.

'The bouncers wanted to beat you up, but Justin and I stepped in and dragged you out here.'

I blushed.

'No one's ever going to forget this one. You've made my drunken train trips look like child's play. Thanks, mate. Now you can be the butt of all the drunken idiot jokes.'

'Thanks for looking after me,' I said. My cheeks were burning.

'Don't worry about it,' Wij smiled. 'You can pay for my dry-cleaning though.'

'That was some birthday present.' Justin had joined us. 'I think you'd better get a new chat-up line if you want to get a girlfriend. That projectile vomiting isn't going to get you anywhere.'

# 13

# Winter blues

*My gums had been bleeding* for the past two months every time I brushed my teeth. This was getting out of hand. I needed to find myself a dentist.

I delayed. The gammy, crooked smiles of my students and the silver-plated grins in the staffroom had done nothing to instil confidence in Japanese dentists. Then one night I had a terrifying dream that all my teeth crumbled to dust and fell out of my mouth. I was suddenly a tooth-less young man with flapping gums who struggled to make himself heard and could no longer pronounce the word 'sausages'.

This was the clincher. I called the local dental surgery and made an appointment for the following Saturday afternoon. After I had waited in his furnace-like reception area for forty minutes, my new dentist, Dr Shimano, got around to seeing me. His surgery was spotlessly clean and reeked of disinfectant. I was puzzled to notice two other patients already reclining in dental chairs and being attended to by dental nurses. It seemed that Dr Shimano was going to treat all three of us at the same time.

Dr Shimano had a quick look around the inside of my mouth and then disappeared to consult his dictionary. He returned looking sombre, and in a grave tone announced, 'You have a disease.'

'Hmm,' I thought, wondering how I would explain this to my mother.

'Yes, you have gum disease.'

I was suddenly very sweaty. What this would mean here in Japan, land of prehistoric dentistry?

'Ah, Mr Hamish, you have a disease,' Dr Shimano repeated in halting English, 'so I will need to perform PMTC on you. Do you know what this means?'

Alas, I did not, but nor did I like the sound of it.

'Yes, Mr Hamish, I will perform PMTC, Professional Mechanical Teeth Cleaning, on you. It will take one hour and it will hurt. Maybe.'

I was getting a lot sweatier now and asked him to turn the heater off.

'Please,' I begged, 'is there no other option? A new toothpaste? Some medicine? Or perhaps even a bag of antibiotics?'

Dr Shimano shook his head gravely. Unfortunately there was no other option available. 'Ah, Mr Hamish, this will take one hour, but when the pain becomes unbearable please raise your left hand.'

I looked at my watch. One hour equalled sixty seconds, counted slowly sixty times. I could handle that, surely. I inquired as to what drill he would be using, so I could gauge whether he would be able to fit the damn thing in my mouth.

'Oh no,' he replied, 'I will use this.' I sighed with relief as he pulled out the old-fashioned pointy scraper that dentists use all over the world. Dr Shimano then proceeded to scratch away at my teeth in the usual painless dentist fashion. A good seventy minutes later the procedure was over and I had not raised my left hand once.

And so my first, and hopefully last, trip to a dentist in Japan was over.

It was mid November, and I was being drawn into staffroom politics. Mr Doi, the deranged woodwork teacher, was slowly but surely losing his sanity, and had become the laughing stock of the entire school as he roamed the corridors in his checked flannel shirts with his trademark cellphone and bright orange plastic cord bulging beneath his woollen vest. His abrasive nature and cocky attitude had earned him a fearsome reputation, and everyone went to great lengths to keep well clear of him.

I took no pity on Mr Doi. However, it seemed he had taken some sort of shine to me. He constantly appeared at my desk, trying to chat me up.

'Mr Hame,' he announced loudly, keen to show all and sundry that he was able to speak English with me, 'what are you doing now?'

I looked up grumpily from my *Harry Potter* novel. I was halfway through the third book in the series and not in the mood for interruptions.

'I see that you have free time now. Why not speak English with me?'

Why not indeed, I thought to myself. 'Ah, Mr Doi,' I replied, 'what, may I ask, are you currently doing on this pleasant autumn morning? As you can see, I am busy reading this English novel while at the same sipping some bitter coffee that is still too hot for my poor delicate tongue.'

Mr Doi blinked. He had absolutely no idea what I was talking about.

'Ha, ha...yes,' he replied. My long-winded and rapid-fire English had not deterred him. 'I am thinking...I have many cars. I have four cars. Did you know?'

'Yes, I have four cars,' he continued. The volume of his voice increased. 'I have a Toyota.'

He looked around, a cocky smirk etched on his flounder-like face. The neighbouring teachers were ignoring him.

'I have a Volkswagen.' He paused. Nobody showed even a flicker of interest.

Mr Doi looked nervous. 'I have a BMW.' His voice rose expectantly. Somebody coughed and turned further away in their chair.

'Ah, and I have a Mercedes. It is a new car!'

Nobody cared.

Mr Doi turned back to me quickly. 'Do you like my cars?' he asked pleadingly.

I shrugged. 'I have three bicycles,' I replied. 'Two of them have baskets.'

Mr Doi blinked. He was still struggling to understand my kiwi accent and rapid-fire responses.

'Ah yes, I think you can use my BMW any time, Mr Hame.' Mr Doi smiled greasily. 'But I am not sure that you are a good driver. Before I give you my BMW I want to see you drive. Yes, why not go for a drive with me sometime?'

It was my turn to blink in surprise. 'Pardon?'

'Let's go for a drive, only you and me. Are you free now? We can go for a drive in the countryside.'

I coughed in alarm. 'I am very busy. I have many classes to teach.' I grimaced. In reality I had a four-hour break until my next lesson, and had been planning to eat chocolate and write an email to my family.

'But I know you want my BMW. It is a great car. I will give it to you. You will enjoy it.'

I stopped smiling. 'Mr Doi, I have three bicycles. I do not want a car. I am happy with my bicycles. Thank you for your kind offer, but I do not need your BMW.'

Mr Doi shrugged. 'Tell me when is your free time. We will go for a drive then.' And with that he departed.

Mrs Takaoka, the friendly second-grade English teacher, leaned over to me quietly. 'Mr Hame,' she whispered, 'I do not think you should go for a drive with Mr Doi.'

I nodded in agreement. 'He's very strange.'

Mrs Takaoka smiled. 'I never talk to him. I always hide when he is in the room. The other teachers think he is strange too. Mr Terada thinks he has mental problems.'

Mr Terada was the head PE teacher, and more powerful and influential than the school principal. All the teachers admired him greatly, and the students loved and feared him. He was the funniest teacher in the school, yet at the same time chillingly strict. Because he was very fair, everyone respected his decisions and judgments.

Mr Terada exuded coolness. In his late thirties, he looked at least ten years younger. His intelligent face was accentuated by a devilish goatee and razor-sharp haircut. He wore the latest fashions and knew more about Japanese pop culture than any of his students.

I had long ago realised that success as a teacher at Kanan Junior High School depended, in part, on being accepted by Mr Terada: it was like getting the blessing and protection of a mafia godfather. Students who misbehaved in your class would be dealt with in PE class by Mr Terada, who would make them run extra laps of the school field, or put them on cleaning detail during their lunch breaks. At the same time Mr Terada would rave about his preferred colleagues to the students, thereby giving those teachers a golden seal of approval.

I had managed to make a good impression on Mr Terada from the start. He had seen me playing tennis with the boys' team after school, and had taken me under his wing.

Sadly, though, Mr Terada's speech was peppered with colloquial Japanese slang and he was possibly the most difficult-to-understand person I had encountered in Japan. He was completely unable to speak English and so we struggled to communicate at anything more than a basic level.

Be that as it may, we had developed a slapstick routine that Mr Terada insisted we perform whenever any students were nearby. We would talk loudly at each other in our respective languages and Mr Terada would laugh loudly, proudly exclaiming that he understood every word that I had said. The students would cheekily call him a liar and he would respond by speaking gibberish at them, which he claimed was fluent English. The students would explode with laughter and Mr Terada would pat me on the back.

Mr Terada's opinion of me had grown fonder following the recent staff party where he had nicknamed me 'dark horse', and he made sure everyone knew what a 'cool guy' I was.

To be offside with Mr Terada, then, was not something to be taken lightly. Mr Doi was in trouble.

Over the next few weeks, Mr Doi's visits to my desk and attempts to arrange a romantic drive for two in his BMW became more and more frequent. He stepped up the pace by inviting me into his office in the woodwork room to sit on his new couch and talk about computers.

I took refuge with Mrs Takaoka and other neighbouring colleagues. They sadly informed me that until Mr Doi was fired, committed or pushed under a bus, there was little any of us could do except listen to him drivel on about his prowess with a saxophone, or how he used to be a great racing-car driver.

By mid December, my list of grievances with Mr Doi stood as follows:

- Telling me I couldn't pronounce English 'plopery'.
- Telling me that I should buy a (faulty) computer from him for $6,000.
- Constantly inviting me to his house so that his children could have someone to speak English to.
- Wiping the school computer's network server so the school was two weeks without internet access.

- Patting a visiting seventeen-year-old Czech exchange student on the leg and telling her I was a nice guy, and that she and I would make a great couple.
- Patting another male teacher on the leg and telling him I had a big penis.

As December approached, the temperature in south Osaka gradually dropped through the floor. Winter had come early to Kanan Town, and the barrages of sleet felt straight out of Siberia.

My apartment's air-conditioning unit was now switched to the heat setting, and tirelessly cranking out hot air. I was sleeping beneath four thick blankets, including my old pink favourite, and never ventured outside without a woollen hat and gloves. I spent numerous evenings huddled under a blanket on my sofa, eating takeaways and watching English movies from the local video store.

I was now well-known at the local eateries. The Chinese takeaway store near the train station served generous helpings of sweet and sour pork. The 'hot lunch-box' shop next to the video store sold a great barbecue beef and deep-fried potato meal. The convenience stores had their own brands of steamed meat buns, to which I had developed something of an addiction. And at least once a fortnight I braved the elements to dine on fresh tuna or marinated eel sushi at the rotating sushi restaurant about ten minutes' walk from my apartment.

At school, the teachers huddled around the two oil heaters in the staffroom. These belched out such overpowering paraffin fumes that it felt as though we were working in a petrol station.

I had a particular problem. My desk was situated closest to the staffroom door, which was constantly left open by scurrying students and less than thoughtful colleagues. Icy winds raced down from the mountains, across the frost-covered school grounds, into the school's entrance hall, along the corridor, through the staffroom door, and up my trouser leg.

I eventually took matters into my own hands and posted a stern bilingual 'Keep shut' sign on the door. My students pointed at my scribbly

Japanese handwriting and giggled until Mr Terada overheard and gave them a good telling-off. From then on the door remained firmly closed at all times.

Conversation about the weather was always a popular topic, but never more so than during my sessions with my Japanese mothers. Mrs Tanaka had caught a cold, and all sorts of home-made remedies and medicines were prescribed. Some, such as mixtures of garlic and pickles, sounded extraordinarily unpleasant, but the mothers assured me that their concoctions were much more successful than the swags of antibiotics dished out by doctors.

Mrs Kiguchi, our polite host, was slowly becoming more confident in her use of English. She would quietly inquire about winter conditions in New Zealand, and what everybody did to keep warm. At this point, Mrs Terauchi would inform everyone that winter was a very hard time in New Zealand as we often had no electricity, and occasionally no food, and walked through the snow to work.

I was becoming less concerned by such misinformation, as it seemed that no one took any notice of Mrs Terauchi's opinions. However, her eccentric nature caused me some distress on the day of our final conversation class for the year. It was raining heavily and bitterly cold, so I had decided to take the bus to work instead of cycling. Mrs Terauchi had promised to pick me up and ferry me to the class.

When school finished, I waited in the rain at the pre-arranged place. Time passed and the rain plastered my hair to my scalp. Mrs Terauchi had chosen an exposed pick-up point, but I had not expected her to be late.

Twenty more minutes passed. Mrs Kiguchi's house was only five minutes' bike ride from the school and downhill most of the way. I decided to take my chances and jogged off down the road.

I arrived at the elegant Kiguchi residence fifteen minutes later, dripping wet and resembling a drowned rat. Mrs Kiguchi hurriedly ushered me in, fussing about my wet hair and clothes. Fresh towels arrived, hot tea was prepared and chocolates and sweets produced.

A shrill voice called out from the living-room. 'Sensei, why are you so wet? Why did you go outside in the rain?' Mrs Terauchi shook her head disapprovingly. 'You should have asked me to pick you up!'

The mothers were keen to prescribe all sorts of sticky medicines and putrid hot drinks. 'Sensei,' they implored me, 'you must take care of your health. In this cold and wet season you can easily catch a chill. You must stay warm and dry.'

I smiled wanly. Yes, I certainly needed to stay warm and take things easy. Life in frozen Osaka would be the death of me. I needed a tropical holiday. Meanwhile, though, I had been invited to the local kindergarten to play Santa Claus for the second year in a row. I wondered what unfortunate events would befall me this time.

The first disaster was completely unforeseen. No crying children or violent audiences, but something much, much worse: Rachel Brown had also received an invitation. She was to play the part of Mrs Claus.

I had been managing to avoid Rachel exceedingly well over the past couple of months. The first part of my strategy had been to screen all in-coming telephone calls. I no longer answered my phone, and had instruc-ted all my friends and family either to leave a message or call my cellphone, which had caller ID. Despite this, Rachel had made persistent efforts to contact me and had peppered my answer machine with whiney problems and bleating requests.

In mid September, she had left a message inviting me to a local café for a cup of coffee. Suspicious of her motives, I had left a message informing her that I was unfortunately preoccupied for the entire fortnight. She had called back and explained that she had wanted me to bring my dictionary and a pen and paper to the café to translate the menu for her. Later she called again, asking if I would lend her my dictionary.

In October she had left more messages, asking me to lend her my microwave oven. 'I'm making cup-cakes' she informed me, 'and my micro-wave is too small to make suitable batches.'

I ignored these requests for two weeks and hoped the matter was resolved. At seven-thirty on a Wednesday night, however, my door bell rang. I opened it without thinking, expecting the visitor to be my landlady or her daughters bringing me fruit or chocolate.

A bedraggled and sour-looking Rachel Brown stood pouting on my doorstep. 'I've come for your microwave,' she snarled without any form of introduction.

'Sorry, I'm using it at the moment.'

'I'll come back tomorrow then. I need it for Friday. I've got friends coming round and I need to bake cup-cakes.'

I shrugged. 'Okay, come round about seven.'

Rachel stuck her head nosily over my shoulder. 'Have you finished that *Harry Potter* book yet? I want to read it after you.'

'Sorry, I've got ages to go,' I dissembled, 'and my friend Justin wants to borrow it after me anyway.'

'Right. Well, I've got it after him then.'

'Sure,' I said coldly. 'Sorry Rachel, but I was asleep. I better go.'

'But it's only seven-thirty.'

'Yeah, I'm tired.' I bowed in polite Japanese fashion and closed the door.

Rachel called out from behind the door. 'I'll see you tomorrow then?'

Since this episode I had managed to completely avoid Rachel. The kindergarten visit was going to make for an unpleasant reunion.

'You're in my bad books at the moment.' We were sitting at our desks in the Board of Education, dressed in our Santa suits, and Rachel was pouting at me.

'Why's that then?' I asked in a bored voice.

'This is all your fault,' she hissed. 'I don't want to do this stupid kindergarten visit.'

'But it's fun,' I protested.

'No it's not. This sucks. I look ridiculous.'

'At least you don't have a fake beard,' I muttered. 'And at least your suit fits you.' Rachel had been given a perfectly sized Santa suit and comfortable black gumboots. I, meanwhile, was again wearing my pint-sized doll costume and rubbish-bag shoes.

'You're weird! This sucks. I didn't want to come, but Mr Horrii said that since you were going I had to. This is all your fault,' she repeated.

I fumed silently. 'Don't worry,' I said coolly, 'it wasn't my idea to invite you.'

I paused, and considered telling her that I could think of nothing worse for the poor children of Kanan Town than having to suffer a surly visit from a grumpy young woman from England. But I held my tongue.

The visit flashed by quickly. The children from the previous year's two kindergartens had been merged into one giant-sized class in order to reduce nervous tension and panicked reactions. The mothers of the fifty-four tiny children had also been invited, in the hope that, as well as providing a comforting presence, they would control the hyperactive demons who wanted to jump on Santa's feet and pull his trousers down.

Rachel and I pranced out on to the kindergarten stage and danced awkwardly to Japanese pop music. Actually, only I danced awkwardly to Japanese pop music. Rachel stood still as a statue and pouted, while the children pointed, laughed, squealed and cheered. After a rendition of 'Jingle Bells' by the tone-deaf kindergarten orchestra, a rapid-fire question-and-answer session ensued, with the children demanding to know where we were from, how we had come to Japan, and where we were staying. Rachel stared out grumpily. I was tempted to tell everyone in Japanese that she had flown in on a broomstick, but charitably rolled out the 'super jet over Europe, helicopter over China, and sled from Hiroshima' story I had invented the previous year.

Then it was play time, and I was dragged off to a play room by the five-year-olds. I chased the kids around a bit and they punched me, pulled off my hat and beard, and one girl pulled my pants down. Remarkably, by the end they all still seemed to believe that I was Santa. As we were leaving, I was presented with a sack full of scribbled lists of toys that the children wanted.

Rachel snorted. 'I can't believe they think you're Santa. You look ridiculous.'

I continued to smile. Rachel's prickly personality was not going to burst my bubble. 'What are you doing for Christmas?' I asked.

'Humph. I dunno. Think I'll be stuck here. What about you?'

'Nothing much,' I lied. 'I'll probably spend the winter holidays studying in the town library.'

Rachel rolled her eyes. 'Man, that sounds boring.'

In reality I intended to follow the advice of my Japanese mothers and escape snow-bound Osaka for a three-week holiday in hot places. I had secretly planned this two months earlier, at the same time telling anyone who was interested that I would be spending Christmas at the library and

then celebrating New Year with the Tanakas in Tokyo. Officially sanc-
tioned international travel would require me to use up precious annual
leave and have my itinerary meticulously scrutinised by the education
superintendent. Study at the local library, on the other hand, was considered beneficial for both me and Kanan Junior High School. I was therefore allowed uninterrupted time away from school, the Board of Education
and Rachel Brown.

I departed Japan on December 19 and spent Christmas and New Year
with friends, travelling through Singapore, Malaysia and Indonesia.

January had arrived, and with it the Year of the Horse. Since I had been
born in the Year of the Horse, my Japanese horoscope informed me that
I was destined for much good fortune during the year, and would prosper
to new levels of happiness.

Things certainly got off to a prosperous start. I had sent Mr Kitahashi,
the mayor, a New Year's greetings card prior to my departure for Malaysia.
Mr Kitahashi had reportedly been blown away by my small gesture, and
had reciprocated by giving me an antique sake jug and matching mugs.

From then on, my level of prosperity increased ten-fold. I arrived back
in Japan from my tropical holiday on January 8 and started work the next
day, only to find that my classes had been cancelled for an entire fortnight
because of exams. I was therefore able to eat chocolate, drink coffee,
finish reading the fourth volume of *Harry Potter*, and grow fat at my desk
while still being paid. Luckily there was a three-day weekend thrown in
along the way. I toiled away, struggling to get through first a three-day
and then a four-day working week of no classes.

My third week back at work rolled around, and after Monday and
Tuesday's lessons had been cancelled due to a timetable reshuffle, I left for
three days of gruelling skiing and snowball fights on the school ski trip.

Mr Kazama, the owl-like principal, realising how demanding this
hectic lifestyle would be on my frail health, gave me the following
Monday and Tuesday off work 'in case you have sore muscles'. Deciding
to make the most of his kindness, I used my recuperation time to jet off
for a four-day holiday in a spa town on the southern island of Kyushu.

On my return, I dragged myself back to the office for a three-day working week, in which all my classes had (unsurprisingly) been cancelled due to examination debriefs. Still worried about my sore muscles, I booked myself and some friends in for a relaxing retreat at a mountain-top temple for the following weekend.

Blake, Matt and I caught a train to Koya-San, the small alpine town where I had admired autumn colours with the Okis over a year earlier. The maple trees and the town were now blanketed with thick powdery snow. Our hosts, a shy group of Buddhist monks, ushered us to our spartan rooms, served us healthy vegetarian meals and invited us to take part in Buddhist chanting outside in the snow.

Following this introduction to monastic worship, we were ushered back to our rooms and left alone to meditate and contemplate the meaning of life. Being sadly devoid of spiritual intention, however, we spent the weekend in epic snowball battles up and down the town's main street and through its enchanted snow-covered forest, during which I managed to dislodge Blake's glasses from over 100 metres away.

Back at Kanan Junior High School, life was not all chocolate bars and *Harry Potter*. My abundance of free time had made me even easier prey for the mentally deranged woodwork teacher.

At our first conversation of the year, Mr Doi was looking tired and stressed. He stood at my desk with slumped shoulders and crossed arms, ready to share his emotional burden and assorted woes. He leant forward slowly and whispered that the other teachers did not like him, but he was very happy because I was his friend and he could confide in me since I was a foreigner and therefore a more open person than his Japanese colleagues.

He went on to explain that the resentment towards him was unfair. The teachers did not understand him. 'I am an energetic man,' he said, 'and do not have much time to spare for this job.'

He lowered his voice and gave me a secretive, knowing nod. 'Yes, I have many other jobs. I am a bodyguard, but that is very secret. I am an ombudsman. I work at a secret chemical laboratory, and I used to be a race-car driver.'

'The other teachers do not understand me,' Mr Doi repeated. 'They have small dreams.' He wandered off mid-sentence to teach thirteen-year-olds how to build stools.

The next day's interruption was even more bizarre, and I was completely baffled by Mr Doi's opening question. 'Do you have any relations with the US military in Korea?' His flounder face was locked in an expression of absolute seriousness. This was not a joking matter.

I scratched my head. I had no idea what this was about and how I should answer.

It transpired that Mr Doi was intending to drive to South Korea, and hoped to obtain the help of the US military in his mission. Doing my best not to laugh, I flicked through my handy *English Teacher Fact File* and produced a map of Korea and some useful statistics, such as the population of Seoul. As Mr Doi shambled off to use the photocopier, I made my escape.

# 14

# My friend Mr Higo

*Mr Higo was my best friend* in the Kanan Junior High School staffroom. On my first day at school he had introduced himself by asking whether I wanted to be part of the group of young single male teachers who regularly ordered the staffroom lunch-boxes.

He was twenty-four years old, and until my arrival at the school had been the youngest member of staff. He had been working as a fully qualified English teacher for only two years, and had never travelled abroad. He spoke halting English and seemed embarrassed by his accent and lack of foreign travel.

It was after many months of working at the school that I learned that Mr Higo's first job after graduating from teacher's college had been working alongside a stubborn, opinionated teacher from England named Melanie. Descriptions painted a picture of a rude, spoiled young woman, not dissimilar to Rachel Brown. I was appalled to learn that Melanie had publicly criticised Mr Higo's English ability and accent in front of his students. Understandably, he had developed a fear of working with foreigners, and was initially shy to approach me.

Mr Higo and I soon discovered, however, that we shared a lot of common interests and a sardonic sense of humour. He was the coach of the school baseball team and a proud supporter of Osaka's Hanshin Tigers.

I was a less-than-average cricket player who delighted in watching the New Zealand team lose to third-world opponents.

This shared interest in sport got our working relationship off to a flying start. We both detested the formal rote learning methods of the Japanese education system, and decided that competitive games and a humorous environment would be more stimulating for our third-grade students. Each week we would arrive at class armed with simple games that we had prepared only moments earlier, and that usually involved groups of students racing around the classroom, making sentences, and then sprinting to the blackboard to be the first group to scribble out their answer. These games produced an excited reaction from the students, and resulted in several head-on collisions and messy spills. However, the accidents were never serious and Mr Higo and I would cheer on the teams and perform theatrical umpiring gestures to rev up the audience.

As well as these physical games, our lesson plans usually included some sort of impromptu comedy routine, in which we would act out a skit or scene relevant to the day's grammar lesson. Often our skits involved making fun of each other or impersonating one of the other teachers, and our daring increased as the months went by. Eventually I felt confident enough to impersonate the super-cool Mr Terada; I stormed into the classroom with Mr Terada's trademark tough-guy glare and yelled at Mr Higo in mafia-esque Japanese.

The students roared with laughter, but Mr Higo went uncharacteristically pale. Sure enough, word of our skit reached Mr Terada, but he merely gave me a mock telling-off in gibberish English, inserting the words 'dark horse' into every second sentence.

As well as poking fun at our colleagues and each other, Mr Higo and I excelled at taking the mickey out of our students. Cheeky or rebellious students were given nicknames, and these would later appear in worksheets or English homework.

The class clown of 3-D was a boy called Yuji Tomiyama. Yuji repeatedly tried to make me blush during class by fluttering his eyelashes and blowing me kisses. Mr Higo began referring to Yuji as 'Tombi', the nickname of Yuji's eleven-year-old sister, and Yuji stopped giving me the glad eye.

Several weeks later Mr Higo presented the class with its term exam. The written section involved the students writing a short story about 'Tombi' Tomiyama, who was waiting at the bus stop. Students had to write about where 'Tombi' was going, and what he was going to do once he got there.

Several of Yuji's good friends decided that Yuji was going to a 'clothes shope' to buy a 'lady wig'. I chuckled as I marked the exam, and Mr Higo and I fell about laughing when we read Yuji's bold scribbling proclaiming that he was going to 'Mr Hamish's house' to see his 'number one boyfriend'.

While I eagerly looked forward to the two days a week I spent teaching classes with Mr Higo, the day I spent teaching alongside Mr Hioki was a different matter entirely. In the year we had been working together, nothing had changed. My only contribution was to act as a human tape recorder. My brain was unplugged from my body and every week I repeated the same pointless, soul-destroying routine:

Trudge to class.

Greet the students.

Perform the prescribed greeting. Do not stray from the prescribed greeting.

'How are you? I'm fine.'

Go and stand in the corner by the overhead projector.

Stare out the third-floor window.

Recite today's grammatically faulty script five times.

'What kind of movie do Yuki like the most?'

'What kind of movie do Yuki like the most?'

'What kind of movie do Yuki like the most?'

'What kind of movie do Yuki like the most?'

'What kind of movie do Yuki like the most?'

Speak slowly.

Do not correct the grammar. Do not change the script. Free thought is banned!

Speak more slowly. Mind-numbingly slowly.

'Does Jim think that studying hard is the most important thing of all?'

Slower.

'Does Jim think that studying hard is the most important thing of all?'

Slower.

'Does Jim think that studying hard is the most important thing of all?'

Slower.

'Does Jim think that studying hard is the most important thing of all?'

One more time. Slower.

'Does Jim think that studying hard is the most important thing of all?'

Do not correct the grammar. Do not change the script. Free thought is banned!

Go and stand in the corner by the OHP.

Stare out the third-floor window.

Wait for the students to repeat the script and fill out a worksheet for thirty minutes.

Stare out the third-floor window. Consider jumping.

Bell rings.

Wait for Mr Hioki to send lazy or unmotivated students to detention.

Farewell remaining students.

Perform the prescribed farewell. Do not stray from the prescribed farewell.

'Goodbye, everybody.'

Do not expect a response. At best, the boy with cross-eyes will mutter 'Goodbye, Mr Hame.'

It seemed I was not alone in despising my classes with Mr Hioki. After only a few months Mr Hioki had managed to kill all motivation and enthusiasm in his twelve-year-old students. The very intelligent ones were stifled and bored, discouraged from advancing themselves in case this proved them to have superior English skills to Mr Hioki. The less intelligent ones were scolded severely for not understanding the pointless English sentences that were bludgeoned into them, and quickly gave up all interest in the English language.

The result of Mr Hioki's monotonous lessons was eventually revealed to him in mortifying fashion when he foolishly conjured up the idea of giving all one hundred and fifty-three students the exercise of conducting an English survey. Each student was required to interview every member of their homeroom class and determine who were the most popular teachers at school, as well as the least popular.

I scratched my head in bewilderment as I could immediately see where these survey results would lead. As well as this, I was astonished at Mr Hioki's belief that the students would even attempt to conduct the survey in English. Sure enough, they rose from their seats and huddled in small groups, interviewing each other in Japanese and copying each others' answers. The findings were collated by the student leader in each class, and then written on the blackboard.

The results across the five homerooms were virtually unanimous. The three most popular teachers in Kanan Junior High School were Mr Terada and Mr Hamish, tied on 100 percent, and Mr Nakata, a physical education teacher, on 95 percent.

Only two teachers featured in the unpopularity ratings. Mr Doi came second to bottom with a 3 percent popularity rating, and Mr Hioki bottom with 0 percent to 12 percent. I did the maths in my head and soon figured out that Mr Hioki's 12 percent support base consisted of a few of the timid, slightly handicapped students who were verging on demotion to the young minnows' stream.

Mr Hioki was outraged when the first set of results was written up on the blackboard, and erased them immediately. The remaining results were read out once, and anyone caught laughing or repeating them was given detention.

While I basked in the glory of my flattering popularity, the survey gave Mr Hioki an opportunity to dent my spirits and put me offside with the students. 'Since Mr Hamish is soooooo popular,' he announced, 'the children should be forced to write English fan letters to him.'

And so the following week Mr Hioki hatched his most boring class of all time. 'Your homework is to write a letter in English,' he declared sternly.

The children groaned, and one severely aggrieved boy was given detention.

'Yes, you must write a letter in English,' Mr Hioki repeated. 'Your letter must be at least one page long.'

More groans. The severely aggrieved boy received a second detention.

'You must write a letter in English,' Mr Hioki chanted for the third time. He paused for dramatic effect. 'And you must send it to Mr Hamish.

You must write a letter to Mr Hamish. You must introduce yourself and tell him a story.'

The students groaned. More detentions.

I seethed quietly. In the students' minds I was now the reason for their having to write a stupid, boring letter in a stupid, boring language. Mr Hamish's popularity rapidly began to wane.

My friend Mr Higo watched me with a smile as I slowly waded through the stack of scribbled, incoherent letters on my desk.

'Ha ha ha,' he laughed, peering over my shoulder, 'that letter is very wrong. Very bad. Very lazy. Ha ha ha.'

His laughter was contagious. I laughed and gave the student 3/10 for effort.

My Higo laughed harder. 'Ha ha ha, 3/10. That is a very bad mark. Mr Hioki's students are not so good. How many students received 3/10?'

'Lots,' I grumbled. I handed Mr Higo a letter that had received 0/10. The boy responsible had simply signed his name at the bottom of a blank piece of paper. He had already been sent to detention by Mr Hioki.

One day Mr Higo admitted that he was learning a great deal about foreign people from our classes. 'I like our classes,' he enthused. 'They teach me about how to work with foreign people. I enjoy that. But there is one thing that I very much want to learn.'

'What's that?' I asked, happy to oblige.

'I must learn how to play cricket. I think that we should play cricket during next week's English class.'

I was delighted but a little reluctant. I had not swung a cricket bat in over a year, and missed the sport terribly, but I was worried that the students would be unable to get the hang of it. However, after the debacle of the students v. teachers running race I had learned not to underestimate them.

Once the rules were straightened out and altered a little, the boys really got into it. The girls, though, were another matter. They appeared barely able to run, let alone quickly. The bowling action proved impossible, as did throwing, catching, underarm rolling, fielding, batting, running and other basic actions that most humans take for granted.

In no time, the boys took control and elected themselves to both bat and bowl. One team was short a player, so I was allowed to fill in. I was eager to get off the mark.

The first ball I faced was wide down the offside and I padded it away with my left leg. This brought loud applause from both the fielding and batting teams. Such a feat of heroics is unheard of in baseball, and I was declared manly for putting my body on the line.

The next ball was pitched short and I was upon it in seconds. The blade of my bat flashed and I struck the ball cleanly. It whizzed through the gymnasium at great speed and struck a girl who had her back turned, clean in the calf. She crumpled into a startled heap and I made a quick single. This brought another huge cheer from the batting side, but the girls were now horrified and sheltering in the corner.

I eventually got back on strike after my partner managed to score a run by hitting the ball with the handle of his bat. The time limit I had imposed meant this would be my last time on strike, and possibly the last time I would play cricket for another year. I decided to make the most of it. The poor bowler was still struggling to throw the ball without bending his arm. I advanced down the pitch menacingly. As I expected, he faltered and the result was a gift of a delivery. Again, I struck the ball cleanly with the meat of the bat. It soared through the air and scattered a bunch of fourteen-year-old girls, before clearing the boundary ropes for six.

February proved to be cold, nasty and surprisingly busy, with little or no time for surfing the internet or reading trashy novels at my desk. I was suddenly required to teach lessons and endure five-day working weeks.

I received many inquiries from family and friends who were intrigued with the misadventures of the unhinged woodwork teacher, Mr Doi. However, I was unable to supply an update as Mr Doi had been mysteriously absent from work for three weeks. During the first three days, the other teachers had assumed he was merely in his office and did not want to disturb him. The students had gone to woodwork class and sat at their desks for an entire period without raising the alarm and alerting anyone to his non-attendance.

After a week had gone by, Mr Doi had phoned to say he was 'injured'
—and then there was silence. After three weeks, rumours abounded as to
what might have happened to him. The students believed he had been
fired, while Mr Higo, who had the misfortune of occupying the desk next
to him in the staffroom, was convinced he had skipped town and was
having a holiday in Shikoku. I, meanwhile, speculated that he had somehow succeeded in reaching the Korean peninsula and was not intending to
return any time soon.

As to the nature and details of his supposed injury, no one had any
idea. Apparently a doctor's certificate had been produced, but no one was
taking it seriously. With the end of the school year less than a month away,
my hopes were high that Mr Doi would be terminated and his contract
discontinued. However, I had a sinking suspicion that my arch nemesis
would be back.

With Mr Doi away, an atmosphere of normality returned to the
staffroom.

My only remaining problem with life at Kanan Junior High School
was Mr Hioki and his mind-numbing classes. Fortunately, though, this
was more than balanced by the two other happy and amusing English
teachers.

Mrs Takaoka and I had developed a popular teaching routine. Our
early lesson in which I had drunk strawberry milk and eaten chocolate in
front of the gob-smacked class was well remembered, and the students,
now second-graders, enthusiastically involved themselves in lessons, and
resented any fellow students who attempted to disrupt and derail the
lessons and games. There was seldom any need for discipline.

I was, therefore, horrified when, on a cold February morning, Mrs
Takaoka arrived at my desk and announced that she had resigned. Mrs
Takaoka had always been a good friend, and had made a special effort to
involve me in the events of the school. Now, however, she had been
nominated to join the Kawachi Nagano City Council and was to start her
new job immediately. In fact, she said tearfully, she had only three days
to say her farewells and prepare for her departure.

The ratio of good and bad English teachers now hung precariously in
the balance. Mr Matsuno, Mrs Takoka's replacement, arrived soon after-

wards. A substitute teacher, he had been unemployed for the past six months. He arrived at the school wearing a dark blue three-piece suit, black horn-rimmed glasses, and a neatly combed haircut that made him look more like an accountant than a teacher.

I was keen to introduce myself and get our relationship off to a cordial start. 'Good morning. Mr Matsuno, isn't it?' I said cheerfully. 'My name is Hamish. We will be working together. Pleased to meet you.'

Mr Matsuno blinked in alarm and started sweating profusely. He mopped his brow with a shaky hand, and stammered out a panicky greeting in Japanese. 'He...he...hello...I have never spoken wi...wi...with a foreigner before. I...I...I am very shy. Pur...pur...pur...please forgive me for not speaking good English.'

I was both surprised and concerned at Mr Matsuno's terrified reaction to my presence. I excused myself, and allowed him to rest his nerves in a foreigner-free environment.

I was scheduled to meet Mr Matsuno the following afternoon to discuss the lesson plan for our first class together. His frayed nerves and terror of dealing with foreigners seemed to have festered and grown overnight. When I sat down in a chair next to him, he started sweating and began to pant nervously. He tried to speak, and his words caught in his throat.

'Excuse me,' he finally gasped, steadying himself against his desk.

I was baffled. What on earth was going on?

Mr Matsuno's panic attack increased. He started shaking, and his face flushed purple.

'Are you okay?' I asked, now very worried.

Mr Matsuno continued to shake and pant. 'Excuse me,' he stammered again. He quickly stood up and walked away.

I sat stone still, stunned by the reaction Mr Matsuno was having to me. Did I smell?

Mr Matsuno was talking to Mr Hioki. Mr Hioki nodded slowly, and then both he and Mr Matsuno walked towards me. Mr Hioki seemed embarrassed. Mr Matsuno started shaking again.

'Hello, Mr Hamish,' Mr Hioki began slowly. 'Um, Mr Matsuno seems to be having problems speaking to you. He has never met a foreigner before and is too shy to talk to you. He has asked if I will talk to you on his behalf.'

'Sure,' I said. 'Please don't worry. We can speak in Japanese if Mr Matsuno would prefer.'

Mr Hioki relayed my comment to Mr Matsuno. Mr Matsuno's panting had stopped, and his sweating seemed more under control. He started babbling incoherently. Mr Hioki blinked in surprise; even he couldn't understand what was going on.

'Shall I talk with you in private?' Mr Hioki asked Mr Matsuno kindly. 'We can talk to Mr Hamish again later.'

Mr Matsuno nodded. He seemed relieved.

I returned to my desk very concerned about working with someone who was unable to be in the same room as me without suffering a panic attack. This was certainly going to impede our performance in the classroom.

Mr Hioki approached me at my desk half an hour later. 'Thank you for being patient with Mr Matsuno,' he said warmly. 'He seems very shy around you. He is very nervous about talking to foreigners.' Mr Hioki paused. His body language suggested that he was as puzzled by Mr Matsuno as I was. 'Yes,' Mr Hioki continued, 'Mr Matsuno is very worried about teaching with you. He does not know how to work with foreigners, so he asked for my suggestions.'

I froze. I could see where this was leading.

'And so,' Mr Hioki began, 'I gave him a copy of some of my lesson plans.' I grimaced as Mr Hioki handed me a copy of his original ABC song and 'How are you? I'm fine' lesson sheets.

'Mr Matsuno really likes these,' he said happily. 'He would like to use my lesson plans in his classes with you.'

The balance of good and bad English teachers was suddenly swinging in a dangerous direction.

Mr Matsuno did not come to school the following day. When I made discreet inquiries, I was told that he had 'taken the day off'.

He returned the day after and approached my desk boldly, head and shoulders erect, with a confident smile on his face. 'Good morning, Mr Hamish,' he remarked casually.

I blinked. Who was this remarkably confident person? Where was the spluttering gasping nervous Mr Matsuno? What miraculous transformation had taken place overnight?

'Ah, good morning Mr Matsuno,' I said carefully, not wanting to frighten him away with any loud noises or sudden movements. 'You were absent yesterday. Are you okay?'

'Ah yes,' Mr Matsuno beamed happily. 'I was drinking yesterday. I drank many, many beers. I like beer. I became very drunk. Now I am relaxed. Now I can talk to you easily. Please forgive my nervousness the other day.'

I was concerned at the Jekyll and Hyde metamorphosis that had taken place with the aid of an overdose of alcohol. This did not bode well for the future.

'Would you like to discuss our lesson plan for tomorrow morning?' I asked.

Mr Matsuno nodded. 'I have already spoken with Mr Hioki. He gave me some very good ideas.'

I commented that the second-grade students spoke a much better level of English than Mr Hioki's small children, and perhaps I should plan the lesson myself.

Mr Matsuno pondered this. 'Yes,' he announced after some time. 'That sounds like a great idea. You make the lesson plan. That is very good. So please, you can do all the teaching. I will sit in the corner and watch you. This way I can get used to working with you.'

The following day proved relatively successful. Mr Matsuno had been out again the night before and was in easy-going mood. 'I went drinking last night,' he enthused as we walked to the classroom together. 'I had very many beers. I became very drunk, so I feel very calm today. I sang lots of karaoke too. Do you like karaoke? I sang many Frank Sinatra songs. Do you like Frank Sinatra songs?'

I nodded. Mr Matsuno's smile spread from ear to ear. 'Perhaps we should go to a karaoke bar sometime?' he suggested. I did not need to respond. We had entered the classroom, and the students were waiting for our lesson to begin.

The second class proved a little more difficult. Mrs Takaoka and I had always had a problem with the students of 2-E class, who were prone to clowning about, and Mrs Takaoka had occasionally needed to reprimand them. Several students talked throughout the lesson and refused to quieten down when I asked them to. I was disappointed to notice that during this Mr Matsuno steadfastly stared out the window.

Sadly, Mr Matsuno's topsy-turvy mental state was to have a negative effect on the students' concentration levels. As the weeks went by, I began to notice that behaviour in Mr Matsuno's classes was slowly deteriorating. The second-grade students had always been my favourites, and had taken part in class eagerly and enthusiastically. Now, after only a few weeks with stammering Mr Matsuno, the girls were chattering and giggling noisily, and the boys were throwing objects at each other and refusing to take part in group activities.

After a month, the second-grade classes had lost all semblance of discipline. While Mr Matsuno or I were talking, boys would walk around the classroom kicking chairs and being insolent. Girls yelled and there was non-stop talking.

It was a Tuesday morning, and I was patiently trying to battle my way through 2-E, the final second-grade class of the day. I was tired, and trying to get the students to follow my lesson plan and complete a grammar worksheet. Before class, Mr Matsuno and I had rehearsed an English dialogue that accompanied the worksheet, and I indicated to Mr Matsuno that it was time for us to perform this.

It was here that Mr Matsuno let me down. Halfway through the dialogue that we had performed so well together during the other four classes, he disappeared out of the room in search of the class roll. I was flabbergasted. The students started yelling and kicking chairs. Shortly afterwards Mr Matsuno returned with the roll book and proceeded to check for absent students. I thrust the dialogue sheet into his hand, and hissed that we needed to continue with the lesson plan. He shrugged: he had forgotten what we were doing.

By this stage, the students had lost interest in the class and were refusing to fill in the grammar worksheet or take part in the game. I finally decided to take matters into my own hands. I stopped the class and instructed Mr Matsuno to come up the front and translate what I said next.

I then rounded on the students in loud, angry English and proceeded to tell them that I was sick and tired of them playing up and being idiots. I insisted that they treat my lessons with more respect, and added that they would never have acted like this with Mrs Takaoka present.

I went on for a while, singling out kids and scolding them in rapid-fire English. I knew they would understand nothing of what I was saying, but I figured that they had never seen me angry before and that my deep scary voice and body language would speak volumes.

No one made a peep.

But then Mr Matsuno tapped me on the shoulder and told me to calm down. 'That's enough,' he whispered. 'Please be quiet, Mr Hamish.' In Japanese culture, to do this was a complete insult. It showed that, in Mr Matsuno's eyes, what I had just said was completely meaningless and that he knew better than I did.

'I'm not finished!' I snapped, and he let go of my shoulder. A girl laughed and I gave her a thirty-second telling-off. She went white and shut up.

I finally finished and Mr Matsuno rushed in to try and 'fix things up'. He began translating my angry lecture into Japanese, but it wasn't until several moments later that I calmed down sufficiently to understand what he was saying.

'Poor Mr Hamish came to this country because he loves Japan and the Japanese people,' Mr Matsuno stammered. 'But his family is very, very far away in another country, and he is now very sad and homesick. We must help Mr Hamish not to be upset and homesick any more. Shall we all try and be kind to poor Mr Hamish?'

I was too tired to object, and not up to conducting an argument in Japanese. The students were still dead quiet. The bell rang and I walked angrily out of the classroom.

Once he was in the relative safety of the staffroom, Mr Matsuno raced over to my desk and apologised profusely on behalf of the students, claiming that the misbehaviour had not been overly serious and should be overlooked. 'I think it was simply a misunderstanding and a difference of cultures,' he declared.

I didn't say a word, but at lunchtime I left the school and ate my lunch in solitude beside the concrete-lined fishing pond next to the town hall.

It took me some time to calm down and return. As well as feeling a mixture of anger, frustration and embarrassment at having blown my top, I was concerned that my reputation with the students as a happy, easy-going teacher would be in jeopardy.

Mr Higo smiled as I entered the staffroom. 'Ha ha, I hear you scolded your students.' He laughed. 'One of the boys in the baseball team told me at lunchtime. He said the students were very naughty and that you became angry.'

I relaxed. Mr Higo's laughter was always infectious. I explained the situation and my concerns about damaging my rapport with the students. Mr Higo pondered this for a moment and then assured me that I was worrying needlessly. 'The students will forget all about this after a couple of days,' he assured me. 'It was good for you to scold them.'

He lowered his voice. 'I hear Mr Matsuno is not such a good teacher.'

I thanked him for his reassurance and resumed my busy schedule of eating chocolate and drinking coffee.

Mr Higo was right. My outburst was soon forgotten and my happy relationships with the second-grade students remained intact. If anything, 2-E now treated me with more respect, and no longer acted up during class. I was relieved that things seemed to be sorting themselves out amicably, and approached my lessons with a positive attitude.

Sadly, though, Mr Matsuno's self-medicating alcoholic binges were no longer calming his nerves and it was only a matter of time before he snapped. This occurred only a week after my outburst, and took everyone completely by surprise.

Everything started calmly enough. Mr Matsuno and I were teaching 2-D, the best behaved homeroom class in the second grade. The students were the brightest and most enthusiastic English students in the school, and they were always a joy to teach. I had not encountered a single problem with 2-D all year.

I was midway through the lesson, and had just finished explaining the rules of a word game I had already played three times with the other second-grade classes. While I was busy writing up the scoreboard on the blackboard, I strayed from the usual teaching plan by just a fraction. I asked the six teams of students to think up team names for themselves.

This harmless request was intended to keep the students quiet and preoccupied while my back was turned writing on the blackboard.

The class managed to produce several team names, most of which were Japanese words, and random and imaginative. One team had called themselves '???' and another team's name translated as 'Sexy something or other'. On the whole there was nothing too outrageous.

I started adding the team names to the scoreboard, and was about to get the game underway when Mr Matsuno, who had been sitting silently in the corner, meekly raised his hand and in a quiet stuttering voice asked, 'Please excuse me for a minute, Mr Hamish.'

Before I could turn to respond, Mr Matsuno had leapt to his feet, and with an insane gleam in his eye thrown a chair across the classroom.

Everyone gasped.

Mr Matsuno rounded on the students, his face purple and his hands twitching. 'And what the bloody hell do you think you're doing?' he yelled.

Everyone gasped again and a few students laughed. Then, in a flash, Mr Matsuno bounded across the room, kicked over a desk and sent another chair sailing into the wall. He towered over the student who had suggested the team name 'Sexy something or other'.

At a complete loss as to how to deal with the situation, I quietly started picking up the scattered classroom furniture and spilled stationery. I was desperately praying that Mr Matsuno didn't start killing anyone.

'What do you think you're doing!' Mr Matsuno thundered again.

Some of the students politely protested that they had just thought up team names as they had been instructed. This seemed to put the brakes on Mr Matsuno's brain implosion for a few seconds, but he soon started ranting and raving about how the team names were no good whatsoever. 'Who on earth came up with '???'? This is completely absurd. This is a crap name.'

I cringed. The name had been suggested by the quietest boy in the class. He seldom spoke, and this maniacal attack would no doubt emotionally cripple him from speaking again in the future.

After he had exhausted his tirade of grievances, Mr Matsuno bowed to me and returned to his seat in the corner. I was left to try and continue the word game with a group of shell-shocked thirteen-year-olds. I did my best and the remainder of the class went relatively smoothly. However, I was constantly checking over my shoulder in case Mr Matsuno took objection to something and decided to throw some more chairs.

The bell rang and Mr Matsuno stormed from the room. Some of the girls started giggling and some of the cheekier boys re-enacted my alarmed reaction to Mr Matsuno's outburst. I chuckled as they performed slow-motion replays of my horrified facial expressions and skilful chair-dodging moves, which had apparently looked like Keanu Reeves in *The Matrix*.

I raced after the girls and tried to dissuade them from spreading this episode around the school grapevine, but I realised this was a hopeless request. Sure enough, by the time I made it to the staffroom, news of Mr Matsuno's meltdown had reached the ears of the 2-D homeroom teacher. She raced in and began lecturing Mr Matsuno loudly about how he needed to get better control of his temper. Mr Terada had also heard the details of the chair-throwing and was less than impressed. He waded into the fray.

Everyone else watched in wide-eyed amazement, and I retreated to the relative solitude of the computer terminal.

Fortunately, I would not have to deal with Mr Matsuno and his mental issues for too much longer: Mr Higo informed me that he would be working as a substitute teacher only until the school year ended in March. He was to be replaced the following term by a full-time, mentally sound teacher.

The spring vacation could not come quickly enough. Only two weeks of working with Mr Matsuno remained. My concentration and interest in school affairs was, by this stage, somewhat lacking. During the past month Blake, Andy, Matt and I had been secretly planning a three-week holiday in Laos and Vietnam for the spring vacation. I had long ago started sowing the seeds of my cover story with the Board of Education. Yet again I would be spending the vacation studying Japanese in the Tondabayashi town library.

There were no tearful farewells on Mr Matsuno's last day in Kanan Junior High School. He seemed relieved that his harrowing encounter with a scary white foreigner was at an end.

# 15

# English wars

*After an enjoyable holiday* in Laos and Vietnam, cruising up the Mekong River, hiking in the hills and staying in mud-floor huts, I returned to Japan. There was just one problem: I was suffering from severe sunburn and losing skin at a serpent-like rate. Every time I stood up, large deposits floated incriminatingly on to surrounding surfaces.

My face was fortunately not burnt, but my back and shoulders looked as though I had been hit by some form of nuclear weapon. My condition soon became an embarrassment in the classroom. As I was studiously helping a second-grade girl correct spelling mistakes in her holiday homework assignment, I pointed at her page and several large flakes of skin wafted out of my shirtsleeve and settled delicately on her pencil case. I looked at the ceiling and mumbled something about a shoddy paint job before quickly walking away.

Fortunately it was the start of the new school year, and the line-up of new teachers and pint-sized first-graders distracted attention from my wizened skin. No one thought to ask how I had become so badly sunburnt while studying Japanese for three weeks at the town library.

Five new teachers were busy setting up their belongings on their new desks in the staffroom. Mr Ishitani, the new first-grade social studies teacher, had a curiously long face, and lips that curled up above his gums when he smiled. A fluffy mop of hair teetering on the top of his head dwarfed his round John Lennon glasses.

Mrs Takeuchi, the new second-grade maths teacher, had a shrill voice and gave the impression of being very strict. Ms Amano was a young, attractive PE teacher straight out of teachers' college. She was a past pupil of Kanan Junior High and lived within walking distance of the school.

Mr Doi was still mysteriously missing in action, and his desk was being temporarily used by a young teachers' college graduate who, Mr Higo informed me, would be employed only until Mr Doi returned.

And finally, a brand new English teacher, Mrs Nakazato, was busy arranging her textbooks and dictionaries. I eyed her suspiciously: the balance of good and bad English teachers was once again going to change, but in which direction? Mr Higo and Mr Hioki were also taking an interest. The new teacher had an air of determination and stubbornness. Mr Higo seemed thoughtful. Our eyes met and he frowned.

Mrs Nakazato's stubbornness and sense of self-importance soon became apparent. In her late forties, Mrs Nakazato was older than both Mr Higo and Mr Hioki. She was, therefore, the senior English teacher in the school, and she used this sudden rush of power to appoint herself the new head of the Kanan Junior High School English department.

I was unsure what this meant. I soon realised, however, that Mrs Nakazato had an empire to build and a school to conquer. Her first decision was to make sweeping changes to the English teaching structure —with one exception: Mr Hioki was to be left alone to continue teaching his mindless, repetitive lessons to his students from the previous year. These children were now in the second grade. They had all grown slightly taller, but seemed intellectually stunted, with little or no imagination. Mrs Nakazato seemed aware of the damage that a year with Mr Hioki had done to them, but did not intend to change things for the better.

Instead, her reformist sights were set firmly on Mr Higo. Mr Higo had been scheduled to continue working as the third-grade English teacher. He and I had been looking forward to picking up the pieces after the departure of Mrs Takaoka and Mr Matsuno. I had been teaching the third-grade students for nearly two years, and enjoyed their company.

They were a mature, enthusiastic, intelligent group who would respond well to my classes and Mr Higo's games and humour.

Mrs Nakazato was, however, reluctant to teach only the new batch of first-graders. Acting in her self-appointed role as head English teacher, she decided to split the first- and third-grade students between herself and Mr Higo. This meant that Mr Higo would now teach only three of the five third-grade classes, while Mrs Nakazato would teach the remaining two.

At the same time, Mrs Nakazato would teach three first-grade classes, with Mr Higo teaching the other two—the ones whose students, according to reports from their elementary schools, were likely to be rebellious and naughty.

Furthermore, Mrs Nakazato announced that she would be responsible for planning the curriculums and lesson plans not only for her classes, but for Mr Higo's as well. It seemed that Mr Higo's age and junior rank were counting against him. Without sufficient teaching experience, he was unable to question or dispute Mrs Nakazato's decisions.

The new school year was now forebodingly uncertain. The comedic freedom that Mr Higo and I had been enjoying for nearly two years was in jeopardy.

米

Mrs Nakazato's first lesson plan was a fine example of things to come. Mr Higo and I cringed through the first planning meeting of the year, as Mrs Nakazato refused to listen to our opinions and suggestions and steadfastly ignored my advice that several of her English texts were ridden with mistakes.

'No,' she scolded. 'We will use *my* English script, Mr Hamish. I used this many times at my previous schools. There were no problems.'

Mr Higo flinched.

'But it's not correct English,' I said softly. 'We don't speak like this. I can write a more natural script if you'd like.'

Mrs Nakazato looked angry. 'No! It's too late, I have already prepared the worksheet. It's too late to make changes to the script.'

'I'd like to play a game at the end of the class,' Mr Higo piped up.

'Hmm, a game. What game did you have in mind?'

Mr Higo and I looked at each other. Perhaps Mrs Nakazato was not totally inflexible.

Mr Higo quickly explained our 'sentence row race game', which involved rows of students racing against each other to create English sentences. Mr Higo and I had used this successfully several times in the past two years, and it had proved a good way to introduce new students to the humour of our classes.

Mrs Nakazato frowned. 'No! I do not like that game. We will play *Battleship*. I have already prepared the game boards—it is too late to change.'

I blinked in confusion as I read Mrs Nakazato's *Battleship* rule book. Everything seemed to be completely wrong.

'Umm,' I began slowly, 'I thought the idea of *Battleship* was to bomb the other person's boats.'

Mrs Nakazato glared at me.

'It says here that the idea of the game is to call out the coordinates of your own boats and be the first person to destroy your own fleet.'

Mrs Nakazato looked back at me blankly. 'So?'

'Isn't that pointless if you can see the location of your own boats? Isn't it kind of easy to bomb them?'

'Aha!' she retorted. 'That is where you are wrong. The students do not 'bomb' their own boats, they 'check' them. I do not like the concept of 'bombing' things. The students can 'check' their own boats by drawing stars or hearts on them instead.'

I was astonished. Mr Higo was speechless.

'But the students will already know where their own boats are,' I pleaded. 'They drew them on their page themselves. The boats are sitting right in front of them. The universally accepted version of *Battleship* involves the players trying to guess where their opponents' boats are hidden. It's no fun if you simply 'check' your own boats.'

Mrs Nakazato looked thoughtful. 'No,' she said at length, 'it's too late now. I have already prepared the game boards.'

I gave up. Mrs Nakazato had won. Her illogical argument was too much for me. Mr Higo and I withdrew to our respective desks. The new school year was going to be hard work.

Mrs Nakazato's first lesson proved predictably terrible. I cringed my way through her nonsensical English script and hated myself for inflicting it on my favourite students.

*Hamish*: I am messy. I don't like cleaning.

*Mrs Nakazato*: I want you to clean your room.

*Hamish*: I am sleepy. I am tired.

*Mrs Nakazato*: I want you to sleep much.

The purpose of this was to teach the students how to give instructions. I shook my head in shame every time I realised that I was now responsible for teaching impressionable adolescents that 'I want you to sleep much' was acceptable English.

I was equally disappointed with myself for trying to force my students to play a namby-pamby, love-heart version of *Battleship*. Fortunately, though, the solid foundations laid by Mrs Takaoka allowed the students to withstand Mrs Nakazato's nonsensical script, and even emboldened them to question her version of the game.

'Excuse me, teacher,' called a nerdy bespectacled boy. 'Why are we bombing our own ships? Won't we lose if we bomb our own ships?'

Mrs Nakazato's face reddened. 'No. You are not *bombing* ships. You must *check* them. You can draw love hearts on your ships.'

The nerdy boy frowned. A rebellious boy sneered. 'What a dumb game.'

Everyone laughed. Mrs Nakazato's face turned purple. 'It is too late to change. Please continue.'

'But I've already finished,' the nerdy boy replied. 'I can see where my own boats are. I've already coloured them in.'

'Then start again and play another round,' Mrs Nakazato snapped.

'Can we play with the normal rules in the second round?' the boy asked hopefully.

Mrs Nakazato's jaw locked. I could feel the tension radiating off her. To admit her mistake now would expose her flawed rules and refusal to listen to my advice.

'Please, teacher, can we use the normal rules?' Several other students chorused. Everyone was looking at Mrs Nakazato hopefully. 'All right then,' she snapped. 'Use the other rules.'

She looked away angrily, muttered about needing to get something from the staffroom and stormed out of the room, leaving me to supervise the first round of real *Battleship*.

Mr Higo chortled when I recounted the events. 'I think the game is very bad,' he said, 'very, very wrong. We will use the normal rules in our class. Also, I feel very sorry for you having to say her English script. Shall we cut it from our class?'

I nodded emphatically.

'Good,' he laughed. 'Shall we do one of our comedy scripts? I think we should impersonate another teacher in our script. Who shall we impersonate?'

We scratched our heads thoughtfully. I looked at Mr Higo. We smiled.

Battle lines may have been drawn in the mainstream English classes, but a new ray of hope was dawning in the young minnows' stream.

I had all but given up on Hiro, Yurika and Teru-Chan and decided that they were unable to learn or retain any new material. Mr Doi's absence had been a huge relief. Not only was I now free from perverted conversation in the staffroom, I was also able to roll up to the young minnows' room with no lesson plan or teaching material. By mid April, I had played *Snakes and Ladders* with them at least a hundred times.

The minnows' short memory spans meant that I could recycle the same game week after week without any complaints. Sadly, though, my hundredth round of *Snakes and Ladders* was more than I could humanly take and my brain refused to play ever again.

For the sake of my sanity, it was time to try something new. I decided to teach the minnows how to play cards. I reasoned that a few games of *Snap* or *Last Card* would help while away our time together.

The first game of *Snap* received a mixed reaction. Hiro's interest in English class flickered back to life and he sat rigidly to attention, on the lookout for numerical pairs or matching coloured cards.

Yurika's chirpiness had never abated, and she was as enthusiastic as ever. Her limited eyesight, however, levelled the playing field somewhat, and Hiro was now able to take part in an activity without being soundly beaten, or shown up by Yurika's superior intellect.

Teru-Chan, meanwhile, regarded the game suspiciously and refused to take part.

Yurika, Hiro and I played a competitive first round, which I allowed Hiro to win. He leapt to his feet, and for the first time since Jun Fujita's departure he started dancing and chuckling to himself. After a few giddy gyrations, he returned to his seat and announced that he was ready for another round.

Yurika loudly demanded that she wanted to play again as well. She seemed bewildered at not having been able to beat Hiro. I started shuffling the cards slowly. I needed to drag this out to use up as much class time as possible before the bell rang.

'Mr Hame, I want to play.'

I nearly dropped the cards. Teru-Chan had spoken. This was, in fact, the first time Teru-Chan had ever spoken to me.

'Why sure,' I stammered, and dealt her a hand. 'Do you understand the rules?' Teru-Chan looked at me and slowly nodded her head.

The game started.

'Snap!'

Hiro had found a pair. He chuckled merrily to himself.

'Snap!'

Yurika had spotted a matching colour.

'Snap!'

Everyone paused.

Teru-Chan was on her feet. She had mashed her large round hand down on a pair of unmatching cards.

Hiro and Yurika looked at me for clarification.

I was frozen with uncertainty. Teru-Chan stood scowling, ready to claim her cards. To let her win a pile of unmatching cards would not be fair on Hiro and Yurika. At the same time though, depriving Teru-Chan of her spoils could result in my being stabbed in the head with the paper scissors.

'Umm...Teru-Chan, I'm sorry but those cards don't match.'

Teru-Chan glared at me.

'He's right!' Yurika said shrilly. 'You need matching numbers or colours. You've got an eight of spades and a four of hearts. They don't match.'

Teru-Chan eyed me menacingly. I looked at her hands. She was currently unarmed.

'Hmphh, all right' she said finally, and sat back down.

Play resumed.

Hiro was on a roll and his pile of cards was increasing steadily.

'Snap!'

Teru-Chan was on her feet again, scowling suspiciously. 'It's a pair,' she proclaimed. I smiled: this time Teru-Chan was right. 'Yes, it is a pair, Teru-Chan,' I said. 'Well done.' For the first time ever, Teru-Chan smiled. She clutched the cards to her roly-poly body and sat down.

Hiro looked across at her and glanced defensively at his own pile of cards.

The game continued. Teru-Chan's confidence grew and she slowly started to win more and more cards.

'Snap!' She clutched the final pile of cards protectively to her chest. 'I won!' she exclaimed in surprise. Her face cracked into a smile. She sat quietly and started shuffling the cards.

'I want to play again,' she insisted and looked at everyone expectantly.

Hiro nodded. He was out for revenge. Yurika looked nervous: her role as class genius was under threat. She nodded slowly. I nodded as well.

Teru-Chan's smile broadened.

The third round was cut short when the bell rang. Teru-Chan scowled and seemed angry. I checked that the paper scissors were safely out of reach and started packing up the cards. We all stood and bowed to one another, and as I left the room Hiro shook my hand.

The following Friday morning I was busy eating chocolate at my desk while reading a trashy English novel from the local library. There were five minutes remaining before the start of the young minnows' class and I was determined to finish the chapter.

A large rotund figure appeared in my peripheral vision, and I sensed I was being watched. I turned around slowly. Teru-Chan was regarding me intently.

'Mr Hame,' she began. 'It's time for class.'

I looked at the staffroom clock. Nope, still five more minutes to go.

'The bell hasn't rung yet,' I replied.

'But I want you to come now. What will we do today?' She paused. 'Will we play cards?'

I smiled. 'Yes, we can play cards if you want, Teru-Chan.'

Teru-Chan smiled a huge smile and balled her fists with excitement. 'Yay! Mr Hame, please come to class early. I want to play many rounds of cards today.'

I put down my unfinished chocolate and half-read novel. Teru-Chan's sudden interest in my classes was somewhat inspiring. 'Okay,' I said, grabbing the pack of cards, 'let's go.'

The game of *Snap* produced many humorous moments. Yurika finally managed to win a round, and Hiro and Teru-Chan battled away trying to produce an overall champion. The scores were still tied when the bell rang, and Teru-Chan insisted everyone return at lunchtime to play the deciding round. We agreed, and Teru-Chan was the happy victor. Hiro was good-natured about his loss and happily congratulated Teru-Chan.

I was stoked. All the students were again taking part in class, and their good natures had returned.

Over the next few weeks, I introduced the young minnows to other New Zealand card games, and they taught me several Japanese variations. I also lovingly designed and created a *Cluedo* murder-mystery game board and playing pieces. I knew it was going to be difficult to teach my three special friends the slightly complicated rules but decided it was worth a shot.

At first it seemed I was being too ambitious. The minnows' attention seemed to be drifting and they weren't picking up the rules at all. But slowly, after two weeks of patient explanations and tentative trial runs, breakthroughs were made and the first successful *Cluedo* game was played. As always, Hiro delighted in rolling the dice and moving a playing piece around the board. Yurika loved the idea of exploring various rooms in a large mansion, and Teru-Chan giggled whenever she had a chance to accuse another person of being a murderer.

I did my best not to win, but the minnows kept dropping their cards, speaking out loud and generally giving the game away. Finally, I could restrain myself no longer: I correctly identified Hiro as the mystery murderer and deduced that he had conducted the sinister act in the ball-room with the dagger.

Yurika laughed gleefully and pretended to sentence Hiro to prison. Teru-Chan, although miffed that she had not won, smiled all the same. Hiro leapt to his feet and pranced around the room, pretending to be searching for an escape route. He eventually gave himself up and returned to his seat to face his punishment. I ordered him to eat a plate of cabbage (his all-time least favourite food) and he clapped himself on the head and wailed with mock misery.

The bell chimed and the children begged me to bring *Cluedo* to the following week's class.

My friend Mr Higo handed me the telephone. I was sitting at my desk, reading a newspaper and eating steamed pork buns. 'I think this is for you,' he said with a curious grin. 'I think it's your friend. I don't understand what she's saying.'

I was confused. None of my friends knew my office number, and they would always contact me at home or on my cellphone.

I put the phone to my ear. 'Hello?'

'Heymishi!' A familiar nasal voice wafted through the phone line.

'Heymishi! What are you doing? Why didn't you answer the phone? Who was I speaking to before? Are you at school? Why aren't you teaching?'

I opened my mouth to answer, but Mrs Oki carried on at her usual rate of knots.

'Now then, Heymishi, what are you doing on Wednesday evening? Please come to our house for dinner. Mr Oki will buy sushi. Do you like sushi?

I assured Mrs Oki that I did, and reminded her that we had visited several sushi restaurants together in the past.

'Hmm...well then, you can come to our house at five p.m. We will have sushi. Do you remember where our house is? Do you know how to get here?'

'Yes,' I replied calmly. 'I've been to your house before. How did you get this number?'

'Good.' Mrs Oki ignored my question. 'See you at five.' The phone went dead.

I frowned as I hung up the receiver. The Okis had figured out how to contact me at work.

I caught a train to the Okis' residence in Sakai at 4.30 on Wednesday afternoon. I had studied the train schedule and knew that this would get me to their neighbourhood station at precisely 4.57. From there it would be an eight-minute walk to their home. I would only be five minutes late, and figured that no one would notice.

Mrs Oki was waiting feverishly when I knocked on her door. 'Hey-mishi, where have you been?' she asked excitedly. 'I thought you were lost, or had forgotten to come. I've been calling your house. Now then, take off your shoes. I thought you were lost. Come in, come in, Heymishi, I thought you were lost. Do you like sushi? We're having sushi for dinner. I was worried you were lost. Have a seat in the living room. Heymishi, do you want a drink? I sent Mr Oki to find you.'

I had still not had a chance to say hello. I checked my watch. I was only five minutes late.

'Sorry,' I said politely. 'I didn't mean to be a problem. Where did Mr Oki go?'

Mrs Oki wasn't listening. 'Mr Oki has been gone for five minutes. He went to the station to look for you. I think he might be lost. Shall we wait here or go and look for him?'

I started laughing. 'Maybe we should wait here. He'll be back soon.'

Mrs Oki continued to fret. 'Heymishi, do you like sushi? We will have sushi tonight. Hmm...Mr Oki has been gone for ten minutes. I think he might be lost. Now then, I need to feed the cat. Here puss puss puss.'

She trailed off in search of the Oki feline and I was left alone with my glass of orange juice. Mr Oki returned home shortly afterwards. He had been cycling around the neighbourhood and was covered in sweat.

'Aha,' he said merrily, slapping me on the shoulder. 'There you are. I've been looking for you.'

'Sorry, I was a couple of minutes late,' I apologised. 'I hope you didn't go far.'

'Huh?' Mr Oki peered at me deafly. He had forgotten to put in his hearing aid.

'I said, I hope you didn't go far,' I repeated loudly.

'You went where?' he replied, frowning.

'No, no, I hope you didn't go far,' I said again. I was well used to dealing with Mr Oki's hearing impediment.

'I was on my bicycle,' Mr Oki said happily.

Hearing her husband's voice, Mrs Oki scuttled back into the room. 'Mr Oki,' she scolded impatiently. 'There you are! I was worried about you. I thought you got lost. You were gone for such a long time.'

'Huh?' Mr Oki chuckled and slapped me on the shoulder again. He had not heard a word his wife had said.

Mrs Oki seemed satisfied with Mr Oki's response and turned her attention to me once again. 'Now then, Heymishi, we will have sushi for dinner. Can you eat sushi? Do you want a drink?'

I nodded at my unfinished glass of orange juice. 'I'm fine, thanks.'

'I think you need a beer,' Mrs Oki lectured. 'Mr Oki, get Heymishi a beer.'

'Huh?' Mr Oki looked on blankly. 'All right, I'll go and get changed.' He rose and left the room.

Mrs Oki had seemingly forgotten about her order to get me a beer. She wandered off to find the cat. It was business as usual in the Oki household.

Kanan Junior High School was now in the midst of a two-week exam period. Mentally exhausted eleven- to fourteen-year-old students sweated and panicked in muggy classrooms as they worked their way through pieces of paper that would decide their entire educational futures.

I, meanwhile, ate chocolate and ice-cream in the air-conditioned comfort of the teachers' room. As always, my lessons had been cancelled for the exam period, and also for the following week when the papers would be returned and the answers explained to the students. Most days I sneaked out at noon and went shopping. I was growing bored with my blank lesson schedule, and toyed with the idea of buying plastic model kit sets and bringing them to school to make in my abundant spare time.

Outside school hours, though, life in Osaka was eventful. The World Cup Football extravaganza floated around Japan, and I surprised myself by getting caught up in the hype. I didn't miss a game and even managed to learn a bit about soccer. However, spending an entire month watching soccer games had made me feel like an unemployed slob. By mid July I felt as though I hadn't done anything productive in years, except for getting paid and eating ice-cream.

With summer approaching, I made a radical fashion decision and had my hair cut short and spiky. I was delighted when students told me how cool I was, and how much I looked like David Beckham. However, my bubble was cruelly burst when Justin, Blake and Matt, who looked nothing like the English football superhero, received similar compliments.

To make matters worse, soon afterwards England got eliminated in the quarter-finals. Suddenly no one cared whom I looked like. Damn, damn and damn.

Although football was certainly the topic on everyone's lips, PE lessons for the students had, for the past month, focused on swimming. It was again time for the school swimming sports. For weeks, the students had been drilled in the arts of freestyle, backstroke and dog-paddling. The school anthem had been rehearsed methodically and the school swept and polished in preparation for the spectators and dignitaries who would attend the big event. Homeroom classes made banners and composed songs and chants to urge on their peers.

I was looking forward to the swimming sports as well. Despite my almost lethal dose of tonsillitis the previous year, I had managed to swim like a super-powered dolphin and had made a name for myself as a swimming superstar. I was determined to do a repeat performance.

The day arrived. I lounged around in the sun, chatting with colleagues and joking with students, as we cheered on race after race of spluttering swimmers. Finally, it was time for the last race—the third-grade boys' relay teams v. the teachers.

Mr Higo, Mr Nakata, Mr Shimizu—another teacher from the single male teacher lunch-box club—and I lined up on the starting line. For the second year in a row I was the teachers' first swimmer.

I took my position on the diving block and waited for Mr Terada to fire the starter's gun.

Bang! I sprang from the diving blocks and executed an elegant racing dive. Splash! I hit the water at speed.

Shit! My swimsuit had slipped down to my thighs, exposing my round white bottom. I frantically splashed around underwater. After what seemed an eternity, I managed to pull the swimsuit up to a respectable level and kicked off to continue the race.

This proved difficult. Whenever I built up speed, my swimsuit would slip down again, so my stroke was constantly punctuated by desperate snatches at my legs with my free arm.

Finally I managed to complete my length of the pool. I tagged off the next swimmer and surveyed the opposition. Mr Nakata was now half a pool length behind the main pack. We were dead last. All hopes of a teachers' victory for the second year in a row were dashed.

Minutes later the race was over. I was standing on dry land, wrapped in a towel, my swimsuit tied firmly under my armpits.

Mr Higo smiled as he lamented our loss.

'Did you see my pants fall down?' I whispered in hushed tones.

'No,' he laughed. 'When did your pants fall down?'

I looked around nervously. Mr Higo was blaring out my embarrassing news at an indiscreet volume. 'When I dived in.'

'Ah! I didn't see anything. I just thought you were swimming badly. Ha ha ha. I must think up a nickname for you. Ha ha ha.' He wandered away, deep in thought.

Luckily, if Mr Higo did dream up a nickname for me he never had the chance to use it. The end of the school term was nigh and eight long weeks of summer holidays beckoned. I had probably taught an average of only ten hours a week for the past several months, but I was desperately in need of an exotic vacation.

The following week, to mark our two-year anniversary in Japan, Matt, Blake and I caught a slow boat to Shanghai.

# 16

# The importance of
# being identical

*I got my third year in Japan* off to a flying start by achieving something that had, until then, seemed impossible. I found myself a girlfriend.

I was still on the rebound, having not fully recovered from Mariko Kitamura's 'just good friends' speech, and in hindsight I should perhaps have taken things a little more slowly, or been a little more cautious, when I bumped into Chie Matsumoto in an inner-city bar on that fateful summer's evening. Neither of us were sober, and I lapped up her breathless assurances that I was tall and handsome and looked like Ben Affleck. I handed out my contact details and made amorous promises that we would meet again the following weekend for dinner.

I was still hung-over the next morning when Chie called to remind me of my romantic invitation and to further remind me of just how attracted to each other we had been the previous night. 'We had so much fun dancing together. It was such a great time,' she exclaimed in a smoky, raspy voice.

'Err...okay. So where exactly did I say we would go for dinner?'

'Oh, I see, you're trying to tease me. You promised to take me to a Mexican restaurant. You do remember, don't you?'

I could not remember anything of the sort. 'Ah yeah, that's right. A Mexican restaurant. I didn't promise anything else, did I?'

Chie didn't answer. 'Don't forget, Friday night at Shinsaibashi Station. I'm really looking forward to seeing you again,' she said.

I sighed as I hung up the phone. All my friends now had girlfriends. I was sick and tired of being the only single guy in the group. Perhaps I should take Chie out for dinner. What was the worst that could happen?

I paused. It was possibly best not to tempt fate by answering the question.

Dinner with Chie turned out to be surprisingly enjoyable. She had dressed up for the occasion in designer clothes, accompanied by a designer handbag and sparkly designer jewellery. We chatted and laughed, and discovered that we had several mutual interests. Chie had always wanted to travel to New Zealand, and she listened intently to my stories about life in Christchurch and holidays in the countryside.

'I think you're very handsome,' she said smokily during the main course. 'You have lovely eyes.' She winked seductively and stroked my hand.

I blushed, and stammered out a feeble compliment in return. 'Ah, you have nice hair.'

We held hands for the rest of the evening, and Chie kissed me goodbye when we parted company. I felt happy and pleased with myself as I rode my train back to Tondabayashi.

I met up with Chie again the following weekend and we dined at a flash inner-city restaurant. She sported yet another designer outfit and we laughed, drank expensive cocktails, and then danced the night away at a trendy nightclub.

A week later, we met again for our third extravagant meal together. Chie sparkled with diamond earrings and a matching bracelet. We drank fine wine and ate imported seafood.

I was enjoying this experience of high society, and was visiting much more exclusive establishments than I ever would have with my drinking buddies. I was therefore rather unpleasantly surprised when, during our oyster hors-d'œuvre, Chie suggested we spend the next afternoon on a shopping expedition to a cheap men's clothing store. 'I want to buy you some clothes,' she enthused. 'I want to give you a present.'

I was tempted to recommend that we instead pay a visit to the local Armani store, where Chie would be more than welcome to select the latest summer suit for me, or perhaps some Italian leather shoes. In the event, though, she choose a pair of skatey pants and a light brown T-shirt, both manufactured in China. I must admit, though, that I rather liked her selection, and felt cool in my new threads.

'You should wear these next weekend,' Chie suggested. 'I want to take you somewhere special. It's a place called Harvest Hill. It's a picnic area. I think you'll really like it.'

'Sure,' I agreed happily. It would be nice to spend a summery weekend outside in the fresh air.

'Great!' Chie clapped her hands together. 'I can't wait. Make sure you wear these new clothes. You'll be the coolest guy there.'

The week passed quickly. On Friday Chie sent me details of how to get to Harvest Hill and where to meet her at the adjacent train station. 'Don't forget your new clothes,' she reminded me. 'You look so handsome in them.'

It was Saturday afternoon. I stepped off the train and surveyed the empty platform.

I checked my watch. I was on time.

I checked my clothes. I had kept my word and was wearing my newly acquired shorts and T-shirt.

I looked around again. I detected movement up ahead. Chie's face ducked out from behind a station pillar.

I smiled. She was being playful and hiding from me.

I approached the pillar slowly. Chiiieeee?' I called teasingly.

Chie leapt out. 'Ta-daa,' she announced proudly.

I gasped in bewilderment. 'What do you think?' she asked expectantly. She pirouetted in front of me and stepped back so I could admire her attire properly.

Words caught in my throat. 'Aaahhh...you look...you look...'

'Just like you!' Chie finished the sentence for me. 'Don't I look cute?'

'I don't know what to say.' I looked around quickly, hoping desperately that no one had seen us together. Chie Matsumoto was wearing exactly the same pair of shorts and T-shirt that I was. To an uninformed observer, we would look like a pair of nutty simpletons.

Chie leapt into my unenthusiastic arms and kissed my cheek excitedly. 'I'm so glad you like it. I think we look great together. We look like such a happy couple.'

A happy couple of morons, I thought to myself. What on earth was going on?

'Ha,' I said. 'This *is* a surprise, Chie. Did you want us to wear the same clothes today, or did you forget what I would be wearing?'

Chie giggled happily. 'I knew, I knew. I planned this all along. After I bought you your clothes last week, I secretly went back to the store and bought myself the same things. I wanted to surprise you. What do you think?'

Chie stepped back and performed her pirouette again. I grimaced. Not only was she dressed in the same clothes as me, but in her haste she had chosen a pair of shorts that were almost the same size as mine. To stop the legs dragging on the ground, she had been forced to pull the shorts up to her chest, where they were clamped tightly around her body with a brown leather belt. The effect was of a pair of spacesuit trousers ballooning out below her breasts and hanging down limply to her shins. A similarly over-sized T-shirt drooped from her small shoulders.

'You look...aaahh... You don't happen to have a change of clothes with you?'

Chie's smile vanished immediately. 'Don't you like this? I wanted to surprise you? Don't you like it?'

I smiled gingerly. 'No, I think it looks very nice. It's a big surprise, trust me. My friends will also be surprised when I tell them about it.'

'Oh good,' Chie chirped, her smile returning. 'I can't wait to meet your friends.'

'Trust me,' I assured her, 'they would love to have seen you today. I can just imagine their happy reactions.'

'Oh good!' Chie clapped her hands together. 'Let's go,' she exclaimed, racing off ahead. 'Harvest Hill here we come.'

I shook my head in disbelief. At what point in our relationship had Chie quietly lost her sanity? What on earth was going wrong with my screening process for potential girlfriends? Why did I only ever seem to attract weirdos?

I plodded slowly after my look-alike girlfriend and her baggy space pants. Harvest Hill turned out to be a large theme park and picnic area, modelled on the Japanese idea of a New Zealand farmyard. It was full to bursting with stores selling 'Hello Kitty' merchandise, a German beer hall, banjo music on loudspeakers, and a sheep show.

Two young men, Matt from Waimate and Ryan from Christchurch, were up on stage. For the first time since being in Japan, I was made to feel truly embarrassed by my New Zealand heritage. Matt was a tough country guy who glared at the audience and had obviously been doing the show so long that he had come to hate Japan, life and the human race.

Ryan, meanwhile, managed to smile occasionally at the audience, which was nice of him, but when he tried to speak Japanese I wanted to cut my ears off. In his ten-minute introductory speech, he managed to mispronounce every syllable of every word. I looked around at the audience. They were studying their shoes.

'What's he talking about?' Chie asked with a confused look.

'He's introducing himself,' I explained. 'His Japanese is a little incorrect though.'

'He's speaking Japanese?' Chie blinked in surprise.

Ryan's awkward introduction came to an end and the audience sighed with relief. It was now time for the sheep show to begin; we settled in to observe life on a New Zealand farm. Matt glared at the audience, yelled at Bess the dog to 'fucking well get up on stage', and swore when the sheep got out of their stall before his cue. Two sheep went AWOL and were never rounded up. The rest of the straggly flock were moved three metres to the next pen, and Matt swore at them until they went through the gate.

Next, Matt hauled a sheep up on stage and proceeded to shear it, a task for which he seemed wholly ill-equipped. As the ragged old sheep got cut and started bleeding, some children in the audience began to sob loudly. Undeterred, Matt told the poor creature to 'stop fucking moving' and 'sodding well quiet down'.

And then, to my relief, the show was over. There was a timid smattering of applause and several children continued to cry. Ryan called out goodbye and then, instead of politely inviting the audience to come and take photos with him and the sheep, ordered them up on stage in crude

Japanese. I quickly raced away before anyone could associate me with Harvest Hill, or mis-identify me as a psychotic New Zealand farmer.

'I had such a great day with you today.' Chie smiled lovingly. We were sitting in a fast-food restaurant, wearing our matching outfits. Chie's shorts were hitched up under her arms.

'It was certainly a new experience for me,' I admitted.

'Oh, I'm soooo happy with you,' Chie said sweetly. 'I can't wait until we're living together in New Zealand. I think we will be together forever and ever.'

Oh, dear Lord. I gagged on my hamburger and started coughing violently. 'Pardon?'

'I said I can't wait until we are living together in Christchurch. We can have fun days like this all the time.'

I slurped some Coca-Cola. The chunk of hamburger was still stuck in my throat. Chie's pants were hitched up under her arms. We were wearing matching outfits. And now she wanted to live with me forever and ever. Why, oh why, had I taken her out to the Mexican restaurant in the first place?

I realised that my relationship with Chie Matsumoto needed to be terminated. Things were moving way too fast. I had known her for only five weeks, but it was only a matter of time before our entire wardrobes were matching.

I decided to let her down gently. Slowly but surely I spent less and less time with her, until at last I was brave enough to send a gently worded email suggesting it would be best if we parted company.

In Chie's defence, her slightly deranged fashion sense had been a misguided attempt at creating a group identity for us. Being part of a group is an overriding aspect of Japanese society. From an early age, children are sternly taught to conform to group culture and ways of thinking. To express an opinion different to that of your classroom group will soon result in social rejection. To be seen as being too intelligent or too stupid, too tall or too short, too fat or too thin will eventually have disastrous consequences. Nobody wants to be different, an outsider left on their own and quietly shunned by their peers.

Mr Doi had achieved this within weeks of his arrival at Kanan Junior High School. There was now no way for him to be welcomed into lunch-time conversations, after-school drinking sessions and staffroom events. That was, of course, if he ever decided to return to work.

Group mentality extended to the sports field. The students in the school's baseball team shaved their heads and adopted a 'tough guy' swagger. The boys in the basketball team were outspoken and cocky. The girls in the tennis team were cute and giggly, while those in the music club were quiet and shy. Even though participation in each of these activities required a certain skill-set, and often a matching personality as well, group consciousness seemingly highlighted and reinforced these stereo-types, and behaviour patterns were altered in order to fit in.

Fashion also served to reinforce your place in a group. School or office uniforms were a badge of honour and showed you had a place within society, a place within a group.

Chic young women sporting matching designer handbags and virtually identical (usually Italian) clothing would parade through town, their gear proudly proclaiming that they were trendy, wealthy, and part of a like-minded group of friends. Even rebels wore group clothing. Punk rockers sported pink Mohicans and gothic girls wore black lacy dresses. These 'free spirits' would hang out in groups of similarly attired friends. Nobody wanted to be alone.

Fourteen-year-old Megumi Uchida was a prime example of what could go wrong when one dared oppose group mentality. She stood in the middle of the staffroom, tears streaming down her face. Her mascara had painted black smears down her swollen cheeks. Everyone was yelling at her.

Megumi was a third-grade student. She was slightly taller than her female peers and also a little plump, making her an easy outcast in such an image-conscious society. Alas, though, poor Megumi was a hopeless romantic and dreamed of one day finding a boyfriend. To attract the attention of her male classmates, she had daringly come to school wearing mascara and a touch of lip gloss.

Sadly for her, this simple act of self-decoration was considered akin to a criminal offence at conservative Kanan Junior High School. Make-up allowed students to make themselves 'different', and so was strictly prohibited. Megumi had been sentenced to parade around the staffroom, stopping at every desk so the teacher could give her a ten-minute telling-off.

During such events, my desk was always bypassed as there was no way I would be able to convincingly scold anyone in Japanese. I retreated to a chair by the computer terminal and kept my head down. Megumi had so far made it past only three desks, had been slapped twice, was sobbing pitiably, and no-one had thought to give her a tissue.

Slap! I looked up. Megumi was being sent back to desk two, as Mrs Otani had something further to say. I began to wonder if the poor girl was going to make it home that evening.

I returned to my emails and tried to think of happy stories to tell my family. Forty minutes later poor Megumi was finally taken away to the 'conversation room' for the remainder of her sentence, which would last another two hours. It was safe for me to return to my desk.

Everyone breathed a sigh of relief. The crisis had been averted. Megumi Uchida had learnt her lesson and would never again wear make-up to school. Order had been reinstated.

Two weeks later, however, a new threat to group harmony suddenly reared its head. The staffroom was thrown into turmoil. There was a new student in the school: Yurika Yurano.

Everyone referred to Ms Yurano by her surname, and this single word seemed to have a terrifying effect whenever it was uttered. The reason was that Ms Yurano had bleached blonde hair, like a Simpsons' character.

I quickly took refuge at the internet terminal and set up a makeshift bomb shelter with supplies of Coca-Cola and steamed pork buns. I waited: World War Three was on its way.

To my astonishment, however, Ms Yurano was allowed to go to class and display her bright yellow hair in peace. Mr Higo explained the teachers' predicament. It seemed that Ms Yurano had an interesting family background, so interesting in fact that the teachers were completely at a loss as to how to deal with her. I made an educated guess that her father was somehow involved in organised crime, and hence Ms Yurano was not to be yelled at, beaten, slapped, and pushed around as anyone else would have been.

As well as having a mafia dad, Yurika Yurano was taller than any of the boys at the school, and almost the same height as me. This made the short male teachers, who usually didn't hesitate to give a female student a good slap, think twice before even raising their voices. Furthermore, Yurika's ten earrings, Barbie-doll make-up and extremely short skirt all served to strike fear into the heart of my colleagues.

There were, nevertheless, a few teachers still bold enough to attempt to reprimand her. The week after Yurika arrived I was walking along the hallway behind her when a short, fierce man leapt out of a classroom and yelled the equivalent of, 'Oi, you there, what are you doing? Walk properly!'

I was fairly convinced that Ms Yurano had been walking normally. She, too, must have realised she had been the target of unjustified criticism. She turned defiantly and proceeded to strut her stuff, flicking her hips so her miniscule skirt bounced up and down, and the boys sitting on the floor got a clear view of her underwear. The short male teacher rapidly retreated, and the boys squirmed.

Lamentably, I was allowed little opportunity to get to know the school's newest member as Ms Yurano repeatedly bunked English class, claiming she had little interest in the subject. However, while walking past my classroom one day, she popped her bright yellow head through the open window, gave me the glad eye, winked, and continued on her way.

The teachers, meanwhile, continued to hold emergency meetings every day to discuss what should be done. This continued for several weeks and, as no course of action was decided on, the spirit of Ms Yurano slowly started to spread. Other girls began to strut provocatively in the hallways, shorten their skirts and give people the glad eye. Rebellion was in the air.

Unfortunately, I was far too busy to dye my hair green or pierce my eyebrows. For the first time in two years and two months in Japan, I finally had a full workload: stacks of first-grade speaking tests to mark, a town magazine article to write, and board games to create for the young minnows. I was forced to stay at school later than 4.30 and even spent a Sunday afternoon working on the magazine article.

Gone were my two-hour-long coffee breaks and extended trips to the convenience store. Gone were the days of being able to read an entire paperback novel in a single afternoon. My carefully ordered pen collection fell into disarray.

In the midst of a society that prides itself on hard work, it was wonderful to at last feel productive and involved in the staffroom 'group'.

After a slight reshuffle in the staffroom seating arrangements, I found myself sitting next to the new woodwork teacher. Mr Yagi was twenty-two years old and now held the esteemed title of youngest teacher in the school. He had a shaved head, a black rap-star T-shirt, and, in keeping with the current rebellious spirit, wore his baseball cap back to front.

I was delighted with the school's choice of replacement woodwork teacher, and Mr Yagi and I rapidly became good friends. One day, however, my bubble burst: Mr Yagi sadly informed me that magnificent Mr Doi had not been fired and was still considered a member of the staff. He was currently undergoing 'job retraining and counselling', and once he'd been given the all-clear he would return. With the new seating arrangements, I could look forward to sitting next to Mr Doi forever. I prayed that his processing would take a very long time.

My run of happy classes with the young minnows continued as the summer months ticked by. Hiro, Yurika and Teru-Chan were now big fans of *Cluedo* and *Snap*, but I was keen to try something new before their interest waned. I stayed late at school for a solid fortnight, armed with an array of felt-tip pens, coloured paper, sheets of cardboard, sloppy glue and a rusty stapler. The end result was a lovingly created imitation of the classic board game *Who's Who?*

I had painstakingly produced four matching cardboard game boards. On each I had drawn a variety of faces encased within small cardboard windows. Each player drew a card from a pack. This portrayed the player's identity, and corresponded to a picture on the game board.

Players then took turns asking each other questions to guess their opponent's secret identity: 'Do you have blue eyes?' 'Do you have glasses?' 'Do you have long hair?'

If a response were affirmative, the faces without the corresponding features would be 'checked off' by closing ingenious little cardboard window-shutters, which were then sealed with little latches made of staples. The players would continue to ask each other questions, until by a slow process of elimination they could deduce their opponent's identity.

As I am no artist, drawing fifty little faces with unique features was quite a struggle. I had managed to draw only five before I realised that my cartooning abilities were limited. Each face had started to look like the previous one—a round head, scraggly hair, googly eyes and a small hook nose. Try as I might, I could not seem to draw anything different.

I resorted to copying faces out of comic books and magazines. This did the trick, and I proudly displayed the four handsome game boards to my bemused colleagues. Mr Kazama, the principal, pored over them intently. 'Ooohh,' he exclaimed joyfully, 'it's so bright and colourful. Ooohh, and look, the little windows have little latches!' He clapped his hands and called for the vice principal to come and inspect my work.

The minnows were completely blown away. Yurika peered happily at the little faces, Hiro fiddled with the window latches, and Teru-Chan inspected the stack of 'identity' cards, gruffly inquiring as to whether this was a new game of *Snap*.

I explained the rules, and we had a practice run. Debate soon flared as to whether red hair could be considered blond or not. Teru-Chan was adamant that it could, and I suddenly realised that Hiro was colour-blind and thought that a quarter of the faces on the board had green hair.

We struggled on with a second practice round and the students slowly got the hang of things. The bell rang and they made me promise I would bring *Who's Who?* to the next lesson so we could have a proper competition.

Group harmony was now fully restored to the young minnows' class.

Group harmony was also very much alive and well during my fortnightly conversation sessions with my mothers. Over the past year we had discussed all manner of things—local weather patterns, festivals, favourite recipes, gardening tips, parents-in-law, children, grandchildren, Kanan Junior High School, Mr Doi, and my life in New Zealand.

I had noticed, however, that conversation was always very polite, and often dominated by the talkative Mrs Terauchi. Occasionally other members would dispute her outlandish interjections, but for the most part they went unquestioned. An example was her response to Mrs Tanaka's news that her son and daughter-in-law were planning a holiday in Honolulu.

'Aha! Hawaiian sumo wrestlers are not so strong. They have weak knees. Most foreigners have weak knees,' Mrs Terauchi raved.

Mrs Matsui nodded in mute agreement. Mrs Tsubota coughed, and pursed her lips.Mrs Tanaka twiddled her thumbs. Mrs Kiguchi murmured a soft 'Oh really?'

I flexed my supposedly feeble knees. It was time to inject some lively discussion into our conversation sessions.

What my mothers needed, I decided, was a formal, well-structured debate. I explained the rules. Each person would take a turn at speaking— defending and promoting their team's theory. The opposing team would then be given the chance to make a rebuttal. Each team was to try to convince me, the judge, that they had the most convincing argument.

I divided them into two teams, old v. young: Mrs Terauchi and Mrs Kiguchi v. Mrs Matsui, Mrs Tanaka and Mrs Tsubota. The first topic was 'The merits of country life v. the merits of city life'. The older team would present the merits of country life.

Mrs Terauchi began. After making some valid points about the beauty and tranquillity of the Japanese countryside, she lost the plot and added some extraneous comments about the history of Kanan Town and ancient rice-farming techniques.

The younger team then made a good response, with convincing remarks about the convenience and abundance of services available in urban areas.

Mrs Kiguchi shyly attempted her reply. Despite tripping over some tricky English words, she managed to explain that a slow-paced country life was better for your health than a hectic, money-driven lifestyle in the city. I smiled and gave her a good mark.

'I have to admit though,' Mrs Kiguchi continued in Japanese, 'that the other team made a much better argument than I did.' She bowed politely. 'I agree with all their points so far.' She bowed again and smiled at her opponents. 'Please do not be offended by my remarks,' she said politely.

I sighed. I should have realised that the mild, courteous nature of my Japanese mothers would never adapt to the cut and thrust of Western-style debate.

The younger team took the floor and Mrs Matsui made some well-thought-out comments about the greater number of employment opportunities and higher level of financial rewards available in the cities. Mrs Kiguchi nodded and hummed along in agreement. 'Yes, yes, good point,' she said, bowing. 'Well done.'

Mrs Terauchi was beginning to realise that her polite friend was becoming a hindrance to their team's performance. 'Shhhh,' she hushed. 'You can't agree with them. You're on my side. Remember, we're the country life team.'

'Oh!' Mrs Kiguchi blushed and covered her mouth delicately. 'Can I change teams then?'

The women exploded with laughter.

The debate ended happily. The younger team had been thoroughly convincing, and Mrs Kiguchi cheerfully agreed when I announced that her opponents were the winners. 'Hamish sensei, I enjoyed our discussion today. I'd like to have a debate next week,' she said, clutching my arm as I walked to the door.

'Oh, I'm glad that you enjoyed it,' I replied.

'Yes, it is very nice to talk about things.' She covered her mouth as she began to chuckle. 'But please, sensei, next time can I have a different team-mate?'

As I wheeled my bicycle down the driveway I looked back. Mrs Kiguchi was bowing and chuckling with Mrs Terauchi, making sure her comments had not caused offence. Mrs Terauchi laughed and bowed. The group closed the door. They would return to the kitchen for a cup of tea.

# 17

# The Great Lake Biwa
# Circumnavigation

*My good friend Justin* was in one of his endearingly enthusiastic moods when I answered the telephone on a warm September evening. 'I've got it,' he began eagerly. 'I've got a map. It's all sorted. I've come up with a winning plan for the best weekend ever. You're going to love this.'

I listened apprehensively. I already knew what Justin was about to propose.

'I've found a map,' he repeated excitedly. 'It was on the internet. It's a road map for the entire Osaka prefecture. It's just what we need for the trip. Whaddya reckon?'

I groaned. 'So you're still keen to go on this trip of yours then?'

Justin could hear the negativity in my voice. 'You bet I am!' he thundered. 'Don't you get cold feet on me now, mate. You told me last month that you were keen to do this. Well, I've found a map. That's all that was missing before. There's nothing stopping us now.'

'Hmmm...' I tried to be supportive. I did not want to dampen my friend's enthusiasm.

Justin had, for some time, been daydreaming of attempting a three-day bicycle pilgrimage, which he claimed would settle an ongoing debate between himself and his Japanese co-workers. Justin's elaborate cycle journey would see him pedalling furiously north from Osaka City, across the Kansai plains, up and over a tall mountain range, and then around Lake Biwa—the largest lake in Japan—before then returning to Osaka.

Justin was convinced that this daring expedition could be completed comfortably within three days. His co-workers argued that the trip was virtually impossible to complete by bicycle, and even if it could it would take at least ten days, assuming the cyclists somehow managed to cross the 'towering' Mount Ise.

Justin had debated this strongly, pointing out that the distance between Osaka and Lake Biwa was not great (seventy kilometres on a map), and that 'pitiful' Mount Ise could be overcome by even an amateur cyclist.

He was, however, reluctant to attempt The Great Lake Biwa Circumnavigation on his own, and his dreams of proving his co-workers wrong started to fade when he struggled to attract any friends who were willing to accompany him. Finally, I had consented to his repeated requests during one of our midweek drinking sessions in downtown Osaka.

'C'mon, mate. You said you were keen last month,' Justin scolded. 'I've found the map now. That's all we were waiting on.' He paused.

'All right then,' I sighed. 'When do you want to do this?'

'Last weekend of October. It's a long weekend: we've both got the Friday off work. I've got everything planned. All you need to do is turn up to my apartment on the Friday morning.

'Honestly, it's gonna be a breeze. We're going to be legends after this. No one's ever tried it before. We're going to show them what New Zealanders are made of. We'll teach these namby-pamby stay-indoors workaholics how to enjoy life.'

Justin's enthusiasm was starting to dispel my nagging doubts. 'So tell me about this map then,' I muttered.

'Excellent. That's the spirit.' Justin's smile was audible. 'Hang on a tick, I'll go and get it.'

I sighed again. What had I signed up for?

The Great Lake Biwa Circumnavigation was just over a month away. I still had plenty of time to get into peak physical condition and razor-sharp mental fitness.

In the staffroom, Mr Higo chuckled as we young single teachers picked away at our lunchtime octopus tentacles and noodle salad. The teachers' relay team had just come last for the third year in a row at school athletics day. This time Mr Hioki was to blame. He had tripped over his own feet in the home straight.

'Say, who wants to go drinking tonight?' Mr Higo asked cheerfully. Everyone nodded enthusiastically.

'Great.' He smiled. 'This will be good training for Mr Hamish's bicycle ride to Lake Biwa. He needs to become very strong.'

My plans of circumnavigating Lake Biwa on a bicycle had quickly become public knowledge after I had shared them with Mr Higo.

'Why do you want to ride a bicycle to Lake Biwa?' Mr Hioki asked. 'It is easier to go by train.'

'Your trip will take two weeks,' Mr Shibukawa lectured. 'Your legs will be very tired.'

I shook my head. I was surprised to find myself becoming as defensive about the bicycle expedition as Justin. 'No, it's not so difficult,' I protested. 'My friend and I will be able to complete it in only three days.'

My colleagues looked at me with wonder. 'You must be very strong to try such a trip,' Mr Omura said.

'Yes,' I replied nonchalantly. 'In New Zealand, people ride bicycles everywhere. The trip to Lake Biwa will not be so difficult.'

My cool self-confidence had seemingly been convincing. My fellow teachers nodded in awed respect. Mr Hamish, the rugged athlete from New Zealand, was obviously very strong.

Later that evening we assembled at a local Korean barbecue restaurant. Mr Higo was keen for a big night out. We hunkered down on tatami mats and he ordered several large plates of beef and ox tongue. I had developed a particular liking for barbecued ox tongue; upon hearing this, he ordered another two platefuls.

I had already been out drinking with this group of young male teachers several times that year. A typical evening would start at a bar-becue restaurant, and then proceed to a karaoke booth for several hours of drunken crooning. After having had enough of howling and singing badly, several married teachers would bid us farewell and depart. Those of us remaining would then adjourn to a pub and drink ourselves even stupider, until, one by one, we would slowly disappear off home.

Tonight was looking to be a typically fun-filled affair. Mr Higo had ordered the young waiter to keep our beers topped up, and to keep the plates of meat flowing until we could eat no more. Everyone was in high spirits, having spent a day outside in the sunshine watching the school sports. We laughed and teased each other as we recounted the teachers' team's loss.

Mr Hioki blushed when his clumsy accident was re-enacted by Mr Nakata, and his face turned a strange purple, a mixture of beer and embarrassment. Outside the classroom and away from our tedious English lessons, I had slowly grown to like Mr Hioki and his bowl-shaped haircut. He was a valued member of the young male teachers' drinking circle, and his hilarious renditions of cartoon soundtracks during our karaoke sessions proved he had a good sense of humour after all. I was also becoming used to his regimented teaching style, and had accepted that my role in his classroom was to act as a human tape recorder.

Mr Hioki seemed to enjoy chatting with me during our drinking sessions, and other teachers would ask him to act as translator so they could ask me personal questions without feeling intrusive. He would be called upon to inquire whether I had a girlfriend in New Zealand, what I thought of Japanese women, and how many former girlfriends I had. He would usually chip in and reply on my behalf, giving exaggerated numbers and ludicrous answers. Mr Higo and Mr Hioki would end up teasing each other in English, and then ask me to judge who had been the most witty and humorous.

Beer was flowing freely and I had consumed a large quantity of barbecued ox tongue and beef. Conversation turned to school—the scandalous attire of Ms Yurano, the mysterious disappearance of Mr Doi, and the bossy attitude of Mrs Nakazato. Mr Hioki was requested to inquire as to my opinion of Mrs Nakazato. I gave a diplomatic response.

'Mr Hame, I do not think you like her so much. Ha ha ha.' Mr Higo laughed. 'Go on, tell the truth. What do you really think? I think she is too bossy.'

I laughed. 'No commento,' I replied in an exaggerated Japanese accent.

Everyone laughed. In a society that prided itself on veiled responses, my elusive comment had provided enough information for the listener to read between the lines.

Mr Higo clapped me on the back and passed me another beer. 'Is it time to go to karaoke?' he asked. Everyone nodded and patted their swollen stomachs. We had been eating and drinking for two hours and the thought of more barbecue beef was making me nauseous. We finished our drinks and staggered down the road to the local karaoke establishment. Mr Hioki paid for a private booth for two hours, Mr Higo ordered a round of beer and we programmed in our favourite songs.

As I am a terrible singer, tone-deaf and unable to hold a note, my karaoke technique consisted of belting out a few well-known numbers so loudly that any imperfections were drowned out. On this occasion I was the opening singer. I performed a hearty off-key rendition of Billy Joel's 'Piano Man', rocked through a duet of Deep Purple's 'Highway Star' with Mr Higo, and squeaked through 'Unchained Melody' by the Righteous Brothers. Mr Hioki was keen to perform a duet with me, so we thrashed out a spirited version of 'I just called to say I love you' by Stevie Wonder.

Despite the continuous supply of beer and sake, my throat was becoming a little hoarse. I decided to take things easy with 'Imagine' by John Lennon. We had now been singing for two and half hours, and were well over our time limit. Several of the married teachers announced that they would need to return home or meet an unfriendly reception.

Four of us remained: Mr Higo, Mr Hioki, Mr Nakata and I. We decided to end the evening with a last couple of rounds at the local pub, Wasshoi. The couple of drinks soon turned into four pints of beer, a plate of noodles and a dish of fried chicken wings.

Starting to feel a little queasy, I decided to head home before I did anything idiotic. I stood up and felt the evening's alcohol rocket to my brain. I staggered slightly and leant against the wall.

Mr Hioki looked at me with concern. 'Are you okay?' he asked.

'Sure,' I assured him. I settled my bill and stepped outside. Foolishly, I had decided to take my bicycle with me in order to get home at the end of the evening. I had not foreseen that we would end up at Wasshoi, and had presumed that our last stop of the night would be further afield. Wasshoi was located only a hundred metres from my apartment building. A narrow, backstreet alleyway led in a straight line directly from the bar to my building.

I swayed drunkenly on the pub's doorstep and peered hazily down the lane. It was pitch-black and there was not a soul to be seen.

'You should bike home!' a voice in my head said. 'It's not that far.'

I hiccoughed and looked left and right. There were no cars, no traffic, no people. I paused and considered. I should cycle home. I needed to get in shape for the great Lake Biwa bicycle ride. This was a perfect opportunity.

I unlocked my bicycle, tripped over the back tyre and fell forward on to the road. I landed on my hands and knees, and stood up again shakily. I brushed off my dusty palms and straddled my bike. No problems so far.

I turned to face my apartment building, and paused to collect my bearings. 'Let's go!' I announced aloud, and peddled off.

My left arm wobbled, the handlebars turned and I veered straight into a concrete wall. I lurched forward out of the seat and my private parts landed uncomfortably on the bike's metal frame.

I slowly found my balance and sat down again on the bicycle seat. I looked back at the Wasshoi doorstep. I had managed to cycle only three metres before colliding with the wall. I would need to concentrate.

I peered into the darkness and visualised myself cycling steadily home.

I set off again. I slowly built up speed. My right leg twitched and my foot slipped off the pedal. I wobbled madly and collided with a beer-vending machine. Still unable to control my right leg, I toppled sideways on to the pavement.

I lay still for a moment, a confused bundle of drunken limbs and bicycle parts. My left trouser leg was caught in my cycle chain. I tugged at it blindly, and eventually it came free without tearing. Slowly, I started to untangle myself from my vehicle and tried to stand up. I looked back at the Wasshoi doorstep. It seemed to be quite distant now: I was halfway home.

I turned, and looked at my apartment entrance. I was nearly there. I was standing outside Mrs Okuda's house. I swayed on my feet and looked carefully at her vegetable garden. I would be in serious trouble if I ran over any of her pot plants.

'Perhaps you should walk?' I heard my brain suggest. I stubbornly picked up my fallen bicycle. I refused to give up. I was nearly home.

I straddled the seat and set off again. As I neared Mrs Okuda's vegetable garden, I wobbled and teetered. My hands were sweaty and I held my breath as I passed her doorstep—nearly home, don't blow it now.

I had managed to pass most of Mrs Okuda's beloved garden. A large sunflower stood to my left. My hands wobbled and I veered dangerously towards it. In an attempt to save both myself and the sunflower, I leant crazily to the right and my bicycle swerved in the nick of time.

I breathed a huge sigh of relief.

Crash! My front tyre struck the kerb. I fell forward, hit the handlebars and bounced on to the ground. My bicycle followed shortly after and landed upside down on my back.

I lay still for a moment, wondering where I was. I looked up. 'Tokiwa Mansion' was painted in large Japanese characters above the apartment building entrance. I smiled. I would be able to walk the rest of the way from here.

The next morning my alarm clock rang.

I came awake slowly.

My head hurt. I grimaced.

I looked around.

I frowned.

I looked down.

I was sitting upright on my sofa.

I was fully clothed. I had spent the night sleeping in a seated position with my jeans and shoes still on.

My head throbbed. I slowly began to recollect the events of the previous evening. I checked my shirt. No vomit stains. Thank heaven for that.

My hands stung. I held them up for closer inspection. They were grazed and dirty. So were my trousers. The hem of my left trouser leg was stained with oil. Perhaps, I pondered, this was the level of stupidity and complete disregard for personal safety that would be needed to attempt the great Lake Biwa bicycle expedition.

One of my Japanese friends had told me about an intriguing tourist attraction in Kyoto. 'It's called Monkey Mountain' she explained excitedly. 'You walk up a big hill and there are monkeys everywhere. They are free to run around wherever they want. You can feed the monkeys fruit. They're soooo cute. Plus, it's a great place for hiking. Do you have places like Monkey Mountain in New Zealand?'

'I don't believe so,' I replied. 'Don't monkeys bite people?'

'No, they're really, really cute. I want to have a monkey for a pet. Do New Zealand people keep monkeys for pets?'

'No,' I replied again. 'Monkeys have diseases and bite people. Plus they throw their poos around.'

'But they're so cute!' my friend protested. 'You really should go to Monkey Mountain. It is a very, very natural place. I think it will remind you of New Zealand.'

I dipped my eyebrows sceptically. Monkey Mountain sounded about as similar to New Zealand as Harvest Hill. However, the idea of spending a day hiking up a big hill appealed. The great Lake Biwa bicycle expedition was now only three weeks away, and my training was yet to get off the ground.

I set off for Monkey Mountain the following weekend. It was an overcast day, so I packed a jacket and jersey in case it started to rain. Monkey Mountain is located on the outskirts of Kyoto prefecture. Like all significant tourist attractions in Japan, it can be easily reached by train or bus.

I arrived at the base of the mountain shortly after midday and began my invigorating trek uphill, my eyes peeled for any sign of the cute monkeys. The trail zigzagged through wooded areas that became increasingly dense as the altitude rose. I could feel my leg muscles straining, and congratulated myself for having chosen such a suitable workout.

I certainly had no need for my jacket and jersey, and decided to take a quick break to catch my breath. I wiped my brow. I was perspiring nicely —my physical training was obviously having an effect.

I looked around. I was yet to see any sign of the cute monkeys. I had been told, however, that they mainly congregated around the feeding station at the top of the hill. A marker suggested that I was only halfway up, and had a steep climb ahead of me.

I set off again. The trail grew slightly steeper and my legs protested. I heard rustling to my left. I peered into the undergrowth. Were the cute monkeys in there?

My eyes adjusted to the shadows. Two scrawny flea-ridden male monkeys with bright-red swollen bottoms stared back. The bigger monkey hissed and made a rude hand gesture. It then bared its fangs and scampered up a tree.

The other monkey ran directly at me. I shrieked, unsure how to deal with an enraged primate. The monkey bounced on to the path in front of me and held up an open hand like a beggar. He looked up at me with imploring eyes. I looked back at him, terrified that I was about to be bitten.

The tree-top monkey hissed again, this time at his companion, and the beggar monkey ran back into the undergrowth.

I checked my pockets. I still had my wallet, cellphone and keys but I had very nearly been mugged by a pair of scrawny monkeys. My friend who had recommended Monkey Mountain was going to receive a stern telling-off.

I decided to press on uphill and seek shelter in the feeding station. I had not come all the way to western Kyoto only to wimp out halfway. I increased my pace and broke into a slow jog.

Eventually, the feeding station came into sight. It was, in reality, a small wooden shack in the middle of a grassy clearing. It was surrounded by hundreds of scrawny monkeys with bright-red bottoms. Wire mesh covered the windows, and a heavy wooden door prevented the monkeys from clambering inside. Human visitors, meanwhile, were free to enter the station, purchase bags of food, and hand or throw the food to the waiting monkeys through the gaps in the mesh. We were sternly instructed not to carry food outside the feeding station, as this was likely to trigger violent riots.

I eyed the monkeys nervously. For the most part they were babies or small skinny females. The babies were certainly cute, performing roly-polys in the dirt, playing games of tag with each other, and clinging helplessly to their mothers.

The large male monkeys, however, were not nearly as adorable. Packs of them had staked out territory in front of the feeding station. They hissed savagely, chased each other, and beat their chests to ward off anything that dared to encroach on their area.

Doing my best to appear bold and self-assured, I strode towards the entrance. The smaller monkeys scattered, chattering wildly, but the dominant males glared at me, baring their fangs and hissing. Several made rude hand gestures.

Inside the shack, a withered old woman sat behind a counter on which were arrayed bags of fruit chunks. I purchased two. 'The monkeys have been very naughty lately,' the old woman warned. 'It's mating season and there are too many males, so there are many fights. Don't take any food out of here with you. They will attack you if they think you have food.'

I gulped. Monkey Mountain was certainly a lot more dangerous than my friend had led me to believe. I pondered the fact that Japanese people were perfectly content to stroll among rabid untamed monkeys, while fretting about potential accidents on escalators, walking in the rain without an umbrella, and contracting mad-cow disease at Korean barbecue restaurants.

I opened my bags of fruit and stepped towards one of the large mesh-covered windows. Sensing movement, the monkeys started yelping. The dominant males rushed to the windows and rattled the wire meshing wildly, biting and clawing each other in the process. I stepped back in alarm.

Short, stubby fingers curled through the mesh, ready to snatch any fruit that might be on offer. I looked around for any needy baby monkeys that may have been brave enough to approach the feeding station. A small pack had gathered to one side. They shivered nervously and looked at me with wide saucer eyes.

I quickly thrust a handful of apple pieces through the mesh to the dominant males. As expected, they rushed forward and fought among themselves over the small pieces of apple. I then bounded across the room and emptied half a bag of fruit pieces through the window to the baby monkeys below. They grabbed as much fruit as their little hands could carry and raced away.

The dominant males gave chase, but the infants had fled to the safety of their mothers, and the males returned testily to the feeding station. The tin roof clanged and banged. The males had scaled the walls. They were now jumping up and down on the roof in protest at my trickery.

'Oh, they're being naughty again,' the old woman said disapprovingly. 'They like to jump up and down on the roof to make a big noise. I'd better go and tell them off.' She stood up, picked up a broom and stepped outside. There was a sudden cacophony of screeching, and the banging on the tin roof ceased. I watched through the window as several males leapt from the roof and fled to the safety of the undergrowth.

The woman returned. She put down her broom and took her seat behind the counter without a word.

I looked at her in amazement. Japan and its people were still managing to surprise me after more than two years. This little old woman, probably in her eighties, spent her days climbing Monkey Mountain and warding off packs of savage male monkeys with a broom.

My physical training was now amounting to little more than cycling to work every day. This thirteen-minute doddle was not going to prepare me for my three-day expedition to Lake Biwa. I needed a more prolonged cardiovascular workout to get my heart and lungs into suitable shape.

My friends had planned a big night out for the following Saturday. I decided that dancing until dawn in a nightclub would count as a good workout, and condition my body to extended periods of exercise.

After the night out with the young male teachers, I had vowed not to touch another drop of alcohol before the expedition. So far so good: I had managed to go two weeks without being invited out and forced to drink beer and sake. When Saturday evening rolled around I staunchly drank only orange juice and water. I frolicked on the dance floor from midnight until dawn, and when my intoxicated friends staggered out the door to catch their respective trains home I was still feeling bright-eyed and bushy-tailed.

I was now with a group of female Japanese friends who had also spent a sober night dancing and were keen to go and get a hearty breakfast. We exited the nightclub and wandered down the road to a twenty-four-hour restaurant. We were in the heart of Shinsaibashi, a district famed for its designer clothing stores, red-light activities and Yakuza-controlled businesses. Several metres ahead of us a large white van was parked on the footpath outside a small jewellery store. Something peculiar about the van caught my attention. I gestured for my companions to be quiet and stop walking.

Suddenly, two masked men brandishing crowbars leapt from the van's side door. They sprinted to the entrance of the jewellery store and attached a thick steel cable to the store's iron grill. One then signalled to the driver of the van, who revved the engine and sped off. The steel cable went taut, there was a large cracking sound, and the entire iron grill was torn off the front of the store.

The masked men raced back, stepped around the shattered security front, and smashed their way through the window. All of this had taken less than 30 seconds.

'Wow!' I said in shock. 'What's going on here then?'

'Do you think they're real gangsters?' one of the women whispered.

'Hmmm...I dunno.' I considered the question carefully. 'I guess they could be. Should we do something?' My friend was way ahead of me. She was holding her cellphone and taking photos of the van and its number plate.

Smashing sounds could still be heard from inside the jewellery store. The masked men were obviously having a lot of fun. The smashing stopped and the men stepped out on to the street.

My friend took a photo of them. 'Um, do you think that's such a good idea?' I stuttered nervously. I suddenly realised that I was the only male in the group; if anyone was going to receive a tap on the head with a crowbar, it would be me.

The masked men froze and stared at my friend angrily. They retrieved their steel cable, leapt into the van and sped away down the street.

One of the other women was on her phone, calling the police. 'There's been a burglary,' she explained calmly. 'A jewellery store has been broken into.' She gave the address. 'The police will be here in a minute,' she announced as she hung up. 'They want us to give evidence.'

We were suddenly very happy. This was proving to be a most exciting start to the day.

Fifteen minutes later, two antiquated Japanese police officers arrived on equally antiquated bicycles. They stopped outside the jewellery store and scratched their heads in bewilderment. 'What happened here?' the skinny one asked his chubby colleague.

'I don't know, sir. It looks like the security grill has been removed. What do you think?'

'Hmm, yes, I think someone has removed the security grill.'

I nodded in agreement. The twisted and buckled security grill was now lying in the middle of the street. It was, quite obviously, no longer attached to the jewellery store.

The two men bent down and examined it. 'It's definitely been removed,' they deduced. 'I wonder who did it?'

'We saw it happen,' one of my friends offered brightly. 'We even took photos of the people who did it.'

The policemen ignored her. They scratched their heads and turned their attention to the shopfront. 'I think someone's smashed the window,' the chubby policeman noted sagely. 'I wonder how they did it?'

'They smashed the window with crowbars,' another woman volunteered. 'Do you want to see a photo of them?'

The policemen ignored her and stepped inside the trashed store. 'Oh, I think they've broken all the display cases,' I heard the skinny one exclaim. 'I think they've taken all the jewels too.'

Several minutes later, the policemen stepped outside on to the street. 'Did anyone see anything?' one asked.

'Yes!' my friends chorused impatiently. 'We saw everything. We even took photos.'

'Oh.' The policemen scratched their heads. 'May we see?'

My friend handed over her phone and the policemen scrolled slowly through the photos. 'I think they attached a steel cable to the security grill,' the chubby one announced. 'That must be how they removed it.'

I was losing patience with the policemen's incompetence. 'That's their white van,' I said, pointing at the photo. 'We wrote down their licence plate.' I handed the skinny policeman the details. 'They drove off in that direction.' I pointed down the street. 'You should look for the van.'

The policemen scratched their heads again. 'I guess we should write a report about this,' they mused. 'Do you think we have enough details?'

We had grown tired of their inane bumbling. It was time for breakfast. Osaka's finest would have to solve the case on their own.

Justin was bubbling with excitement over the telephone line. It was the night before our keenly anticipated departure for Lake Biwa. 'It's all set,' he enthused. 'We're good to go. I've got two bikes ready and waiting at my place. I've checked the brakes and pumped the tyres. The weather forecast is good for the next few days—sunshine and blue skies all the way to Lake Biwa and back. I've booked accommodation for Friday and Saturday nights, and I've plotted our route all the way from Osaka City to Kyoto.'

'What about the rest of our route?' I asked. 'How do we get from Kyoto to Lake Biwa?'

There was a pause on the other end of the line. 'I'm not so sure about that bit,' Justin admitted. 'I couldn't find a map for that section. But I've done the trip by car, and I think I can remember most of the way.'

'Hmmm,' I grumbled.

'Don't worry about it,' Justin said reassuringly. 'We can stop and ask directions at convenience stores and petrol stations. It's honestly not that far. We'll be fine. Remember, we're from New Zealand.'

I listened apprehensively as Justin repeated our three-day schedule.

Day One, Friday: Cycle north from Osaka, cross the Kansai Plain, up and over Mount Ise, and spend the night in Otsu City. This would take only six hours. Apparently.

Day Two, Saturday: Cycle around most of Lake Biwa. Spend a couple of hours sightseeing at a local castle, and then spend the night in an inn overlooking the lake. Possibly an eight-hour ride.

Day Three, Sunday: Complete the circumnavigation of Lake Biwa, cycle back over Mount Ise, cross the Kansai Plain and return to Osaka. Get home nice and early and have a good night's sleep before starting work on Monday morning. Possibly ten hours.

'It's going to be a piece of cake,' Justin said. 'I can't wait to see my co-workers' surprised faces on Monday.'

'How's your training going?' I asked.

He laughed. 'What training? I haven't even cycled to work for the past three weeks. I ride the train. We don't need any training for this. Apart from crossing the mountain, it's going to be dead flat all the way there and back. Not a hill in sight. Anyone could do this. Look, don't worry about a thing. Just turn up at my place nice and early tomorrow morning.'

I spent a nervous night fretting about the upcoming trip. I had visited Lake Biwa with Mr Tokunaga the year before. We had driven around the lake in Mr Tokunaga's trusty campervan and returned to Osaka in a single day. However, we had encountered numerous traffic jams and the trip had taken thirteen hours. It had been a long exhausting drive. I was not looking forward to repeating it on a bicycle.

I arrived at Justin's apartment shortly after nine the next morning. He was waiting impatiently. 'Good! You're here. We should get going. You choose which bike you want. Have you had breakfast? Good. We should get a few hours' cycling under our belts and then stop for lunch once we're well and truly out of Osaka.'

I looked at Justin's pair of bicycles. Both were gearless 'old lady' antiques. This was going to add a challenging aspect to our mountain crossing. I chose the silver bicycle, stowed my backpack in the basket on the front and hoisted myself into the seat.

Justin took one last look at his map, folded it, and stowed it securely in his trouser pocket. 'Let's go!' he roared and we pedalled off down the road. The Great Lake Biwa Circumnavigation was finally underway.

I was suddenly very excited. Justin and I were embarking on an ambitious adventure. We were attempting the apparently impossible, and I was on my way to being able to smugly prove Mr Higo and Mr Hioki wrong. The sun was shining brightly, and Justin's forecasts of blue skies and no headwinds seemed to be on the mark.

Justin cycled merrily ahead. He sang to himself loudly and grinned from ear to ear. It was difficult not to share in his happy mood. He had memorised the local street layout, and was cheerfully heading in search of a quiet, well-marked cycle lane that ran northwards alongside the Yodogawa River, bypassing the mind-boggling mazes of central Osaka and the snarled inner-city traffic.

We made good time and found the cycle lane with ease. Just as Justin had promised, it was beautifully smooth tar seal, completely devoid of traffic or bewildering intersections. We zipped along with the wind in our hair, and my enthusiasm rose.

After an hour and a half, the delightful cycle lane came to an end. We had left Osaka City far behind and were now in the northern suburbs. Our surroundings had changed dramatically. We began to encounter an increasing number of chemical plants, and smoky factories with dirty chimneys. Residential areas were limited to run-down, grimy concrete-block apartment buildings.

Justin reached into his pocket and pulled out his map. 'This is the tricky bit,' he said slowly. 'We need to find Expressway 127, which will take us up towards Kyoto. We follow it most of the way and then veer off towards Mount Ise. I think we're here,' he stabbed his finger at the map, 'and Expressway 127 is over here.' He traced a line across a maze of suburban streets to a bold straight line that had been highlighted with yellow marker pen.

'How far do you reckon it is to Expressway 127?' I asked. I was impressed with the distance we had covered thus far. Judging by our current location on the map, we had covered a great deal of ground.

'Probably only another hour I reckon,' Justin replied pensively. 'We should grab a bite to eat along the way. Once we hit Expressway 127, there may be nowhere to stop until we cross the mountain.'

I nodded. 'There's a family restaurant over there,' I suggested, pointing down the road. 'Do you want to grab an early lunch now?'

Justin agreed readily. 'Hey, they've got a buffet special. And it's only 800 yen. Good spotting, mate. See, I told you we'd have a great weekend.'

We cheerfully locked our cycles outside the restaurant and settled in for a three-course meal of soup, salad and sushi.

We emerged from our gluttonous feast an hour later, keen to make up for lost time. 'We need to head north-east,' Justin announced, looking up from his map. 'If we head down that road over there and keep cycling in that general direction we'll be fine.'

He chuckled happily. 'We're doing great. I can't believe how far we've come already. We'll be there and back before we know it.'

This optimism soon proved sadly unfounded. It started to feel as if we were getting further away from the mountains, rather than closer. After some anxious studying of the map it became apparent that Justin had misread our position, and we had been cycling in the wrong direction. We now needed to make an hour-long detour to catch up with Expressway 127.

Tempers flared and we cycled in silence. The sun was still shining and the skies were still blue but we no longer cared. Justin stopped singing and humming, and his broad grin was replaced with a confused frown.

'Hey! Mate, I think we've found it,' he suddenly shouted. 'This must be Expressway 127 up ahead.' He pointed wildly.

I caught up with him. 'Yep, there's a signpost,' he said with a huge sigh of relief. '1...2...7. We've made it. We're back on track. Gimme five.' I clapped Justin's hand, and took a photo of him standing in front of the signpost.

Our joy and relief at having finally stumbled across Expressway 127 was short-lived. We now realised we were two hours behind schedule. There was not a moment to lose. We hopped back on our 'old lady' bicycles and pedalled furiously.

As we progressed north across the Kansai Plain the scenery changed once again. Rice paddies dotted the countryside, the long stalks basking in the last few weeks of sunshine before the autumn harvest. The Shiga mountains studded the horizon, and we could make out Mount Ise to the north.

We were unable to enjoy these picturesque surroundings for long. Expressway 127 had, up until now, been accompanied by a peaceful pedestrian footpath, which had allowed us to sit back in our seats and gaze around, while sailing alongside the busy road. Now this luxurious trail had disappeared and we were forced out into the middle of the road, where we needed all our wits to battle through noisy, fume-ridden traffic.

We braked and looked at each other hesitantly. 'It might get a bit scary from here on,' Justin said nervously. 'Look, we'll just take our time, and pull over for a rest if the traffic starts getting too fast or overwhelming.' I nodded uneasily.

We pushed off and almost immediately had a brush with disaster.

Expressway 127 now led us through a passage of small rolling hills. As well as being deceptively steep in parts, these hills were spring-loaded with lethal blind corners. As we sailed slowly downhill enjoying the respite from pedalling, we leant to our left and cruised around a long sloping bend.

HONNNNKKKKK!!! A concrete mixer roared around the corner, missing us by a whisker and nearly throwing us under its wheels with its slipstream.

Justin braked, and I narrowly avoided crashing into him. We were both white-faced. 'Do you think we should walk down the rest of this hill?' I suggested, pointing to the secluded safety of a muddy ditch that ran alongside the road. Justin agreed without uttering a single word.

We finally managed to reach the turn-off to Mount Ise just as the sun was setting. However, since we had no lights, no helmets, no reflective clothing, and had been narrowly missed by several more oversized trucks and construction vehicles, neither of us were particularly keen on crossing Mount Ise in the dark.

We eventually decided it would be safer to cycle around the base of the mountain to Kyoto and spend the night there. We had failed in our attempt to cross both the Kansai Plain and Mount Ise in a single day, but we were not overly disappointed. The distance could easily be recovered if we started cycling again early the following morning, and perhaps scrapped our sightseeing plans for Shiga Castle.

Buoyed with the relief of not needing to cross the mountain in the dark, we made good speed and were again in high spirits as we raced down Expressway 24 into Kyoto City. I spied a group of well-dressed young women strolling ahead. 'Watch this, mate,' I nodded to Justin. Speeding up, I whizzed past the women, intending to perform some sort of unrehearsed acrobatic feat.

I squinted my eyes to get a good look at their faces and make sure they weren't high-school students. Bang! The front wheel of my bicycle slammed into the side of the gutter. I bounced out of my seat, soared over the handlebars, and slid along the pavement for several metres on my stomach.

The young women were unimpressed and passed me by, and I was left to pick stones out of my bloody palms and dust off my favourite pair of shorts, which now sported several large holes. Fortunately, though, the bicycle's ancient design had saved me from serious injury. My backpack, which had been stowed in the front basket, had fallen out and landed between me and the concrete pavement, acting as an impromptu airbag.

I patted myself down, checking for broken bones and missing limbs. Nothing. I checked again. Apart from a bit of lost skin and a large dent in my pride, I was unscathed.

Justin was at my side in seconds. 'Are you okay? Are you okay? Are you okay?' He was seemingly more traumatised than I was. 'Where'd you hurt yourself? Are you bleeding?' I assured him I was fine, showed him my grazed palms and holey shorts and explained how my backpack had saved me. To be on the safe side, he raced across the road to a convenience store, and returned minutes later with a packet of Hello Kitty Band-Aids.

'You're bloody lucky,' he said sternly. 'That was your crappiest attempt at a chat-up ever!'

It was dark by the time we finally arrived in downtown Kyoto. We sorely needed somewhere to rest our exhausted, sweaty bodies, but the sudden change in our itinerary meant that we had arrived in an unplanned destination with no hotel reservations. All hotels were fully booked: it was both a national holiday and the start of a three-day weekend.

We slumped down in a hotel car park to discuss our options. I was grumpy and my palms were stinging. I had realised that my favourite pair of shorts were now ruined, and the fact that we had failed to cross Mount Ise was suddenly very depressing.

Justin seemed equally gloomy. 'We could always go home for the night,' he suggested in a tired voice.

'What!' I thundered. 'Go home!'

'We could leave our bicycles locked in Kyoto Station, catch the train back to my place and sleep there for the night. It's only two hours by train. We could be back here first thing in the morning on an early express. Think about it, we'd get a good night's sleep for free.'

'No way,' I said angrily. 'I'd rather sleep on a train-station bench. There's no way I'm catching a train back to Osaka. It would make today's efforts completely meaningless.'

Justin sighed. 'Shall we have one last look around the block then? We may find some place we hadn't noticed before.' I nodded weakly, and we plodded off down the road.

A dim neon bulb flickered faintly above the entrance to an old wooden guest-house. No doubt 'No vacancy' would be posted above the door. We blinked. Nothing. It would appear there was a free room for the night. The Bible tells of how Mary and Joseph, struggling to find accommodation, stumbled across a tiny inn in Bethlehem. What it doesn't mention is the sheer relief they must have felt when they were finally able to relax and put their feet up.

Justin and I were ecstatic: we had found our own biblical inn. We quickly checked into the last remaining room, took a long leisurely soak in the inn's piping-hot bath, and strolled down the road for a late dinner. Later, back in our room, I fell asleep the moment my head hit the rice-filled pillow.

We awoke with agonisingly stiff legs. I struggled to make my way downstairs to breakfast, and my bottom felt bruised and chafed when I mounted my bicycle.

Justin had managed to acquire a detailed Kyoto street map from our kindly innkeeper, and was poring over it. 'We're in luck,' he announced. 'Our detour to Kyoto may have been the best thing that could have happened.' I looked at him quizzically.

'It's actually going to be easier and flatter to cross the mountains from Kyoto than if we'd gone over Mount Ise last night.'

He pointed eagerly at the map. 'Look, we're here at the moment. We can just go across this bit here, and bang, we've reached Lake Biwa. I've already spoken to the innkeeper; he reckons it won't be very steep at all. He reckons it'll only take a couple of hours.'

Justin's smile was broader than ever. 'In fact, he's the only Japanese person I've met so far who's said that it's possible to cross the mountain range on a bike. He reckons it won't be that hard.'

I eyed the innkeeper suspiciously. He was possibly insane and had been filling my naïve friend's head with nonsense. We paid our bill, thanked him for his words of encouragement and set off.

The morning's cycling went smoothly. The road out of Kyoto was lined with footpaths, and these continued to shelter us from the traffic as we started our ascent of the mountains. Our innkeeper's advice was proving to be valid, and after an only mildly difficult hour and a half of cycling, the road started to plateau off and Lake Biwa came into view.

As we paused to take in the grandeur of the next leg of our journey, it was dawning on Justin just how much further we had to go. 'Phew! That's one massive lake,' he said pensively.

We coasted down the other side of the mountain and arrived at the lakefront shortly before lunch-time. Justin sat quietly as we munched on our filet-o-fish combos. 'That's one massive lake' he repeated to himself. I could hear doubt creeping into his voice. 'Do you reckon we can bike around it in a single day?'

I looked out at the lake. It was already noon. We were going to struggle to get even halfway around it before the sun set. 'I think we've arrived a bit late in the day,' I replied. 'We're going to have a massive ride back to Osaka tomorrow if we only get halfway around the lake today. We'd still have to cycle the length of the lake just to get back here, and then go over the mountain, through Kyoto and back home.'

Justin sighed. 'Shall we call it quits?' He looked at me dejectedly.

'How about we go for a cycle ride out into the countryside near here,' I suggested. 'There are some interesting-looking temples we could visit. Plus there's a hot spring where we could relax and unwind later. We could even go to the movies.'

Justin was smiling again. 'That sounds like good fun,' he said happily. 'I read about that famous temple. We should go check it out. Plus, it'll be a fairly decent bike ride there and back.'

He paused. 'You know, I still reckon we'll be able to prove our co-workers wrong. They all thought it would be impossible for us to get this far. Well, they're wrong. And we *could* have cycled round the lake in a single day—we just didn't start early enough. We only needed a few more hours, not weeks like those namby-pamby workaholics said.

'Plus, since we're adventurous New Zealanders we can cope with a change in our itinerary and not get hung up about sticking to schedules. Well done, mate, we should be proud of ourselves.'

I agreed enthusiastically. Justin was right: we'd done incredibly well for a pair of podgy white guys, whose combined physical preparation had been cycling home drunk from pubs, dancing at nightclubs, and climbing a small hill to look at rabid monkeys.

Justin and I spent an enjoyable Saturday afternoon cycling around Otsu City, visiting temples, playing video games and relaxing on the lake front.

Sunday dawned. It was time for the return journey, the longest and most dreaded part of the trip. Justin had chosen the most direct route, Expressway 171, from which, he assured me, we would be unable to stray and get lost.

We set out in high spirits early in the morning, but our tired, creaky bodies barely managed to propel us back over the Kyoto mountain pass. Expressway 171, when we reached it, cut straight through the heart of Kyoto City. It was a smoggy highway complete with freshly laid asphalt, construction work and stinking, teeming traffic.

We cycled in gloomy silence alongside a tall grey concrete wall that blocked residents from Expressway 171's constant noise, but prevented motorists (and frazzled cyclists) from enjoying even the slightest view of the surrounding countryside. After the first couple of hours, I was in a very bad mood. Motorists veered alarmingly close to our footpath, and several times I was nearly clipped by side mirrors. My skinned palms rubbed painfully against my handlebars: the Hello Kitty stickers had grown slick with sweat and fallen off long ago. My bruised knees throbbed and my legs cried out for rest.

I spent the final hours of the great Lake Biwa bicycle expedition yelling at cars, telling ignorant motorists where to go and what to do once they got there. When I arrived home at eleven o'clock that night, I fell into the comforting embrace of my pink futon. Justin and I had cycled for twelve hours, most of them alongside Expressway 171's monotonous grey wall. I had reached the wise and well-informed decision that I would never again cycle on a Japanese highway.

# 18

# The enforcer

*I turned on the staffroom compute*r. It flickered slowly into life, and I sipped delicately at my cup of coffee. It was a Mr Higo-made brew, bitter and burning.

I connected to the internet and opened my email account.

An email from my mother.

An email from my friend Steve in the US.

An email from a family friend, Bev Dewar.

I opened Bev's email. 'How are things going in Japan?' she asked. 'Heard from Mr Doi recently?'

I started my reply. 'Nope, no news from Mr Doi. Absolutely no idea where he is these days.'

There was a tap on my shoulder. I put down my cup of coffee, turned around slowly and blinked. Mr Doi was standing right in front of me. He was sporting a green velvet smoking jacket and a goatee, and drinking casually from a white coffee cup that appeared to be empty.

He shook my hand firmly and gave me a knowing wink. I was unable to wink back, or say anything in reply.

Mr Doi smiled toothily and stroked his new goatee. 'So, have you got your licence yet?' he asked in a low whisper.

I racked my brains, trying to figure out what licence he was referring to.

'Yes, everything is at hand,' I replied confidently.

Mr Doi was delighted. He slapped me on the back, shook my hand once again, and informed me that everything was going well. He then leaned forward ever so slightly and in a stern voice said, 'December 15 will be a very important day. I have made good progress. I think the relationship with South Korea is a very good one.' A quick tap on the nose, a wink, and the message was conveyed.

In a breach of security, I started laughing, but luckily recovered my composure before anything could be leaked to the enemy. Mr Doi wished me well and strode off to continue his mission.

Ms Yurika Yurano had barely been at school for the past month. Things had finally come to a bit of a head in early November, when the teachers had decided to crack down on her bright yellow hair and miniscule mini-skirts. In protest, she had loudly declared that she would not come to school ever again.

I figured this would be the last I ever saw of her. Four nights later, however, at the supermarket I spotted ahead of me in the aisle a tall blond Japanese female, Ms Yurano—and her mother. Mrs Yurano had hair the colour of the mandarins in my shopping basket, and was wearing camouflage trousers and a hip-hop hooded sweatshirt.

I caught up and said hello to Yurika. She smiled meekly and looked at the floor. Obviously a little shy in front of her mother, I thought to myself. Mum, meanwhile, flashed me a big smile, a quick wink and, unless I imagined it, a lingering look.

Three days later I was sitting at my desk reading *The Daily Yomiuri* when I heard someone shouting. I swivelled around in my chair and came face to face with an enraged Mrs Yurano. She had clearly turned up to give the teachers a hard time for picking on her daughter, and I was the nearest to hand. Luckily, though, she immediately recognised me as the warm-hearted foreigner from the supermarket, and diverted her rage to everyone else.

'Where are my daughter's belongings? Why is my daughter being picked on? Where is that dickhead Mr Hisada? Why does he refuse to start a class until my daughter has been packed off to sick bay? Why is my daughter being denied her right to an education?'

One of the male teachers timidly stood up and asked Mrs Yurano to calm down. She screamed in fury and started banging the wall with her fists.

As I picked up my newspaper and studiously informed myself on the state of the Greek economy, the teacher escorted Mrs Yurano into the hallway. This just served to increase the volume.

Only the school's scariest staff member would be able to deal with Mrs Yurano. Sure enough, Mr Kobayashi appeared at the staffroom entrance in a flash. He was in attack mode, and looking extremely menacing.

Mr Kobayashi's job within the school was officially listed as 'counsellor'. In reality, though, he was the discipline enforcer, responsible for taking naughty students into the 'conversation room' and bouncing them off the walls until they learnt the error of their ways. He was the one Japanese man of whom I was mortally afraid. I had witnessed his bouts of corporal punishment on several occasions, and was astounded that such acts were permitted. It seemed the school and the community turned a blind eye, and everyone agreed that Mr Kobayashi's mere presence was often enough to keep the students in line.

Mrs Yurano, however, was no pushover, and seemed unconcerned by Mr Kobayashi's arrival. Although he attempted to firmly guide her in the direction of the 'conversation room', she swatted his arm away like a harmless bug. Mr Kobayashi stepped back in surprise. I wondered if this had ever happened before. Eventually, Mrs Yurano allowed herself to be escorted to Mr Kobayashi's office, but I doubted that she would be the one bouncing off the walls.

My sudden spurt of busyness had come to an end as abruptly as it had begun. I no longer needed to stay at school later than 4.15, or give up part of my weekends to mark homework assignments. Meanwhile, the Kanan Town Board of Education continued to pay my wages.

I started to feel guilty about my lack of productivity and paid a visit to my old friends at the Board of Education to catch up with their news, and remind them that I was still a necessary part of the town's education system.

Mr Horrii, my supervisor, seemed less than thrilled to see me: a visit from Mr Hamish no doubt meant I needed money or wanted time off. He scattered papers over his desk to give the illusion of being preoccupied.

That was fine by me: I had really hoped to catch up with Magnum, Mr Smiles and kindly old Mr Fujimoto. Magnum was out, apparently fixing drainpipes at an elementary school. Mr Smiles, though, was both present and overjoyed to see me. He listened avidly as I recounted the tale of my bicycle ride to Lake Biwa, and called for the office ladies to come and listen.

Mr Smiles added to my narration by performing an exaggerated mime of my spectacular crash in Kyoto. 'You are high tension!' he exclaimed loudly, clapping his hands. 'Very, very high tension. I am high tension too.'

Mr Fujimoto appeared in the doorway, panting and out of breath. He had recently been transferred to the town's tax department, but on hearing that I was visiting the Board of Education office, he had rushed upstairs to tell me his latest news. He was carrying one of his trusty New Zealand travel pamphlets and a large road map of the South Island.

'Mr Hamish,' he began, 'how do you say this place-name?'

'Lake Tekapo,' I pronounced slowly.

'Te-ka-po. Hmmm…I will go there next month.'

'What?' I asked in surprise. As far as I could tell, Mr Fujimoto hadn't taken a holiday in years.

'Yes.' Mr Fujimoto was smiling happily. 'Yes, I will go to New Zealand. I enjoyed talking to you about the travel pamphlets so much that I decided that I should go and see the places for myself. I was eventually able to convince my wife to come too, and was finally granted some time off.'

I was overjoyed for my friend, and quite moved that he had been so inspired by our pamphlet-reading sessions during my first summer in Japan. It turned out he had been secretly planning his trip for two years, studying every travel pamphlet about New Zealand that he could get his hands on. At long last he had memorised the locations and pronunciations of all the lakes and mountains he wished to visit, and was set to go.

'This is my first time to go overseas,' he explained nervously. 'I have a brand new passport. I'm looking forward to visiting your country.'

I shook Mr Fujimoto's hand and wished him safe travels.

Mr Fujimoto and his wife visited New Zealand in December that year. They spent a week travelling through the South Island, and even managed a chartered flight to Mount Cook. They returned to Japan in love with the New Zealand countryside, and raving about all the delicious food they had eaten. Mr Fujimoto replaced the travel-brochure pictures of Milford Sound, which had decorated his desktop at the office for the past two years, with real photos he had taken himself.

Mrs Oki called. She was talking quietly and I could hear little of what she was saying. I finally intercepted the words 'Mr Oki has been ill' and suddenly realised that things might be a little grim in the Oki household.

I was confused by the conflicting accounts that Mr Oki was now receiving his meals through an intravenous drip, while at the same time being back at work at his shipyard office. A jumble of words spilled through the phone line, and I struggled to make sense of them.

It eventually became apparent that Mr Oki's health had stabilised but he was no longer allowed to drink alcohol. Mrs Oki sounded sad when she informed me of this point. 'We would like you to come around for dinner sometime soon,' she announced finally.

'I'd love to,' I replied. 'Please give my regards to Mr Oki.' Mrs Oki bade me a quiet goodbye and hung up the phone.

She called again the following week. Her voice was as chirpy as ever. 'Heymishi, how is your mother these days?' she asked. 'She wears lovely clothes. She is very beautiful, isn't she?'

I reluctantly agreed. 'I think she misses her lovely sons,' I suggested. 'I live in Japan and my brother lives in France.'

'Oh, your mother has gone to France?'

'No, not my mother, my *brother*.'

'Who?'

'My brother, Al. You've met him, remember?'

There was a slight pause.

'So your brother is in France?'

'Yes.'

'Hmmm.'

The phone clicked and went dead.

Mrs Oki called again the next night. It seemed she had suddenly remembered the abrupt ending of our previous call, and was now keen to finish the conversation. 'Now then,' she asked, 'who's coming to Japan, your mother or your brother?'

I shook my head in frustration.

'How's Mr Oki?' I asked.

'Oh, he's very well. When are you coming round for dinner then?'

I frowned. Had I been invited?

'How about next Wednesday?' I suggested.

'Okay, be at our house at 4.30.'

'But I don't finish work until 4.15,' I protested. I had explained this fact to Mrs Oki numerous times. 'The earliest I can get to your house is five o'clock.'

Mrs Oki paused, digesting this new information. 'Okay then, five o'clock.'

She hung up the phone.

When Wednesday afternoon arrived, I dashed frantically from school to the Tondabayashi train station. I was determined to catch an earlier train than usual, in order to arrive at the Okis' house before five. I didn't want Mrs Oki sending out her sickly husband on another search mission.

Mrs Oki answered the door with surprise. 'Heymishi! You're early,' she scolded. I checked my watch: 4.55.

'Oh well, come in, come in.' I stepped into the Oki home.

'This is the entrance hall,' Mrs Oki informed me. 'Yes, there we are. Now I'll turn on the light so I can see. Ah yes, now I can see.

'Now then, where are the slippers? Heymishi! Put on some slippers. That's right, take your shoes off first. Okay, I'm putting on my slippers. Heymishi, have you put on your slippers? Ah yes, you have. Now then, where's the cat?' She wandered away.

I made my way to the dining room. Mr Oki was waiting patiently.

I froze and did my best not to look surprised. Mr Oki had shrunk. He was very thin, and had lost a lot of weight around his face and shoulders.

'Hello,' he said in his deep voice. His smile was as warm as ever.

I smiled, and sat down next to him. Mr Oki had dressed up for the occasion. He was wearing his old woollen jersey from New Zealand, which had a fluffy white sheep knitted into the front.

'We're going out for dinner,' he announced.

'Do you like sushi?' Mrs Oki asked, entering the room. 'We're going to go to a sushi restaurant.'

I nodded quietly. Mrs Oki had obviously forgotten the contents of our previous meal together.

The Okis had booked a table at a local restaurant where we had often dined in the past. The plump lady behind the counter greeted us happily. 'It's so good to see you again sir,' she said smiling at frail-looking Mr Oki. 'I've reserved your usual table.'

Mr Oki chuckled and ordered us a plate of sushi and a bowl of fried scallops as an *entrée*. Mrs Oki grumbled and clucked away about how Mr Oki was not allowed to eat deep-fried food.

'Hamish can eat it then.' Mr Oki winked and clapped me on the shoulder.

Mr Oki was in a mischievous mood. He persisted in ordering artery-clogging food for the rest of the evening, piling it on my plate while he quietly nibbled on slices of raw fish and a green salad.

Mrs Oki watched us both anxiously. 'Mr Oki, you mustn't eat any of that! That's right, give it to Heymishi. Heymishi, can you eat that? Can you eat sushi?'

Mr Oki inquired how I was enjoying school. I informed him of my recent cycle ride to Lake Biwa and back. He snapped his fingers at once and signalled for the waitress. 'A jug of sake!' he thundered. 'We must drink a toast straight away.'

'You can't have sake,' Mrs Oki chirped. 'The doctor said so.'

'I don't care,' Mr Oki replied sternly. 'We must celebrate Hamish's cycle ride. It would be very rude not to.'

The waitress paused. 'Are you sure it's a good idea?' she asked cautiously. Mr Oki shot her an angry glare. 'Yes! A pot of sake.'

I did not want Mr Oki to drink alcohol either, but it seemed that trying to convince him otherwise would only make him irate. A small jug of warm sake was eventually produced, and Mrs Oki carefully poured a tiny drop into Mr Oki's cup. She then poured an especially large quantity into both my cup and her own, and placed the jug firmly out of reach of Mr Oki.

Mr Oki sat back and smiled. 'It would be impolite for me not to drink a toast to you, Hamish,' he said happily. 'I wish you very good health. Well done on your cycle ride to Lake Biwa.'

I blushed. 'Thank you, Mr Oki. I wish you very good health as well.'

'Heymishi,' chipped in Mrs Oki, 'can you drink sake?'

Mr Oki and I laughed. Mrs Oki continued to stare at me inquisitively until I nodded. Mr Oki drank his drop of sake slowly, savouring what was to be his last taste of alcohol for some time. He grinned broadly. 'That's very good,' he said. 'It makes me feel a lot better.'

Mr Oki drove me home at the end of the evening. 'We'll climb Mount Kanan again one day,' he said with a smile as I stepped out of the car.

'All right,' I replied and closed the door.

# 19

# The Japanese mothers

*Mr Oki's health fluctuated terribly* as the cold winter months rolled in. I would often receive frantic phone calls from Mrs Oki, insisting that I come for dinner the following week as Mr Oki had temporarily recovered, or had completed his latest bag of pills and medication. Without fail, though, these invitations would be cancelled the following day. Mr Oki was apparently 'too cold' or 'not so good' and we would postpone my visit to a more suitable date.

I began to worry that I would not be seeing Mr Oki again for some time, if at all. I was still unable to understand his wife's rambling explanations and had no idea what was wrong with him. However, given the reluctance of Japanese doctors to keep patients informed of their illnesses, it was likely that the Okis were just as ignorant as I was.

I did my best to put Mr Oki's health problems to the back of my mind, and buried myself in my Japanese textbooks. I was scheduled to sit the Japanese language proficiency exam in early December.

I had spent most of November preparing myself for this big day. I was determined to leave Japan with some form of recognition that I could speak the language better than when I arrived. I had made little effort to participate in formal studies, having decided that conversation sessions with my Japanese mothers, evenings drinking with the young male teachers, and interpreting for my friends at bars were much more practical forms of learning.

I was now devoting every waking moment to memorising Japanese characters and grammar patterns. My colleagues were delighted with my diligence, and took turns quizzing me on obscure vocabulary and collo-quial expressions. My students would often stop by my desk to offer advice for memorising the stroke order of certain characters and the linguistic background of certain words.

I sat the exam on December 7. Although it was by no means easy, I felt satisfied that I was on my way to a passing grade. Results were not expected until mid February, so I would need to sit through the Osaka winter with my frozen fingers crossed.

One week later the Arctic wind was in full force, blowing frost into Kanan Town and sending flurries of snow down from the mountains. I looked out my apartment window and smiled. It was Tuesday morning, but I did not need to go to work. I turned back to my steaming bowl of instant noodles and started watching the first of the five videos I had hired for the week.

I stretched and yawned. I was in perfect health. My apartment was snug and warm, and I was equipped with enough junk food to see me through until spring. School had been cancelled. In fact, school had been cancelled since the previous Thursday as twenty percent of the students had influenza.

Having the flu in Japan has similar social repercussions to having the bubonic plague in fourteenth-century Europe. Nobody wants to catch the flu. People start wearing gauze medical masks in public as soon as an outbreak is announced in the media. Anyone coughing or sneezing is eyed suspiciously, and left on their own during lunch breaks and train rides.

At school, the teachers were petrified. There were news reports of a particularly nasty flu strain that was apparently circulating in Osaka City. Emergency meetings had been called to formulate a contingency plan in case the school became infected. It had been decided that as soon as the absentee rate reached twenty percent in a homeroom class, the remaining students would be sent home so the germs could be passed no further.

I contemplated this bizarre system. Those who were fit and well would be rewarded with a day at home playing video games. And while some classes would get to go home early, other classes with an absentee rate of perhaps only 10 or 15 percent would have to stay at school and do maths. It didn't take the naughty boys long to figure out that if they acted a wee bit ill and went to the sick bay for half an hour, the whole class could go home and watch TV.

Finally, on Monday afternoon, the teachers had resorted to closing the school completely, hence my long sleep-in. I now had several gloriously lazy days to spend reading books, drinking coffee and eating chocolate. Admittedly, though, this was not too dissimilar from my normal working day at school.

Classes eventually resumed on Friday morning, and the acceptable absentee rate was lifted to forty percent. I noticed that several of the naughty boys were still off 'sick' and making the most of their teachers' paranoia. I arrived at my conversation session with my Japanese mothers the following Monday, chortling about their cunning, and bragging about my relaxing hibernation.

However, everyone seemed ominously subdued. Mrs Kiguchi, our polite host, sat quietly, her face downcast and sad. She barely made any contribution to the conversation, and while she was away making a pot of tea I asked Mrs Tsubota if something were wrong.

'Mrs Kiguchi is a little sad,' Mrs Tsubota whispered confidentially. 'This time of year is the anniversary of her husband's death. She always feels a little lonely.'

My funny stories and cheeky tales suddenly evaporated. I was deeply saddened to hear that Mrs Kiguchi was so upset. It was a shock to see her in such low spirits, as she had always been so enthusiastic and energetic.

I sat quietly through the rest of the conversation session. Mrs Tsubota, Mrs Tanaka, Mrs Matsui and Mrs Terauchi chatted among themselves, and I made only token interjections.

Mrs Kiguchi sat silently. I was becoming sad just watching her. I was desperate to try and cheer her up.

'It's Christmas soon, Mr Hamish,' Mrs Matsui exclaimed. 'Will you do anything special this year?'

A light bulb went on inside my head. 'Yes!' I said excitedly. Everyone looked at me in surprise. I blushed: I hadn't meant to speak so loudly.

'Yes,' I repeated, more quietly. 'I think we should have a Christmas party—next Monday. I'll bring some food, and we can sing Christmas carols. You are always cooking food for me. Well, now it's my turn to cook some food for you. It'll be good fun, and we can all get into the Christmas spirit.'

Mrs Matsui clapped, Mrs Tanaka chuckled, Mrs Tsubota gasped and Mrs Terauchi began to prattle on about how foreign people ate reindeer for Christmas lunch.

'Oooh, I'll bring a plate of okonomiayaki pancakes,' Mrs Tsubota exclaimed. 'Sensei, you should not do all the cooking on your own.'

'And I'll bring some fried rice,' offered Mrs Tanaka.

'I've been making mulled wine,' said Mrs Matsui secretively. The women gasped in eager anticipation.

Mrs Kiguchi smiled and looked at me shyly. 'Sensei, so you will cook for us?'

'Yes,' I replied boldly, suddenly realising what I had gotten myself into. I had no idea what dish would be appropriate for such an occasion. Even if I knew, I would probably have neither the recipe nor the cooking skills to make it.

Mrs Kiguchi's small smile widened. 'Oh sensei, that is so lovely of you. I'm so happy.'

Back home, I flicked desperately through my one recipe book. Nothing suitable leapt out at me. The dishes were either too small, too boring or too difficult for me to cook.

But I had promised Mrs Kiguchi. I did not want to disappoint her. I flung open my pantry door hopefully. A single can of New Zealand baked beans stared back at me.

During lunch break the next day I decided I would prepare the one dish with which I had had relative success at pot-luck parties—Thai Green Curry. I had hoped to be a little more adventurous, but this tried and true favourite would have to do.

In the event, I surpassed my expectations. The curry, although starting off grey, ended up the right shade of green and tasted fantastic. I managed to find a bowl big enough to transport it in, and the success of the cooking experience began to give me ideas about opening a restaurant that specialised in green curry and baked beans.

On the day of the party, everyone was in high spirits. Mrs Tsubota was fussing around, making sure that her pancakes were being kept warm. Mrs Tanaka was setting the table. She had brought a big bowl of fried rice and a large platter of pickles. Mrs Terauchi was already sitting expectantly at the head of the table, rattling on about the state of her garden and how cold the weather had been recently.

Mrs Kiguchi stepped into the room from the kitchen. The festivities had seemingly brought her back to her good-humoured self and it was obvious that she was enjoying the hustle and bustle in her living room. Her eyes twinkled. 'Sensei, what have you cooked for us?'

I pulled out my bowl of green curry and opened the lid. The women craned forward to get a whiff of the exotic aroma. 'Oohh, sensei,'they chorused, and daintily concealed their mouths while they chuckled among themselves.

'You are such a good cook, sensei!' Mrs Kiguchi exclaimed, clearing a place in the middle of the dining table for my bowl.

Everyone took their places and we tucked into our Christmas banquet. Despite my warnings that my green curry was spicy, the mothers gave themselves large servings. I tried not to smile as they broke out into a sweat and had to take off their sweaters. We made our way through the mountains of food and a large quantity of Mrs Matsui's mulled wine. By the end of the meal, all the women had pink cheeks and flushed complexions.

'Oh this is fun!' enthused Mrs Tsubota. 'Merry Christmas, sensei.'

'Merry Christmas everyone,' I replied in Japanese.

Mrs Terauchi started singing a religious hymn to the tune of 'Silent night'. I snuck a glance at Mrs Kiguchi. She was laughing and covering her mouth while she watched her old friend Mrs Terauchi sing. I smiled. It seemed that her loneliness had been forgotten.

Mrs Terauchi reached the end of her impromptu Christmas carol and thanked us for listening. Mrs Kiguchi nodded at her, and at the same time I noticed Mrs Matsui and Mrs Tanaka exchange secretive glances.

'Ah yes, of course,' Mrs Terauchi trumpeted suddenly. 'Sensei, how have you been recently?' She leaned forward and looked at me intently. I noticed Mrs Matsui and Mrs Tanaka scurrying from the room.

'I'm fine,' I said hesitantly, wondering what was going on.

'And what have you been doing at school lately, sensei?' Mrs Terauchi asked with exaggerated interest. She seemed determined to hold my gaze and prevent me noticing the absence of her friends.

Mrs Matsui and Mrs Tanaka returned. They sat down, discreetly tucking a pair of mysterious parcels under the table as they did so.

With her friends safely back, Mrs Terauchi now lost all interest in our conversation about school life. 'Is it time yet?' she asked Mrs Kiguchi.

Mrs Kiguchi nodded. 'Sensei,' she began slowly, 'since it is a Christmas party we would like to give you some presents.'

I smiled. I had expected there might be a small exchange of gifts, and had come prepared. 'Aha!' I announced triumphantly. 'I have some gifts for you as well.' I had written each of my Japanese mothers an individual letter and greetings card in Japanese.

They delicately opened the envelopes and read the messages aloud. Mrs Terauchi corrected a couple of missed strokes on some of my kanji characters. Mrs Kiguchi read her card to herself in a whisper. She looked up with misty eyes. 'Thank you for my Christmas card,' she said softly.

Mrs Terauchi was growing impatient. 'It is time for sensei's presents,' she said crossly. 'Quickly, we must give them to him.' Mrs Kiguchi nodded to Mrs Tanaka, who produced a bulging plastic bag from beneath the dining table.

Three beautifully wrapped parcels were emptied out before me, and I began opening the nearest one.

A bag of apples.

Mrs Tsubota blushed. 'These are from the tree in my garden. I hope you enjoy them.' I assured her that I would.

I opened the second parcel. A jar of home-made marmalade.

Mrs Matsui coughed nervously. 'Ah yes, I made that at the same time I made the mulled wine. I was enjoying cooking so much that I made many different things. Do you like marmalade?'

'Sure,' I said, 'this will go well on my toast.' Mrs Matsui smiled.

The third parcel was heavy and oddly shaped. I fumbled with the wrapping paper and clumsily tore it open. It was a tile from a nearby temple. This was perhaps one of the more bizarre gifts that I'd ever received.

Mrs Terauchi's eyes twinkled. 'I knew you'd like it. It will bring you good luck.'

Everyone oohed and aahed as we examined the temple roof tile. My other Japanese mothers were impressed with Mrs Terauchi's gift, and assured me that the temple it had formerly decorated was very prestigious, and that this tile was, therefore, very special.

I thanked Mrs Terauchi and she bowed happily. 'Thank you, sensei, thank you. I am so happy that you like my present.'

I looked at my Christmas gifts and thanked everyone once again. The women smiled and looked at Mrs Kiguchi. She nodded to Mrs Matsui, who produced another parcel from beneath the table.

I looked at the thin flat package that now sat before me. I reached forward and untied the purple cloth wrapping. I paused. The contents of the package made little sense to me.

The women sensed my confusion. Mrs Kiguchi leaned forward and began to explain. My Japanese mothers had just presented me with my own handmade kimono.

I listened, stunned. Each of them had played a part in its design, and they had pooled their resources for its creation.

Mrs Tanaka had chosen the pattern. Mrs Matsui had gone out and bought the silk. Mrs Tsubota and Mrs Terauchi had procured the necessary sewing tools, and Mrs Kiguchi had painstakingly sewn the kimono.

I felt close to tears. 'Thank you,' I finally managed to stammer. 'Would you like me to try it on?'

They burst into laughter. 'No, no, sensei, this is not for you to wear,' Mrs Terauchi said. 'Wait for Mrs Kiguchi to finish her story.'

Mrs Kiguchi clasped my hand. 'You are such a nice man, sensei,' she said. 'One day you will be a wonderful husband for a young lady. This kimono is intended as a gift for your future wife when you become engaged.'

# 20

# Lost Valley of the Dinosaurs

*It was the end of January.* My life in Japan had now passed the two-and-a-half-year mark. Only six more months remained in my employment contract.

I looked at my calendar. Six months seemed worryingly short. Misgivings about my future swirled through my mind. What would I do for the next chapter of my life?

I shivered. It was freezing cold. Concerns about my future were temporarily forgotten. I had just stepped back into Arctic Osaka after a three-week Christmas vacation in the humid climes of Malaysian Borneo. This had been my last Southeast Asian getaway, and the last time I would make use of the 'studying Japanese in the town library' cover story.

I had thoroughly enjoyed hiking up Mount Kinabalu, trekking in rain forests, catching glimpses of wild orangutans, and travelling overland across Brunei in a beaten up old bus. This T-shirt-and-shorts lifestyle had come to a crashing end the minute I touched down at Osaka International Airport. There was a good five centimetres of snow on the ground.

What's more, I had developed a huge backlog of washing, and while my washing machine worked overtime to catch up I had to wear the same chalk-covered polar-fleece jacket and olive track pants to school every day. A large damp pile of washed clothes slowly accumulated in the corner of my laundry. There was no way to dry them. By the end of January, my grubby jacket and olive pants were being 'recycled' for the second week in a row.

Fortunately, none of my fellow teachers seemed to notice. They were too busy panicking about the daily snowstorms. Not only would the entire town apparently catch the flu, but countless numbers of students were predicted to fall over and break their necks on the icy footpaths. Hence, the teachers spent extra hours in the early morning, and again late at night, ferrying students to and from school.

Meanwhile, I continued to cycle to school. I refused to take the bus from Tondabayashi Station, as this would require getting up ten minutes earlier each morning. And cycling meant I could be as late to work as I wanted, as I could use my mode of transport as an excuse.

Everyone claimed I was crazy, and several people pleaded with me not to go outside in the snow on my bicycle any more. I replied by telling them that in New Zealand people walked barefoot to school across snowy mountain ranges. This boosted my strong-guy image, and to boost it even further I grew a week's stubble and recycled my rugged, outdoorsy clothes for yet another week.

The young minnows class was now an enormously popular hour of my week. At the end of the year, I had rashly promised my small group of special friends that I would make them one more super-duper board game before they graduated the following March. I had later hoped that the minnows' usually short-term memories would let me escape from fulfilling the promise, but it seemed they had written it down in their diaries and I was duty-bound to come up with something special.

So, throughout the month of December, I had painstakingly put together a huge *papier-mâché* board game, which included a large conical volcano, small round hills and a big Mayan-style temple. I had left the board in my apartment to dry for a week and had then brought it into school to be painted by the young minnows themselves.

Teru-Chan was absent on 'painting day' but Hiro and Yurika were frothing at the bit. Hiro was put in charge of painting the Mayan temple.

He dobbed globs of grey paint all over the temple, the surrounding *papier-mâché* hillside, and his own jacket.

While I painted the rolling hillside and smooth playing-field grass, Yurika was charged with colouring the slopes of the conical volcano. Her poor eyesight led to a couple of brown stripes being added to the grunge on my polar-fleece jacket.

The bell rang, and we stepped back to admire our handiwork. I was happy: the game board was shaping up well. The minnows, though, were baffled: why had we just wasted an hour painting an oddly shaped fruit basket, in which the green hills were apples, and the volcano a pineapple?

I chuckled secretly and returned the game board to the safety of the staffroom to dry. Next day I went shopping at the Jinaimachi toy shop and bought a packet of plastic dinosaurs—four Tyrannosaurus rexes, a funny-looking Brontosaurus and a bright pink Pterodactyl.

I then constructed an ingenious set of small playing pieces. Each had a miniature photo of a young minnow player emblazoned on both front and back. I hoped this personal touch would endear the minnows to the game. Although I had copied both the idea and the rules from a popular board game called *Lost Valley of the Dinosaurs*, these playing pieces were entirely my own concoction.

Several days later, when the game board was completely dry, I added the finer details with felt-tip marker pens: playing squares, red and orange-streaked lava flows, temple bricks and steps, and dinosaur caves in the rolling hills. It was time to present my creation to the team.

Hiro and Yurika were completely bowled over by the dramatic trans-formation. Hiro danced around the room, and Yurika tugged on Teru-Chan's sleeve. They all sat down with bulging eyes, keen to learn the rules and start playing.

The first round of *Dinosaurs* was a success. I was eagerly invited to bring the game back to the waka-ayu room during lunch breaks, or whenever I had a free moment.

The idea of the game was simple. Players had to move their counter through the valley of the dinosaurs to the temple. Once there, they had to pick up the treasure and carry it back to the start, all the while dodging lava flows, Tyrannosaurus rexes and the bright pink Pterodactyl.

At first, this proved to be a nice exercise in teamwork and everyone worked together to bring the treasure home. However, things slowly started to go wrong and I noticed a new atmosphere developing among the team.

After two weeks, everyone was out for themselves. Yurika inadvertently revealed that she was planning to make a treaty with Hiro and then, after he had obtained the treasure, drop him in the lava flow. Hiro, meanwhile, surrounded Teru-Chan's counters with menacing dinosaurs and laughed happily when Teru-Chan got eaten. Teru-Chan called us all names and grumpily swore she wouldn't come back to school again.

A few more days of this and tempers were flaring dangerously. Yurika couldn't figure out why everyone knew what she was up to. Hiro and Teru-Chan were no longer speaking, and it was a race to kill the other person's playing piece. The original object of the game was forgotten, leaving me with an unobstructed route to the finish line.

It was Sunday, February 9, and the South Osaka Prefecture Half-Marathon Running Event was about to begin. My foggy breath was evaporating in the frosty air in front of me. I clapped my body to keep warm and jogged on the spot.

Mr Higo panted up. 'Are you ready?' he asked nervously. His nervous gaze suggested he did not have much faith in my running ability.

'Yes,' I answered uncertainly. My stomach felt like jelly.

He smiled. 'Good luck then.' He jogged off to check on the condition of the rest of our team members.

I tried to calm my jangling nerves and concentrate on the race at hand. What on earth was I doing this time? I thought back to the fateful lunch break in early December when Mr Higo had announced he was wanting to put together a four-person relay team to compete in the big race in February.

'I thought you were sick of running long distance?' I had asked suspiciously, remembering all too clearly Mr Higo's reluctance to compete in the previous year's school athletics day. 'You will be taking part yourself, won't you?'

'Yes, of course,' he had replied defensively. 'I think this will be a good event for staff members. It will be good for our health, and good team bonding.'

Not only had I allowed myself to be pressured into joining the team, before I knew what had happened I had been given the great responsibility of being the team's opening runner. This would apparently give our team international credibility, and it was earnestly pointed out to me that the New Zealander who walked barefoot over snowy mountains would surely be strong enough to endure the longest stretch of the race.

I had spent much of December training seriously for the big event, including spending every afternoon on a running machine at the local community centre. Unlike the lead-up to The Great Lake Biwa Circumnavigation, I had managed to get into fairly decent shape and was quietly confident that I would be able to complete my 4.6-kilometre leg within a respectable time.

The race day had turned out to be relatively warm. Although the frosty air was stinging my ears and fingers and my nose was running, there was no snow on the ground and hardly any wind.

At the starting line I checked out my rivals. Most contestants were decked out in snazzy gear—ultra-brief running shorts, space-age shoes and T-shirts emblazoned with the names of past marathons or running races. I was wearing my smelly olive track pants, now in their third week, my Thai beer T-shirt, and old shoes with holes.

About seventy teams had turned up. On my right was a young man with Down's Syndrome and a bald man who, I suspected, had leukaemia. Their presence gave me hope of coming, at worst, third to last.

Mr Terada, the PE teacher, was yelling advice from the sideline, ordering me not to sprint off at the start, as I had done in the school races. This made me nervous. I felt my shoulders tense.

All the runners bent forward into their starting positions—except me. Clamped tightly by the crowd, I couldn't bend down and was left standing rigidly upright.

I started to sweat. The starting gun sounded and the runners sprinted away like a pack of horses. Following the PE teacher's advice, I ran at a moderate pace and was soon passed by pretty much everyone, including the Down's Syndrome man, who raced by in a cloud of dust.

After the first 800 metres I had slipped to the back of the pack—with the bald guy, one of a group of five struggling runners. It was at this point that we struck the first hill. I had completely omitted hills from my training routine, figuring that having grown up in a hilly suburb in Christchurch would have more than adequately prepared me. Alas not. Out of the corner of my eye, I saw the bald guy shoot ahead.

I was breathing pretty hard by now, and sounded as though I'd dropped a lung somewhere along the course. As we passed the spectator section, I came to the mortifying conclusion that I was dead last.

To make matters worse, everyone in the crowd seemed to know my name. The mayor, Mr Kitahashi, was there. My principal, Mr Kazama, was there. My supervisor, Mr Horrii, was there, and it seemed that most of the people who read my monthly town magazine articles were there too.

I looked behind. I was alone. Everyone was chanting my name. Sudden terror of being lapped propelled me onwards and I somehow finished my leg of the race without walking.

At the end of the day I found to my astonishment that I had managed to run the 4.6 kilometres in 20 minutes and 46 seconds, only three seconds more than my target time. Our team had managed to come in sixth to last overall, a not inconsiderable achievement.

It was February 14, Valentine's Day. In my first year in Japan, I had received five boxes of chocolate from elderly well-wishers. One family had even gone to the expense of buying me a grey polar-fleece jacket and special milk chocolates from the northern island of Hokkaido. My landlady's pre-school daughters had given me a cute gift-wrapped piece of chocolate and two scribbly portraits of me picking flowers. Some of the boys at school had parted with bubblegum cards of their favourite girl singers.

The following year I had received an astounding eleven boxes of chocolate from an assortment of students, old ladies and others. In Japan, however, February 14 is merely the day on which women give gifts to men. One month later, in March, the men are compelled to return gifts of five times the value to the women. I was diligently saving for my spring vacation in Laos and Vietnam, and my strict budget left me with little to eat other than instant noodles and bread. The prospect of having to buy eleven boxes of expensive chocolate was too terrible to contemplate. I resorted to pint-sized chocolates, and shuffled off to Vietnam before anybody could complain.

However, this penny-pinching had not gone unnoticed. This year I had received only three boxes of chocolates and a few cards. Nevertheless, I happily gobbled down the chocolates.

My exam results had turned up: I had scraped a pass in the Japanese proficiency exam, and was now fully qualified to communicate in Japanese.

February drew to a close. Less than five months remained of my life in Japan.

# 21

# Love at last

*My dream of meeting a girlfriend* in Japan had all but faded away. With only five months left, I had decided it was time for me to stop looking and hoping, and simply get on and enjoy my remaining time with my friends. I even made a formal announcement to Justin, adamantly stating that my search was over. I was convinced I would never find true love in Japan.

With my search now officially at an end, I was free to meet up with my mates for a boys' night out at one of our favourite bars. It was there that I met Akko.

Akiko Taketoshi, or Akko, as she introduced herself, was a tall slim beautiful girl who had caught my eye the second she entered the bar. I had tried my best to keep my eyes off her, and to remain focussed on the conversation at hand. However, my self-restraint had sadly been lacking and I had caught myself glancing in her direction, hoping to snatch a glimpse of her from across the bar.

Wij and Matt were laughing about something and Andy was on his phone, desperately checking the final score of an English soccer match.

The beautiful girl on the dance floor vanished. I snapped myself back to reality and rejoined the conversation. Andy was excited. His team had won. It was time to buy a celebratory round. We downed tequila shots, shared stories, laughed and drank some more.

The music was loud and catchy. My feet started tapping on their own, and in a trance I drifted away from the table to the dance floor. I danced happily with my eyes closed. It was good to be out with my mates. The beer and tequila were putting me in a relaxed, carefree mood.

I opened my eyes. The beautiful girl was standing in front of me. A spotlight was shining down on her, illuminating her pretty face and long flowing hair.

She looked at me. I looked back. We both smiled.

Without thinking I stepped forward. We both spoke at the same time.

'Hi.' The world stood still. Everything felt smooth. Everything felt fluid. I knew that people were moving around us, but I couldn't see them. I knew the music was playing, but I couldn't hear it.

Akko. The beautiful girl was called Akko. She spoke no English, but she laughed at my Japanese jokes and wanted to talk to me. We stood in the middle of the dance floor. Talking. Smiling.

I offered to buy her a drink. We moved to the bar. People parted for us. She drank a cocktail and I drank beer. We talked and laughed. We talked about everything. We talked about nothing. We talked about my life in the countryside. We talked about her life in the city. We talked about life. We talked about Mexican food. We talked about movies. We laughed about Michael Jackson.

My friends were watching me. From across the bar, they smiled and waved, and gestured that I should keep talking. Just keep talking no matter what.

Akko's girlfriends came to check on her. Who was this tall foreigner she had been talking to for so long? She laughed and waved them away.

We kept talking and laughing. Hours passed. Akko had a soft laugh and a soft voice. She blushed and said that she was usually very shy, but felt comfortable with me as I was easy to talk to. She added that my Japanese was very good.

I waited. The usual request for me to act as a translator so Akko could chat up one of my friends never arrived. Akko wanted to talk to me.

We danced and drank. Hours passed and the bar closed. It was seven a.m. We went for breakfast, arranged to meet up later for dinner. We went to dinner, and promised we would meet the next day for dinner as well.

Our time together flowed effortlessly and quickly. We talked. We laughed. We started to fall in love.

Sunday dinner gave way to Monday dinner. We met again on Tuesday. And again on Wednesday, Thursday and Friday. There was never a need to nervously ask permission to see Akko again. Fate had finally dealt me a winning hand. Before we realised it, we had known each other for an entire week.

We went for dinner at a restaurant that Akko had chosen. The food was tasty and unpretentious. The surroundings were fun. We chatted as if we hadn't seen each other in months. So much had seemingly passed in the hours that we had been apart.

We met up with Akko's friends for drinks in a quiet backstreet bar. Everyone was drunk. Akko held my hand. I felt warm. We looked at each other quietly. The world was standing still again.

Akko blushed. Her eyelashes fluttered. Her pretty mouth curled. I felt warm all over.

We walked to the station. We were holding hands. We stopped walking. I kissed her. She kissed me back.

Sadly, even love and intoxication could do nothing to protect me from the barbs and thorns of the local taxation system. At the end of the previous year I had received a hefty tax bill about which my supervisor, Mr Horrii, had failed to forewarn me. This sudden blow to my finances had knocked me for six, and I had been left with just enough aluminium coins to scrape together a diet of instant noodles and bread to tide me over until my next pay cheque.

From then on I had been keen to avoid a similar debacle, and so, after a few words with my supervisor, it had been decided that the calculation of my tax returns would become the task of the Junior High School staffroom secretary, Mr Yoshimura. Mr Yoshimura was an incredibly efficient office secretary, but he also epitomised the stereotypical bureaucrat. I had once borrowed a pen from him and been forced to write my name on a piece of paper so he could be sure of getting his property back.

I had often watched with amusement as Mr Yoshimura rounded up bands of male teachers to help shift heavy office furniture or appliances. Each teacher would be required to change into a pair of work overalls and don a pair of heavy-duty woollen gloves. Teachers were also forbidden to lift the office printers without the protection of appropriate safety clothing.

However, there was no way that I would be able to fill out my tax returns by myself. The Japanese tax form is a labyrinth of mind-bending Japanese characters and requests for complicated and detailed information. Mr Yoshimura would be ideally suited to carrying out the task on my behalf. At the same time I was concerned that his fine-tuned attention to detail and stubborn refusal to cut corners would turn the already confusing process into a nightmare.

Sure enough, Mr Yoshimura soon began turning up at my desk on an regular basis, wanting to look through my payslips, bank books and various tax records. I had little time for his stammered attempts at explaining the Japanese tax system, and took absolutely no enjoyment from lengthy tales about his pastime of reading accounting and computer textbooks.

However, in early March Mr Yoshimura wandered over to my desk to deliver some good news. 'Ah, Mr Hamish,' he began, adjusting his glasses, 'I have finished your tax returns. I think there was a mistake last year.' He paused. 'Yes, last year there was a big mistake. You paid too much tax.'

My mind flashed back to the impoverished weeks of instant noodles.

'Yes, I think Mr Horrii filed an incorrect tax return for you. So I think you received a very large tax bill.'

Steam started to come out of my ears. 'Go on,' I said.

'Yes,' Mr Yoshimura said cheerfully, seemingly unaware of my escalating anger, 'you paid too much residential tax. I have filled in a form for you. You will be able to receive a residential tax repayment.'

My anger vanished and I shook Mr Yoshimura's hand. 'Thank you, thank you,' I said warmly.

Mr Yoshimura was overjoyed with his accounting breakthrough. 'We should go to Tondabayashi Tax Office this afternoon,' he announced. 'You will need to fill in some other forms there to receive your repayment. Are you free this afternoon?'

I nodded. I had already taught my two classes for the day. The thought of suddenly being eligible for a tax repayment had put a grin on my face. Fill out a few simple forms and the money would be mine.

I ate my lunch as quickly as possible and Mr Yoshimura and I drove off to the tax office.

Here we struck an entire building full of Mr Yoshimuras, each with his own special colour armband, rubber stamp and pen collection. Luckily, Mr Yoshimura seemed perfectly at ease. 'Please follow me,' he said quietly. 'We will need to find the right person to talk to.'

I nodded. There was little I could do but follow my guide through the bewildering rabbit warren of corridors and queues of people. The man in the reception area referred us to a second man, who referred us to a third man, who referred us upstairs to a fourth man, who made us wait for a fifth man, who gave our papers to a sixth man, who scratched his head and went and got a fat lady in a purple jersey.

The fat lady in the purple jersey frowned grumpily while she slowly scrutinised my tax forms. After humming and haahing, she decided that yes, I would be eligible to receive a 30,000-yen repayment from the Tondabayashi City Council. 'However,' she announced in a stern voice, 'this will take two months to process.'

'No problem,' I said happily. My money was on its way.

I glanced at Mr Yoshimura. He seemed thoughtful. 'Oh dear,' he said anxiously, 'Mr Hamish is leaving in July. Maybe there won't be enough time to process his repayment?'

An obnoxious smile crept over the fat lady's face. 'Oh well, in that case, we can't pay him.'

'But that's nearly five months away,' I erupted, knowing full well that five months was longer than two months.

The woman looked over my tax form again and shook her head. 'We'll try and pay you,' she said coldly, 'but I can't promise anything. What's more, it seems you didn't pay enough income tax last year and owe us 4000 yen. Please pay that in two weeks' time.'

I had a mental image of crushing the purple lady with a concrete mixer, but did my best to remain outwardly calm. Raising my voice or making a scene might see my repayment being cancelled, and yet another bill added to my account.

'I'll try and pay my taxes this year,' I muttered to myself, 'but since I'm leaving in five months I can't promise anything.'

I arrived at school the next morning to find my friend Mr Higo waiting at my desk. 'I have an idea,' he said with his trademark smile.

I listened. 'Not another running race?'

'No, no. This will be much more enjoyable.' Mr Higo laughed. 'Next week will be the end-of-year graduation ceremony. But before that, the teachers will hold a farewell party for the third-grade students. The graduation ceremonies are always so sad, we think it would be nice to have a happy farewell party as well.'

I nodded. I was already well aware of the plans for the farewell party.

'Yes,' Mr Higo continued, 'at the farewell party some of the teachers will sing and perform dances for the students.' He paused, working up the courage to make his big suggestion. 'I would like to do a stand-up comedy routine with you. I think we can be very funny and make the students laugh. What do you think?'

'That sounds great,' I concurred. 'Will we do the routine in English?'

Mr Higo went quiet. 'Ah, no. I was thinking that we can do a *Japanese* comedy routine. I have already written the script.'

I paused. I suddenly realised what I had just signed up for.

The Japanese sense of humour is rather different from the Western. The usual Japanese comedy routine consists mainly of puns or slapstick gags. For example, I would hit Mr Higo on the head with a rubber hammer, or he would poke me in the eyes and stamp on my feet.

The puns are even more painful. Take, for example, a joke Mr Yoshimura told me after we had returned from the tax office:

'Excuse me, Mr Hamish.'

'Yes?'

'As you know, I study computers' (this was the most amusing part of the joke for me) 'and I was reading my textbook. Look, this is a task bar.'

'Yes, it is.'

'But you see, I thought it was a *tusk* bar.'

'Nope, it's a task bar. Task means job.'

'Oh, but you see I thought it meant *tusk*, like an elephant's tusk. You see, it's a joke.'

I suddenly realised that in just a few days I would be standing on the stage before a crowd of five hundred people, delivering jokes that would usually be reserved for Christmas crackers. Plus, the entire comedic routine would be in Japanese. This scared me the most. I hadn't seen Mr Higo's award-winning script, but I had a nasty feeling it would be full of jokes I didn't understand.

I had faith in Mr Higo's sense of humour, but if I couldn't understand the gags, or made even a slight mistake with my pronunciation or accent, I would end up being an idiot on stage talking about elephant tusks and computer textbooks.

The farewell party was still a week away. I needed to sit back and relax. I had another important performance to get through in the meantime. The following Friday the third-grade students would graduate. These were the kids I had been teaching since I arrived in Japan. They had started out at the Junior High School only a few months ahead of me, and I had been surrounded by their smiley faces almost every day for the past two and a half years. Now only one week of classes remained.

I was feeling emotional and wanted to make my final class something special. I locked myself away and studiously wrote a ten-minute speech in Japanese, saying how much I'd enjoyed teaching everyone and what a friendly, funny group of students they had all been.

I passed it by Mr Higo for some final Japanese proofreading. He appeared at my desk an hour later with teary eyes. 'This is a very wonderful speech,' he said solemnly. 'Did you write it yourself?'

I nodded. 'Were there lots of mistakes?'

'No, no.' Mr Higo sniffed. 'I think the speech is very fine. The students will be very moved.' He handed it back to me and quickly moved away to make a cup of coffee.

I shrugged. Perhaps Mr Higo was feeling a bit emotional about graduation day as well.

Monday arrived. I walked slowly down the hallway. It was my final day teaching the third-grade students.

First on the schedule was 3-C class. The first forty minutes of the lesson were spent playing games. I reproduced one of the most popular team games, and everyone roared with laughter as they tried to memorise and place an order for a lengthy and confusing list of fast-food items.

The game finished, and everyone clapped. Only ten minutes with my long-time companions remained. A sombre mood descended on the classroom.

I started my speech slowly, making sure I pronounced every word correctly. I reached the two-minute mark in my notes and had just finished explaining how much I had enjoyed getting to know everyone during our respective first years at the school. I recounted some of the funny moments from our first classes together, and my first impressions of them all.

I looked up. All the girls burst into tears simultaneously.

I blinked in surprise and resumed my speech. I struggled through to the bottom of the next page, and suddenly all the boys were crying too. My voice was croaky and my eyes were moist. I carried on, biting my tongue and pinching the webbing of my fingers to stay calm.

I could hear myself thanking my students for being such diligent pupils, and encouraging them to keep studying English and to travel abroad if they had the opportunity. I thanked them for being my friends and for having made me feel welcome in a foreign country. I told them that I was sad to be leaving Japan in July, and would miss them all very much.

I paused. My speech was finally over. I looked up. Everyone was crying, even Mr Higo. He stood in the corner dabbing his eyes.

The bell rang on cue and everyone clapped. The students lined up to shake my hand and give me a hug goodbye.

I retreated to the staffroom to calm my nerves and prepare myself for the rest of the day. I still had the task of going around the remaining third-grade classes and repeating my speech four more times. It felt as if I were going to a funeral.

By the end of the day, everyone who had been present in my lessons had been reduced to tears—including me. Word of this magical speech that was making everyone cry quickly spread through the staffroom. The owl-like school principal, Mr Kazama, made numerous copies of my script and proudly posted them out to all the students' parents to make them cry too.

I pedalled home slowly. My body felt tired and cold. I was emotionally drained. This had certainly been a memorable day.

米

It was Tuesday, and Mr Higo was back to his happy humorous self. We were sitting in the secluded confines of the school's audiovisual room, practising and rehearsing for our performance at the farewell party.

My fears of inflicting a pun-laden yawn-fest on our audience were gradually being allayed. Mr Higo had obviously gone to a lot of trouble to produce a well-written and witty script that resembled something out of a Monty Python sketch.

We had been practising vigorously for the past few days whenever we had both had a free moment. We were confident that our routine was going well and flowed naturally. I was managing to get my tongue around most of the tricky lines, and was actually confident of getting some laughs.

One line still bothered me though: 'Atatamemasen ka?' ('Shall I heat this up for you?') I needed to pronounce this at speed, raise my voice expectantly at the end, and act like a brain-dead convenience store clerk. Even a slight mispronunciation (which I continued to make, despite Mr Higo's stern advice) would see me spouting gibberish.

Our skit was loosely based around Mr Higo buying a pornographic magazine at a convenience store and then robbing a bank. I had initially been unsure about the content being suitable for an audience of twelve- to fifteen-year-olds, but the skit seemed almost pedestrian compared to the other teachers' routines, which included dressing up in drag and showing off knickers and fake breasts. The proposed student-teacher routine devised by a teacher called Mr Hattai involved numerous lewd puns and two giant balloon penises.

Wednesday arrived. Mr Higo and I were the second act in the farewell party. Once Mr Omura had finished his routine, which involved him dressing up in a schoolgirl's uniform and parading around stage with a vibrating cellphone, we were given our cue to get ready.

Both of us were dressed in dark suits. I had a blue shirt and tie, while Mr Higo wore crimson. Matching oversize handkerchiefs stuck out of our jacket pockets. We looked like a pair of music-hall vaudevillians.

Mr Terada introduced us with a great deal of fanfare, and we bounded out on to the stage. We were greeted with whistles and a loud applause, and from then on everything went swimmingly. We got laughs at the jokes. We got laughs at the hitting-each-other-on-the-head bits. We got laughs at my facial expressions. We got laughs at my 'Atatamemasen ka' joke, and we got laughs at all the lines I still didn't understand.

Mr Higo purchased his pornographic magazine and I proceeded to heat it up for him in the store's microwave. We moved seamlessly into our bank robbery skit, in which I was the bumbling criminal who demanded a bag of pesos before hamming up the getaway. Mr Higo, acting as my intelligent accomplice, cuffed me around the head and scolded me for my stupidity.

We then performed some impersonations of teachers in the audience and were given a standing ovation as we ran offstage.

It seemed that bringing happiness and goodwill to the people of Kanan Town was my current role in the universe. Not only had I touched the hearts of my students by making them cry and laugh, but I had apparently inspired the town by having sat the Japanese Proficiency Exam. The event, about which I had written in my monthly town magazine article, had generated a lot of interest, and I had received my first-ever piece of fan mail—from a ten-year-old boy whom I had never met—wishing me good luck. In my March article I had, therefore, added a small comment saying that I had received the results of my exam—a pass—and wished to thank all those who had supported me.

It seemed that passing an exam in Japan carried similar social status to becoming an All Black in New Zealand. People called out to me on the street, and complete strangers approached to congratulate me. At the convenience store, a young female shop assistant giggled and told me how happy she was that I had passed my exam. I gave her a benevolent smile for good measure.

However, my emotional rollercoaster of tears and laughter was set to take one last weepy dip.

On graduation day I arrived at school early in my black suit and new Korean wool overcoat. It was a crisp spring morning, and the sun was shrouded in wispy grey cloud. I took my seat in the gymnasium and watched while the students, parents and town dignitaries filed in for the solemn ceremony.

The high-roofed building was freezing, and I shivered uncontrollably through the formal speeches from the town mayor and the principal. The speeches finally drew to an end, and the music teacher took her seat at the piano. It was time for the individual certificate presentations to begin. A sombre piano solo filled the frosty air as the graduating students began to slowly shuffle on to the stage. When Hiro walked up on stage to collect his certificate I bit my tongue and pinched myself. He bowed proudly to Mr Kazama and returned to his seat looking sad. Hiro was now on his way to join his former classmate, Jun Fujita, at the special-needs school in Tondabayashi.

Yurika had also graduated. She would continue on to a normal high school by herself. Teru-Chan had not wanted to attend the graduation ceremony. She had stayed at home.

I never saw Teru-Chan or Yurika again.

At the end of the presentations, all the homeroom teachers were invited to walk up on stage. Not being a homeroom teacher I stayed firmly in my seat, still trying without success to keep warm. Behind me, the self-appointed head English teacher, Mrs Nakazato, leant forward and urgently whispered into my ear that I should follow the other teachers on to the stage. 'Go on, Mr Hamish. You need to go on stage. You were one of the main teachers too.'

'Really?' I asked in surprise. 'I thought only the homeroom teachers were invited?'

'No, no,' she assured me sternly, 'you must go too. Quickly, they are waiting.'

I glanced at my colleagues on stage. They were all standing rigidly to attention. Nobody seemed to have noticed my absence. 'Quickly,' Mrs Nakazato hissed. She clenched my arm in an attempt to spur me on.

I stood up dumbly and wandered up on to the stage. I had no idea what the homeroom teachers were doing, but assumed that we were all going to give the departing students a standing ovation as they filed out of the gymnasium.

A murmur went up from the audience and I noticed a few people frowning and pointing at me. I glanced around. Mr Omura was standing next to me. He had a confused look on his face.

I looked back at Mrs Nakazato. She smiled and gave me an enthusiastic thumbs-up. I continued to stand rigidly to attention until I suddenly realised to my horror that the homeroom teachers were being presented with bouquets of flowers. I did a quick headcount and realised there was one bouquet too few. I was not supposed to be on the stage at all. I turned bright red and shuffled back to my seat, seething with rage and humiliation.

Akko was waiting for me at my apartment when I arrived home. She listened quietly as I ranted and raved and provided a detailed description of my humiliation at the graduation ceremony. Eventually I ran out of steam and sat still, sipping the jasmine tea she had made.

'You poor thing,' she soothed comfortingly. 'No one gave you any flowers.' She chuckled, and I swatted her playfully with a cushion.

'Shall we go out for dinner?' she suggested. 'I feel like sushi. Let's go to the rotating sushi restaurant. Go on, your tummy would like that.'

Akko leant forward and patted my stomach. 'How is my dear Pooh-san today?' Over the past few weeks, she had noticed that I had been developing a slight paunch, and had decided to nickname it the Japanese equivalent of Pooh Bear. I had been loathe to agree with her, but she was right. Since my pitiful performance in the South Osaka half-marathon, my exercise and eating habits had fallen off the wagon spectacularly, and I had slipped back to my regime of two chocolate bars a day and as little physical activity as possible.

Akko and I spent a happy evening at the restaurant and my anger about the graduation ceremony dissipated. After dinner we strolled through the backstreets of Jinaimachi, enjoying the tranquillity and the warm spring evening. Back at my apartment we sat up late into the night discussing how we would spend the coming spring vacation. Akko planned to take as much time off work as possible.

The break was a truly happy and romantic three weeks. Akko and I spent nearly every day together. We picnicked in the hills of Kanan Town, eating sandwiches and cream cakes beneath glorious cherry blossom trees. At night we climbed to the viewing platforms on top of tall buildings, enjoying the twinkling panorama.

We went to movies, dined at restaurants, shopped, ate ice-creams in the park, and snuggled indoors watching videos when it rained. We spent hours crooning cheesy love ballads in our own karaoke booth.

We went to an amusement park in north Osaka. The Japanese-sized seats and restraining bars on the rollercoasters were several sizes too small for me: not only could I not breathe properly, but my testicles were mashed at every hair-raising dip and curl. After three rides I felt physically ill, but continued to accompany Akko as she gleefully bounced from one rollercoaster to the next. By the end of the day we had managed to ride every damn rollercoaster, pirate ship and giant teacup in the park, and I had narrowly avoided throwing up a dozen times.

The final week of the vacation was spent at a much more relaxed pace. We hung out in my apartment, watching videos and cooking meals. I was usually put on cooking detail, while Akko would venture out to the doughnut store next to the train station to buy dessert.

The three weeks had flashed by in a lovesick blur. Suddenly the world stopped standing still. It was Sunday night, and I was mentally preparing for my return to work. Akko had cooked dinner and selected the evening's viewing, a romantic drama. We held hands and watched the story of a young man who met a young woman, fell in love with her, and then watched as she died tragically from cancer.

Neither of us spoke as the credits started to roll. I moved forward to stop the video player. Akko was crying. 'It's all right,' I said. 'It's just a silly movie.'

Akko stood and left the room. I found her weeping in the kitchen. 'I'm sorry,' she said, trying to hide her face. 'I'm just so sad.'

I gave her a hug, and she melted into my arms. 'I've had such a happy time with you,' she whispered between tears. 'I've had such a happy time visiting your apartment and doing fun things with you.' She started crying again. 'But soon all of this will end, because you can't stay here anymore.'

I listened quietly, and held her close. Tears rolled slowly down my cheeks. I was running out of time in Japan. I was running out of time with Akko.

I slept poorly that night, and was strung-out when I arrived at work the next morning. It was the first day of the new school year, and there had been a fair number of changes. Mr Kazama, the owl-like principal, had retired. In his place sat Mr Nagano, a toady little man who wasted no time informing me that he didn't like *The Lord Of The Rings* movies because they were too imaginative. I disliked him immediately.

There were ten more new faces dotted around the staffroom. The closest to the internet terminal was a middle-aged woman dressed in Gucci and sporting a flash haircut—the new office secretary. Poor nerdy Mr Yoshimura had been booted off to count beans somewhere else.

Two seats along was the new woodwork teacher, the school's fourth in three years. Mr Doi had not returned from his counselling; he had apparently gone into retirement. Shaven-haired Mr Yagi had been relocated and I had not a chance to say goodbye to him. The new teacher was an odd-looking person. His little chin and big moony glasses gave him the hybrid appearance of Elton John out of Brains from Thunderbirds.

My own seating arrangement was unchanged. I was still at the far end of the room, in the cold dank corner next to the door where I was able to act as a draught-stop for my colleagues.

That in itself was not a problem, but what I had not anticipated was that my new neighbour would be Mr Kobayashi, the school enforcer. I could look forward to spending my last four months sitting next to the scariest person in Japan. Gone were the days of turning up forty minutes late, eating chocolate and then sleeping until four...

There had been a few other changes, but by far the saddest was the departure of my good friend Mr Higo, the man who had lost long-distance running races with me, who had introduced me to karaoke, who had daringly impersonated fellow teachers, and with whom I had performed stand-up comedy.

In its infinite wisdom, the Osaka government had decided that Mr Higo had been at Kanan Junior High School long enough. He had been transferred to a school in the rough part of town, where kids sported fluorescent hair and threw chairs through windows.

His desk sat empty. A replacement English teacher would arrive the following day.

# 22

# Lost and found

*It was May. Only two months remained* of my life in Osaka. I had marked the occasion by contracting a virulent head cold, and would have gladly spent my spare time sleeping at my desk and recovering, had it not been for Mr Kobayashi's alarmingly intimate presence. Instead I brewed pot after pot of strong coffee and sought solace at the staff internet terminal.

Life continued its predictable routine. I finished work every day at 4.15 and packed up my gear. I wheeled my bicycle out of the bike sheds, and stopped to chat with the large groups of students who milled about at the school gates. I teased the girls for having crushes on various male students, and shared stories of my latest outings with Akko. I joked with the naughty boys, and received advice as to the latest and coolest Japanese rap stars.

I would then mount my bicycle and ride past the town tennis courts, waving to the boys' tennis team. I would pass the town hall and try not to wobble off my bike as I waved enthusiastically to Magnum and Mr Smiles, who would be enjoying their afternoon cigarette on the Board of Education balcony.

I would meander down the familiar track through the rice fields, and call out goodbye to the gaggle of students reading porn magazines. I would yell hello to the two pensioner rice farmers tending their crops, and they would put down their tools to wave and stare as I rode past.

My rice-paddy path would eventually rejoin the busy main road, and I would sail down Terada Hill with the wind in my hair. Without fail, I would pass a group of elementary-school students in bright yellow hats coming the other way. As the children sweated and panted their way uphill, they would call out to me and practise their breezy rendition of 'Hello, aloha, nihao.'

At the base of the hill I would have two options. If in need of groceries, I would continue down the main road to the supermarket, competing fiercely with concrete mixers and heavy-duty construction vehicles. At the supermarket, I would receive smiles and polite bows from old people whom I had never seen before in my life, and would chat briefly with former students who were now working as checkout girls.

If, however, I had planned ahead for the evening meal and stocked my pantry, I could forego the supermarket, leave the busy main road and pedal down a quiet secluded backstreet. I loved this backstreet trail, which I had stumbled across while working on the town pamphlet project two years earlier.

The trail began as a thin path through the rice paddies, forking away from the main road at the base of Terada Hill. It followed a bubbling brook through a small settlement of elegant homes built in traditional Japanese style before weaving past bushy vegetable patches, straw-stuffed scarecrows, ornate stone walls, beautifully manicured bonsai gardens and my personal favourite, a run-down old house whose front room doubled as a pokey little stall for savoury octopus balls.

The trail finally rejoined the main road to Tondabayashi at the Ishikawa River bridge. Here, I would cross the polluted river, leaving behind the peaceful countryside town where I worked and entering the concrete city of Tondabayashi, where I lived. After battling the traffic jam caused by lunatic drivers and endless roadworks, I would ride the last leg of my journey through my 600-year-old neighbourhood of temples and old wooden warehouses.

At least that's what I had planned for the afternoon of May 16. I suddenly remembered, however, that my pantry supplies were running low, and grudgingly decided to skip my secluded backstreet ride in favour of the busy main road that would take me past the supermarket.

As always, I had barely entered the supermarket before I was spotted by smiling pensioners, who thanked me for teaching the town's young folk and recommended that I try the latest crop of melons, which were apparently very juicy. I smiled, and bowed politely. I didn't want to admit that I was not particularly fond of overpriced Japanese fruit.

I completed my shopping and left the supermarket with four heavy bags of groceries. Unfortunately I was riding my mountain bike, which did not come equipped with a trusty shopping basket. I balanced the grocery bags precariously on the ends of my handlebars, crossed the busy road, and was just getting up to speed when someone called out 'Excuse me!' loudly in Japanese.

I carefully looked around, not wanting to overbalance and get clocked by a concrete mixer. A smiling man was leaning on a bicycle on the other side of the street. He called out again and asked me to stop. Figuring I must have dropped some of my groceries, I pulled over. The man rode blithely through the hurtling traffic and came to a stop directly in front of me, crashing into a lamppost.

I guessed that he must be a relative of one of my students, or perhaps a reader of my town magazine articles. His bike was now completely blocking my path. He twiddled his fingers and looked off into space. It suddenly occurred to me that he might be bonkers.

'What's your name?' he asked. I told him. He stared off into space and repeated the question. I changed my name to 'Hey'. He grinned.

I asked him what his name was, and received an incomprehensible stuttering machine-gun response.

Introductions now out of the way, it was time for me to answer a few questions.

'How do you say "cat" in English? How do you say "oranges" in English? How do you say "traffic light" in English? How do you say "lamppost" in English?' He stammered on, clicking his fingers and doing a good impersonation of Robert De Niro in *Awakenings*, while I answered as best I could.

Eventually, though, we struck some problems when he resorted to asking me to translate every single shop name that he could see.

'How do you say that shop?'

'Honda.'

'How do you say that shop?'

'Mitsubishi.'

I started to realise that if I were to translate every imaginable noun my new friend could conjure up, I wouldn't be getting home any time soon. I had groceries to put in the fridge and dinner to prepare. I moved my bike off the footpath to indicate that I was eager to leave.

Seeing this, he rolled his bike forward to block my way, and started a new line of questions.

'How do you say my mother Keiko's name in English?'

'Keiko.'

'How do you say my father Toshio's name in English?'

'Toshio.'

I was starting to lose my New Zealand patience and could feel myself becoming a bit more American.

'Now then,' I said firmly, 'I have to go.'

I paused. I did not want this lunatic following me home. 'I have to go now—to the library.'

'Great,' he exclaimed. 'Let's go!'

He took off, beckoning me to follow. I didn't move, hoping he would forget who I was and find someone else to chat with. Alas, my escape was not going to be so easy. He stopped again and beckoned furiously. I took off down a side street, hoping to lose him in the maze of winding streets near my apartment. Alas, though, four grocery bags were a cumbersome load and I was forced to pedal delicately so as not to drop any of the contents. Hence, my excited friend had no trouble keeping up with me.

'No, no, the library is this way,' he called out in alarm, and before I could attempt to outmanoeuvre him he blocked off my planned escape route down an alley. As we carried on around the corner he suddenly stopped, leapt off his bike and jumped in front of me, forcing me to either stop or run him over. I skidded to a halt.

He raced up to the door of a nearby house and it was at this point that I noticed that he was wearing blue plastic toilet slippers. He banged on the door excitedly. 'Mum, mum, come quick!' He jammed his finger on the buzzer, and I could hear the bell clanging inside the house.

Ding dong ding dong ding dong ding dong ding dong ding dong ding dong.

Mum finally opened the door. She looked rather cross. 'What's going on? Why are you so excited?' she grumped.

'Look look mum mum! What's your name, mum? How do you say your name in English, mum?' Mum didn't know and looked baffled. Then she noticed me and looked even more baffled.

'Are you friends with my son?' she asked.

'Hmmm…no, not really,' I replied.

Mum's face changed from confusion to suspicion. 'I just met your son. He found me on the road,' I explained.

'Oh.' Suspicion was replaced with pity.

'Tell her tell her tell her tell her tell her! How do you say my mum's name in English?'

'Keiko.'

My friend was overjoyed. 'How do you say my father's name Toshio in English?'

Mum cut in. Where was I from? Was I enjoying my job?

Her son temporarily quietened down, but after five sentences he was off again, asking me to translate his entire family tree.

At last I could stand it no more and started to pedal off. The young man made to climb back on to his bike, but fortunately mum could see what was going on. 'But we're going to the library,' I could hear him exclaiming as I waved goodbye and pedalled away. I quickly decided that I would no longer be talking to strangers.

A week went by. I continued to take the secluded backstreet route home. The relaxing ride beside the bubbling brook was pleasantly devoid of people who wanted me to repeat their parents' names.

May 25 was overcast and drizzly. I left school quickly, keen to get home before the ominous-looking black clouds forming over the mountain range could blow into town. Magnum waved from the town ball balcony as I sped through the rice paddies. There were not many cars on the road, and I zipped down Terada Hill at breakneck speed.

As I veered on to my secluded trail I scanned the road ahead, keeping an eagle eye out for potential crackpots. I reached the banks of the

Ishikawa River and darted through the traffic, across the bridge. A small furry shape moved in front of me. I braked. The small furry shape tripped and wobbled on unsteady legs. I looked closer. A tiny, fluffy kitten was moving intently towards the edge of the footpath, its dazed eyes staring blankly at the busy centre of the road.

The kitten's pitiful cries could barely be heard above the roar of the traffic. It teetered to the brink of the footpath, seemingly intent on crossing the road. I jumped off my bike, raced forward and scooped it up, just as it staggered on to the road.

The kitten mewed softly, and looked around. It went limp in my hands, and made no protest as I bundled it into the folds of my jersey. It shivered slightly, and went to sleep.

I looked around helplessly. Where on earth had this puny kitten come from? It had no collar and there were no houses nearby. I could not bring myself to leave the poor little thing to its fate in the middle of the Ishikawa bridge. With no better idea springing to mind, I cycled home with the sleeping kitten still tucked securely within my jersey.

The kitten came awake when I lowered it gently on to my kitchen floor. It curiously examined my fridge door, seemingly unconcerned by its sudden change of environment. I poured a saucer of warm milk, but it seemed unsure what to do with it.

I conjured up an ingenious solution: I would feed it by soaking the milk in a paper towel. I held the dripping towel enticingly to the kitten's lips. The kitten paused and sniffed. It licked the towel inquisitively. It was obviously famished. After it had sucked the towel clean, it finished off the rest of the milk in the saucer.

I suddenly wondered where my guest would relieve itself. I brought in one of the pot plants from my balcony, ready to scoop up the kitten and place it on the soil if it started acting suspiciously. The kitten mewed happily, and looked up at me with big needy eyes. My heart melted. I gave it a delicate pat on the head.

I fetched a cushion and sat the kitten on top. It stretched out and fell asleep. I watched its skinny ribcage rise and fall. What on earth was I going to do now? With less than two months left in Japan, I had just adopted a weak orphan kitten.

There was a noise on the street outside. My landlady, Mrs Fujita, and her daughters were returning home. Mrs Fujita was a resourceful woman. She would know what to do. I checked the kitten: it was sleeping soundly. I raced out the door.

'Ah, hello,' I called out breathlessly as Mrs Fujita struggled up the stairs, her arms loaded with grocery bags and Fu-Chan's pink tricycle.

She looked at me with a tired smile. 'Hello, Mr Hamish. How are you?'

'Ah, yes, well, I've found a kitten,' I said nervously. Pets were strictly forbidden in Tokiwa Mansion.

Fu-Chan clapped her hands. Mi-Chan shrieked. Mrs Fujita frowned. 'Where was it? ' I explained the story.

'Can we see, mummy? Can we see?' Mi-Chan tugged Mrs Fujita's sleeve.

'Can we keep it? Can we, can we, can we?' Fu-Chan tugged Mrs Fujita's other arm.

Mrs Fujita brushed them away impatiently. 'We should have a look at it. It probably needs to go to a vet.' She looked at her daughters. 'Girls, do not touch the kitten. It might be sick.'

The girls' smiles turned to teary looks of anguish. 'Will it be okay, Mummy?' they chorused as the four of us entered my apartment. 'Will you and Mr Hamish be able to fix it?'

I grimaced. Mr Hamish was suddenly feeling very distraught about the health of his kitten.

Mrs Fujita looked at the kitten carefully. It came awake and wobbled around the kitchen. 'Oh, it's soooo cute,' Mi-Chan chirped. 'I want to keep it. Can we, mum?'

Mum was frowning. 'It looks very weak. I think it has been living on its own for a long time. It is so thin. I think it will not live for very much longer.'

My face fell. I looked at the girls for support. They were on the verge of tears. 'Is there a vet nearby?' I asked hopefully.

Mrs Fujita considered. 'Yes, but it is a very expensive place. You would need to spend a lot of money. A *lot* of money. And I don't think this kitten can be saved. And if it can, what then? Where will it live?'

Everyone felt like crying.

'What about the SPCA?' I asked desperately. 'Won't they take it in?'

Mrs Fujita looked at me blankly. There was no such thing as an SPCA in Tondabayashi.

The kitten tripped and fell. It picked itself up on shaky legs. Mi-Chan started crying. Fu-Chan hid her face.

I looked at Mrs Fujita gravely. 'I'll figure something out,' I said.

The Fujitas departed and I was left alone in my kitchen with my wobbly kitten. I watched it sadly as it tottered around my apartment. It reacted with surprise to the coarse tatami mats. It clawed my old blue cushions, and tried to investigate the gap between my sofa and the wall. It had a soft tortoise-shell coat, and a big round face with pointy ears and blue eyes. It mewed softly whenever it discovered something new, and looked at me happily.

I sat down on my sofa, placed the tiny kitten on my lap, and gloomily watched the evening news. There was nothing I could do for the kitten. I was about to leave the country. I could not take care of it, and it certainly could not return to New Zealand with me. I would need to find a home for it.

I stood up, wrapping the sleeping kitten in my jersey, and set off on foot to explore the neighbourhood. I roamed the streets, hoping against hope that I would find an orphaned animal centre. Alas, the streets were empty, and the homes and warehouses were tightly shut against the approaching storm.

I returned to Ishikawa Bridge, desperately praying that I might stumble across the kitten's owner. There was no one around. The black clouds rumbled overhead. A cold wind blew in off the mountains. The kitten mewed miserably in my jersey.

Suddenly my hopes lifted. Lights were on in a small medical centre down the road. I started walking towards it briskly. Perhaps the doctor there could help me? Perhaps he could help me find a good cheap vet or an animal welfare centre?

I stepped inside the clinic. The nurse looked at me in alarm. The clinic was about to close for the night.

'Can I see the doctor?' I asked urgently. 'It's an emergency.'

The nurse looked at me suspiciously. I wasn't bleeding. My limbs were not broken. What was wrong with me?

'I've found this kitten!' I thrust the small animal towards her. 'Do you think the doctor can help?'

The nurse's heart melted. 'Oh, it's so cute,' she enthused, 'and so small. Wait here, I'll get the doctor.'

She returned shortly afterwards with a bewildered-looking man wearing a white coat.

'Ah, Mr Hamish.' The doctor had recognised me. 'You taught my daughter English for two years. Now she is in high school. She said you were a good teacher. How can I help you?'

I explained my story. The nurse clucked and sighed and gave the tiny kitten pitying looks.

The doctor looked at the kitten intently. 'I think it is very sick,' he said slowly. 'There is nothing I can do. I am not a vet.' He paused. 'But I think I can help. I recognise this kitten. I think it belongs to the old lady down the road. I see her feeding her cats every day. Here, let me give you the address.'

He grabbed a pen and piece of paper and began scribbling numbers and Japanese characters. He held it out to me. 'Thank you again for teaching my daughter.' He bowed. The nurse bowed. I bowed back. The kitten mewed.

I raced down the road, overwhelmed with relief. The old lady's house was close by. I looked back at Ishikawa Bridge; the kitten had done exceedingly well not to have been run over during its long journey.

The cat lady's house was dilapidated. A broken gate opened on to a small front garden full of weeds and overgrown plants. The place reeked of cat pee. I approached the entrance apprehensively. The house was dark, with no lights. I rang the bell.

A cross voice called out from behind the filthy screen door. 'What?'

'Excuse me, madam, I've found your cat,' I called back.

'Don't want it. Not interested.'

She had obviously mistaken me for a door-to-door salesman or religious nutter.

'I'm not selling anything,' I pleaded. 'I've found your little kitten. It was on the bridge. The doctor down the road thinks it's yours. I've brought it back for you.'

There was a pause. 'I don't want it. Go away. Leave me alone.'

Footsteps sounded, and the woman disappeared deeper into the dark house. The wind howled. The clouds rumbled ominously. I was left on the doorstep with a crying kitten.

Back home, I had one last idea. I grabbed a tea towel from my kitchen and made my way to the local Buddhist temple. I wrapped the kitten in the tea towel and placed it delicately in the donations box outside the temple exit. I said a quick prayer to an unspecified god, hoping that the kind-hearted Buddhist monks would take care of the little sick kitten.

I started to walk away. The clouds rumbled and burst. Rain splashed down.

The kitten cried. The rain increased and grew louder and louder, until I could no longer hear the kitten's feeble calls.

The rain plastered my hair to my scalp and glued my shirt to my back. I walked home feeling sick and heartless and miserable.

Over the past couple of months there had been a rash of naughtiness and indecent shenanigans at Kanan Junior High School. The first episode had occurred in late May, when someone had spray-painted three large Japanese kanji characters on the wall of the boys' toilets. The characters were merely the name of the culprit's home class but the school had gone into crisis mode, made worse by the fact that Mr Kobayashi was out of town on a business trip.

When Mr Kobayashi returned the following day, the students were rounded up, yelled at, and threatened for an hour in the school gymnasium. As no one came forward and confessed, they continued to receive a twenty-minute yelling session each day for the next week. But the culprit mysteriously remained unfound.

The behaviour of the 'tough' boys degenerated even further. There were several large-scale brawls in the locker bays, and numerous cases of bullying. Even I was forced to become involved in settling disputes, and had to make a large fat boy in 2-E give a little skinny kid back his calculator. I threw the fat kid's books in the rubbish bin, and impressed upon everyone that only the tall white guy may do the bullying.

But then something happened that would only ever happen in Japan. I went to third-period class as usual, still half asleep and wondering what to have for dinner later that night. The students were straggling in slowly after a swimming class. However, it soon became clear that only the boys were straggling in. The girls were nowhere to be found.

Looking out the third-storey window, I had a good view of the school grounds. The girls were milling around near the pool entrance. Something fairly frantic was going on. Teachers were running here and there, and even the new principal was taking part.

Meanwhile, the boys were growing restless and calling out rude words to get the girls to hurry up and come to class. Eventually the girls arrived, but there were seven empty seats. I was told not to ask why.

After fourth period I raced down to the staffroom to collect my octopus-tentacle lunch-box, and found all my colleagues waiting impatiently. Finally, someone broke the news.

Some half-baked lunatic, presumably with a penchant for pre-pubescent girls, had taken it upon himself to sneak into the girls' changing room during swimming class and relieve seven female students of their uniforms and underwear. Five elderly police officers had raced down from the Kanan Town Police Station on foot, and were now interviewing everyone.

In due course, a middle-aged man in a blue jersey was identified as the suspect, and Mr Kobayashi flew into a rage, punching the wall and slamming doors, before leaving to kill anyone who looked middle-aged and was wearing blue clothing or anything that resembled a jersey.

## 23

# Sayonara

*Three weeks remained of my life in Japan.* I was nervous, scared, excited and sad, all at the same time. Not keen on long farewells, I was hoping to keep my head down and slip quietly out of the country. Goodbyes could be said the night before I left, or at the airport as I slipped through the metal detectors. I did not want to be reminded that I was about to leave my happy life in Osaka, possibly forever, and embark on a totally unplanned chapter of my life back home in New Zealand.

What would New Zealand be like after three years living in Japan? Would my friends still be there? Would we still get on? Would we still have anything in common?

I knew I had changed, but how much? Was I still the same person whom people back home knew and remembered? Was I still the fresh-faced guy who had staggered down main street of Kanan Town in a black woollen suit on a scorching summer day three years earlier?

And what would I do for a job? I had done very little work for the past three years. I very rarely arrived at school on time in the mornings. Was I still employable?

And what about Japan? Would Kanan Junior High School notice my absence, or would I be forgotten like poor Mr Doi? Would anyone even care that I was gone? Would I ever see my Japanese friends again?

*Would I ever see my girlfriend again?*

Akko had arranged to visit me in New Zealand four months after my return. We were both excited about her trip but realistic about our future together. A long-distance relationship was a daunting and heart-wrenching prospect.

I lay awake on my pink futon. It was three in the morning and I couldn't sleep. I was scheduled to meet with Mr and Mrs Oki for dinner the following evening. Mr Oki had insisted that, on my final day in Japan, he would drive me to the airport and help me with my bags. In the meantime, though, he and Mrs Oki wanted to take me out for one last meal together.

Mr Oki had called several times, making the arrangements. 'What do you want for a present?' he had asked sternly.

'Pardon?' I replied cautiously, sensing the determination in his voice.

'Your present!' he repeated impatiently. 'I'm going to buy you something. What do you want? Any budget is possible.'

'Hmmm,' I pondered aloud.

'Any budget is possible,' Mr Oki repeated. His voice was eager and sounded strong. I wondered how his health was these days, but did not want to ask.

I finally settled on a male kimono. There was, I reluctantly decided, no way I could possibly sneak a plasma television on to the plane in my carry-on luggage.

Mr Oki sounded disappointed. 'All right then. Come round to our house after school tomorrow at five o'clock. Make sure you bring your appetite.' He hung up before I could thank him.

The Okis were waiting as impatiently as ever when I arrived at their home the following evening. Mrs Oki had done her hair and put on big round earrings. Mr Oki was wearing a suit, the most formal attire I had seen him in. I glanced at him quietly in the car as we drove to the restaurant. He no longer appeared frail. His hair was thick and silver, and his voice and gaze steady. It was reassuring to see him in good health again.

Mrs Oki chatted to herself happily as we drove. She commented on the oncoming vehicles, the colour of the traffic lights, and what direction Mr Oki should take at intersections. She inquired about my mother and what I wore to school. 'Heymishi, what grade students do you teach?'

I answered her questions and inquired about our choice of restaurant for the evening. She refused to answer. 'It's a surprise.' She blinked and adjusted her glasses.

Mr Oki laughed. 'I chose this restaurant just for you. I want you to eat as much as you can.'

Mrs Oki told him to turn left. We arrived at a large wooden building. From the street it looked like an ornate log cabin.

Mr Oki clapped me on the back. I think you will like the food here. I hope you are hungry.'

He ushered us inside. The log-cabin look had vanished, and we were in a regal dining hall. Plush crimson carpet lined the floor, and dark oak tables were set with sparkling silverware and wine-red napkins. Waiters dressed as penguins bustled around silently. Bowing obsequiously, they guided us into a private room with their white satin gloves.

Mr Oki smiled. His reservation had apparently been made some time in advance. Three huge ornate chairs sat around a thick oak table. A waiter pushed the chairs in for us as we sat down. My chair had large wooden arms and a tall carved back. I felt like a king sitting on a throne.

The Okis were seated on either side of me. Mrs Oki's head was barely visible above the tabletop. 'I'd like a cushion please,' she squeaked. The waiter bowed and disappeared silently.

'You must order anything you want,' Mr Oki commanded. 'Any budget is possible.'

A man and a woman appeared at the doorway. The man wore a chef's hat and an immaculately white jacket. The woman wore a black tuxedo. 'These are our very own chef and waiter,' Mrs Oki said eagerly. She was now propped up on a plush red cushion. 'You must order anything you want.'

I was given a menu and started making my way through it. Everything was beef: beef sashimi, beef steak, barbecued beef, prime Kobe beef—a delicacy, a very expensive delicacy. My eyes watered as I looked at the prices.

Mr Oki was watching me closely. 'Any budget is possible,' he repeated. 'You must eat as much as you can.'

The waitress brought us drinks, while the chef waited patiently. Eventually I ordered a fillet steak. Mr Oki peered at me suspiciously. 'Are you sure that's all you want? Why not have two steaks?'

I explained that one steak would be more than enough. Mr Oki frowned. 'I don't think so.' He turned to the chef. 'I'll have your largest steak please, medium rare I think.'

It was my turn to frown. 'I didn't think you liked beef,' I said quietly. 'Did the doctors say you can eat meat now?'

Mr Oki laughed. 'I ordered the steak for you. I'll just have salad. You must eat as much as possible tonight. This is our last meal together.'

He smiled weakly. 'Yes, our last meal.'

Across the table Mrs Oki gurgled on her glass of red wine. She spluttered and coughed. 'Heymishi, what did you order? Did you order enough food?'

Our chef got to work on the large hot plate that was built into the table-top. The three steaks were carefully cooked and then placed on three ornate plates in front of us. Mr Oki deftly scooped his steak on to my plate before I could protest, then sat back to watch me eat.

There was little point arguing. I now had over half a kilogram of meat on my plate. I cut off a dainty mouthful. The beef looked succulent and juicy. I put it in my mouth. It was one of the most delicious pieces of meat I had ever tasted.

'Isn't it delicious,' Mr Oki agreed. 'I knew you'd like it. Do you want another steak? Will two be enough?'

Mrs Oki eyed me. 'Heymishi, do you like medium rare? I only like well-done. Do you want the chef to cook your steak some more? Is it cooked enough?'

I shook my head. 'This is delicious,' I said enthusiastically. 'Do you want to try some?' Mrs Oki blinked in confusion. 'But I only like well-done.'

I tucked in. I could feel Mr Oki watching me. He seemed thoughtful. I eventually demolished my two steaks. My stomach was full; I could not manage another bite.

The Okis had been waiting for me to finish. 'Have you had enough, Heymishi?' Mrs Oki peered up at me from the depths of her massive chair.

'Yes, thank you. That was the best steak I've ever eaten,' I said truthfully.

Mrs Oki smiled. 'I'm glad you liked it. And Mr Oki is glad too, aren't you, Mr Oki? Mr Oki?'

There was no reply. We turned and looked at Mr Oki. He sat in his chair, crying quietly. He looked at me with sad red eyes. 'This is our last meal together,' he said in a small voice. 'I am glad you came to Japan. I am sorry we did not climb Mount Kanan again together, but my health was not so good.'

I started to protest, but he waved me away and dabbed his eyes. 'If you ever need any help in Japan or anywhere else in the world, please call me. Please come back to Japan again one day. I would like to see you again.' He looked away and hid his face.

I didn't know what to say. I had never expected to see Mr Oki so upset. He had always been Mr Oki—calm, noble, slightly deaf Mr Oki. I had never seen him display any emotion other than happiness. I had not expected my departure to upset him so greatly.

Mrs Oki leaned close to me. 'Mr Oki likes you very much.'

We sat in silence in our little room. Our chef and waitress had both stepped outside. 'Thank you both for looking after me in Japan,' I said at length. 'Thank you for taking me sightseeing and for taking me out for dinner. I always enjoyed visiting your home.'

Mr Oki chuckled. He seemed to have recovered his composure. 'Don't mention it. You looked after us when we visited New Zealand. You were very young but you were a good tour guide and interpreter. It is the least we could do to repay your hospitality.'

Mrs Oki nodded. 'Thank you for looking after us when we visited you in New Zealand, Heymishi.'

I did not know how to reply. The Okis still seemed to feel deeply indebted to me and my family for a small act of kindness nine years earlier.

'I bought you a present,' Mr Oki said. 'I wanted to buy you something bigger, but you only wanted a kimono.' He passed me a gift-wrapped parcel.

'Please open this in New Zealand,' he said with a wink. 'And if you think of anything else that you would like, please let me know.'

I bowed and thanked the Okis for my meal and for my new gift. They pretended not to hear.

Mr Oki drove me to the train station. 'I will drive you to the airport on the day of your departure,' he said as he dropped me off. 'See you then.'

I closed the car door and they drove away. I could just make out the top of Mrs Oki's head as she peered back at me, waving.

The train rumbled slowly through the night. I looked around in a daze. Bored passengers sat gazing out the windows, reading newspapers and staring at cellphone screens. For them it was just another day in Osaka, another day at work, another train ride home. For me, it was my *last* train ride home from Omino Station. I did not have many days left. How many more times would I get to ride a train?

I was suddenly scared. Riding a train was part of my life in Japan, an experience I took for granted. There would be no commuter trains to ride back home in Christchurch. How many other everyday experiences was I about to lose?

I started to panic. A part of my life was about to disappear. Time was robbing me of experiences and sensations that I would never be able to recreate.

The train stopped. Tondabayashi Station. I stepped off, desperately trying to capture and remember every sight and smell: the glare from the soft-drink vending machine; the shrill train whistle; the train conductor with his white satin gloves and robotic manner; the hum of the ticket gate and the polite bow of the station attendant; the empty solitude of Tondabayashi after dark; the soft street lighting of the backstreets; the smell of fried food as I passed Wasshoi pub; the warm summer night air; a neighbour dressed in jandals and a singlet walking his tiny dog at midnight.

I walked around the block. I walked past my apartment. I kept walking. I walked around the block again.

I didn't want to go home. Home meant sleep, which meant another day was over. I walked through the ancient streets of Jinaimachi. I wanted to see all my secret trails. I needed to reassure myself that everything was still as I wanted to remember it. I walked past temples, past old wooden warehouses, past old shops that had been boarded up for the night.

I found myself on the bank of the Ishikawa River. I stared out into the blackness that was Kanan Town. The air was warm and thick. I did not want to go home.

My Japanese mothers were waiting for me in Mrs Kiguchi's dining room. They ushered me to the head of the table.

'Sensei, sensei,' Mrs Terauchi crowed, 'this will be our last meal together. How do you feel?'

They looked at me expectantly. I smiled weakly. 'I am sad to say goodbye to you all. I will miss our conversation sessions very much.' It was true.

Mrs Terauchi clapped her hands. 'Oh sensei, I am glad you enjoyed our time together. We will miss you very much as well.'

Mrs Kiguchi looked at me thoughtfully. 'What has been your favourite memory of Japan, sensei?' she asked softly. I paused. The question could open an emotional can of worms if I weren't careful.

'The people,' I said finally. 'Everyone has been so kind and welcoming. I have made many good friends.'

Mrs Terauchi clapped again. 'I'm so happy you could meet nice people in our country, sensei, and that you could form happy memories here.'

Mrs Kiguchi looked at me with a smile. 'We have enjoyed getting to know you, sensei. You have given us very good memories as well. We are your Japanese mothers. If you ever need help in life, please call us.'

I stammered out some thanks in reply, and stared at the table. I was starting to feel a little choked up.

Mrs Kiguchi raised her glass. We said 'Konpai!'—'Cheers!'—in unison and took a mouthful of beer. My Japanese mothers were not shy about drinking beer in the middle of the afternoon.

The farewell banquet had been lovingly prepared. Mrs Matsui had prepared her delicious savoury pancakes. Mrs Tanaka had brought a huge platter of fresh sashimi. Mrs Tsubota had made a large salad. Mrs Kiguchi had prepared a batch of fried chicken and Mrs Terauchi had brought the beer.

The beer flowed, and we slowly worked our way through the mountain of food. At the end we pitched in to clear the plates away. I was then shooed out of the kitchen, and told to wait with Mrs Terauchi while the others cleared up.

Mrs Terauchi sat quietly and stared out the window. I was surprised by her sudden silence. The others returned and sat down. No one spoke. 'I've made you some presents,' I said, and produced a bag of small parcels from under the table.

I had created a small photo album for each of the women. They smiled in surprise and opened them quietly, adjusting their glasses.

'Oh, sensei,' Mrs Terauchi laughed. 'That's a photo of all of us.'

I nodded. 'Yes, that was my first time here. Do you remember that day?' Everyone nodded.

'And that's when we all went to visit the temple in Kankoji. That's the time we cooked okonomiayaki. That's our Christmas party.'

'My eyes are closed in that photo,' Mrs Terauchi said shrilly. 'Oh, I look so foolish. Sensei, why did you include this photo?'

Everyone laughed.

Mrs Kiguchi took off her glasses and dabbed her eyes with a tissue. 'Sensei, thank you for these wonderful memories.'

I nodded. 'I've written a goodbye speech,' I said. After my final meal with the Okis I had decided I should prepare myself better for my farewell outings. I had come up with a speech in Japanese that I hoped would suitably express my gratitude and deep thanks for people's kindness and hospitality over the past three years.

Silence descended. The women looked at me encouragingly. I unfolded my notes and looked down at the table. I took a deep breath and tried to start my speech.

The words failed to materialise. I coughed. 'Take your time, sensei,' Mrs Kiguchi said softly.

I looked back at my notes. This was my final meal with my Japanese mothers. This small group of cheerful women had been some of my best friends in Japan. They had welcomed me into their homes and shared their lives with me. They had complained about their husbands and divulged their sorrows and secrets. They had given me advice and comforted me in times of my own unhappiness. We had laughed and gossiped together. Happy memories of Monday afternoon conversation sessions flashed through my mind. Now everything was coming to an end.

Suddenly I started crying. Tears rolled down my cheeks and splashed on to the table. I could hear my Japanese mothers crying as well, but I could not look up. I sniffed and started reading out my speech.

'This will be my last meal with you all.'

Mrs Terauchi sobbed.

My lip quivered. I was completely overwhelmed by my sudden emotional breakdown. What on earth was wrong with me? I clenched my fists, fighting to get control of myself.

'Sensei.' Mrs Kiguchi was looking at me kindly. 'Sensei, please take your time. Do not hurry with your speech.' She smiled.

I laughed, a choking, embarrassed laugh, and dabbed my eyes.

'Do not be sad to leave, sensei,' she said soothingly. 'You had a good life in Japan, but you cannot stop time. Nobody can. You should not be afraid of change: it is part of life. You are experiencing life. Do not be sad for the past. Look forward to a happy future.'

I paused. The intense sadness that had enveloped me lifted. I suddenly felt calm, clear-headed. The emotional dam that had been building over the past few months had finally burst. I had been dreading my departure for so long that it had taken on enormous proportions in my mind. Every time I had looked at the calendar over the past few months, I had been subconsciously counting down my remaining days and tying myself in knots.

This sudden outpouring of emotion had been therapeutic. 'Sorry about that,' I said shyly and wiped my face. My cheeks were streaked with tears and my eyes felt puffy.

I looked at my notes again. 'This will be my last meal with you all,' I said. 'Thank you all for being such good friends to me over the past few years.'

My Japanese mothers laughed and dabbed their eyes. 'Please continue your speech when you are ready,' Mrs. Kiguchi said softly.

I recounted funny episodes from our conversation sessions. Thanked everyone for cooking for me. Thanked everyone for inviting me into their homes. Thanked everyone for sharing their stories with me. Thanked everyone for sharing their lives with me.

I finished. All the women were smiling. I folded my notes and put them back in my pocket. I smiled at Mrs Kiguchi. 'Thank you for your advice.'

She shrugged. 'Don't be silly. Now then, who would like a cup of tea?'

As I wheeled my bicycle down Mrs Kiguchi's driveway for the last time, my Japanese mothers stood by the letterbox, waving. I looked back, waved, and started cycling away.

Mrs Kiguchi was right. I should stop worrying about the future.

In the next two weeks I was taken out for dinner every night and put on three kilograms. The Isoi family took me to a sushi restaurant in Nara. Ryohei, the son, had grown noticeably taller. He had not, however, lost his obsession for me; he gazed at me affectionately and tried to hug me whenever a chance presented itself.

I went for dinner with Mr Tokunaga. We reminisced about our six camping trips together, and ate at a Korean barbecue restaurant for old times' sake. Mr Tokunaga still dreamt of one day retiring to a log cabin in New Zealand. He promised he would visit me as soon as he was given leave from his job.

I had lunch with the Board of Education staff. Magnum told stories about our dancing the night away at the town festival, an event that Mr Smiles then re-enacted in a typically enthusiastic mime performance.

The lunch finished and the education superintendent paid the bill. As I was leaving, Magnum quietly took me aside. 'This is a small present,' he said, presenting me with a parcel, 'to say thank you from all of us.'

I shook his hand and opened the parcel. My mouth fell open: the Board of Education had give me the latest, very expensive palm-top Japanese electronic dictionary. I felt embarrassed that I could only stammer out a feeble 'thank you' in reply.

I had a goodbye picnic with my friends on the banks of the Ishikawa River. We played cricket, laughed, drank beer, and recounted our adventures from the past three years. I was mocked for vomiting on trains, in karaoke booths and in nightclubs. Wij was mocked for falling asleep on trains and ending up in neighbouring prefectures. We laughed about our evenings out drinking, and the tales we had told so we could sneak away on holidays together to the tropics.

We were about to go our separate ways. Blake, Andy and Wij would return to England. Matt would travel to Canada. Only Justin would stay in Japan. He had married a Japanese woman, Kimi, and wanted to stay in Osaka for a while longer.

I had now farewelled some of my closest friends, but the list of people from the local community who still wanted to say goodbye seemed to be growing by the day. I visited the mayor in his office, and the staff at the town magazine. I went for dinner with the Tsuboi family. I went for dinner with the Matsumoto family. I went for dinner at Wasshoi and said goodbye to the owner and bartender. People on the street stopped to ask me when I was set to return to New Zealand. They wished me well and thanked me for coming to Japan.

I was starting to amass a sizeable collection of presents. People appeared to feel I had a great need for paper fans. By mid July I had accumulated enough to be able to return to New Zealand and open a paper fan emporium. My friends and family could look forward to receiving them as gifts for their next several dozen Christmases and birthdays.

People seemed to materialise from everywhere. Two of my former students waited for three hours after school to give me some home-made origami. My hairdresser made me a CD filled with all the music on which I had ever commented while having my hair cut.

My colleagues at the school had decided to throw a farewell party on my final Saturday night. I assumed it would be small and knew of only eight people who had said they would attend. I grew slightly nervous, thinking the party would be a surefire flop. I was, therefore, pleasantly surprised to turn up and find a packed banquet room. As well as the thirty teachers with whom I currently worked, there were another fifteen with whom I had worked but who were now at other schools.

Mr Yagi, the shaven-haired woodwork teacher, was there with his baseball cap still back-to-front. Mr Kazama, the principal, had come out of retirement for my big night, and was sitting in a corner, dressed in a three-piece suit and grinning broadly. My good friend Mr Higo was wearing a Canterbury rugby jersey, and had bought me a matching one as a gift.

I looked around. I was surrounded by friendly smiling faces—but someone was missing. Perhaps Mr Doi was off building bombs or driving flash German cars in North Korea?

My colleagues had made an interesting choice of restaurant: our banquet room was beside a vast aquarium teeming with fish and crustaceans. The waiters explained that we could point at anything we liked the look of, and they would scoop it up with giant nets. The hapless fish or shellfish would then be taken out to the kitchen, banged on the head, and set on a plate so we could eat it before it stopped flapping.

For customers who preferred their shellfish cooked, small Bunsen burners were supplied so the poor blighters could be roasted slowly before our eyes.

Despite the gruesome nature of the cuisine, the party was one of my happiest nights in Japan. I was deeply touched to learn that so many people had enjoyed my company: I had often wondered if they had secretly resented my chocolate-eating indolence.

It was especially good to catch up with Mr Higo. He had initially had a rough time at his new school, where he had been put in charge of a particularly rebellious class. I listened in shocked disbelief to his stories of pregnant teenagers, wannabe gangsters and classroom brawls. One day he had been forced to break up a fight between two boys armed with knives. After a few difficult months, however, his good humour had started to rub off on his students and he now found his classes very rewarding.

'I enjoyed our classes the most though,' he rapidly added, worried that I might be offended.

Everyone had brought me a present. There were more paper fans for the emporium, two T-shirts and a male kimono. Including the Okis', it was the fourth male kimono I had received.

I stood up and called for hush. It was time for me to deliver my farewell speech. As I began I tripped over a few words. Mr Higo called out something cheeky. I ignored him. Mr Hioki called out something in my defence, and called Mr Higo a rude name. Laughter.

I continued. I thanked everyone for attending my party. It was a night I would never forget. They had been kind and pleasant colleagues, and I had greatly enjoyed working with them. I finished by suggesting that Kanan Junior High was the best school in Japan. Thunderous applause.

Another round of drinks was ordered. The night was just beginning.

It was now my last week at Kanan Junior High School. It was also the last week of term; most classes had been cancelled in preparation for the school swimming sports on Thursday and the 'Sayonara, Mr Hamish' assembly on Friday.

Thursday rolled around, and with it the teachers v. students swimming relay race. Haunted by memories of my accidental striptease, I fretted feverishly and tied my togs with a double reef-knot. I was to be the fourth and final swimmer in our team. Sadly, all teachers who could swim half-way decently had been transferred to other schools: we were completely lacking in élite athletes.

Mr Hioki, the swimmer before me, needed a kick-board just to complete his length. By the time he gasped and spluttered to the end of the pool, our team was a length and half behind.

I sighed and dived in. My swimsuit didn't come off, or even slip down slightly. Not only that, I seemed to have been magically transformed into Ian Thorpe. I carved my way through the water to the other end without even taking a breath. The crowd went wild.

The 'Sayonara, Mr Hamish' school assembly took place the following morning. For only the third time in three years, I wore a shirt and tie. I stood on the stage at the front of the gymnasium with the new school principal. No one pointed. No one giggled. This time I was supposed to be there.

A couple of teachers made complimentary speeches. The principal coughed and handed me the microphone.

I started in a loud clear voice. 'I am sad to leave this school. This is a very good school. You are all very lucky to work and study here.' Students started to cry. I pinched myself. Not again!

I continued speaking. My voice boomed out of the loudspeakers, and as I got to the end I remembered that hot summer day when I had given my 'Oha!' welcome speech. Surely I should finish things the way I had started?

'Oha, everyone!' I shouted slickly. Everyone laughed. I bowed. My speech was over. It was time for me to leave.

Mr Kobayashi stepped forward and barked at the students. They leapt to their feet and formed two long straight lines, a guard of honour. I walked out of the gymnasium, shaking students' hands as I went. Someone thrust a bouquet of flowers at me. I continued along the avenue of students to the staff changing room.

I was alone at last. My bags were already packed and I had cleared my desk the previous day. It was time for me to leave the school grounds. I picked up my backpack, grabbed my flowers and began to walk to the bike sheds.

I stood stock-still in surprise. The entire school had regrouped and were now lining the walls of the bike sheds. 'Goodbye' banners, and an archway of coloured cardboard had been hurriedly attached above the school gate.

I placed my flowers carefully in the basket of my bicycle and wheeled it slowly towards the exit.

'Sayonara, Mr Hamish,' they cheered. I smiled and waved, blinking back tears.

'Goodbye,' the teachers were calling.

'Goodbye,' I called back.

'Goodbye!' My once tiny pupils stood in rows. They were third-graders now, tall and oily.

'Goodbye!' Yurika Yurano waved. I laughed and called out a farewell. Yurika had finally come back to school. She had dyed her hair chestnut brown, removed most of her earrings and was attempting to compromise with the teachers by not wearing make-up.

I paused at the school gates and waved to the students one last time.

'Goodbye, Mr Hamish!' I looked behind me. Nothing. I looked up. Across the road, Magnum and Mr Smiles were waving furiously from the balcony of the Board of Education.

I waved and mounted my bicycle. It was time to go home. I still had one last goodbye to make.

Akko was waiting patiently. 'How was your day?' she asked as I put my bouquet of flowers into a vase.

'Tiring,' I replied. 'I think I've said goodbye a million times this week.'

Akko giggled. 'And is Pooh-san tired too?' I swatted her with a cushion and chased her on to the balcony. We hugged and looked out across the rooftops of Jinaimachi. Neither of us spoke. We realised this was our last night together.

'Thank you for such happy memories these past few months,' I said softly.

'Thank you too,' Akko replied, and nuzzled my shoulder. 'I'll see you in New Zealand.'

I smiled and stroked her hair. 'Yes, I'm looking forward to it.'

'Shall we go for dinner?' I asked. She nodded. I had booked a table at a local restaurant in Tondabayashi. We had eaten there many times in the past, and had decided it would be a nostalgic place for our final meal together.

I had not written a farewell speech for Akko. Neither of us wanted to spend the evening being reminded that we were about to be parted. Saying farewell was too final. I had faith in the durability of our relationship. Tonight was all about enjoying ourselves.

We walked hand-in-hand through the Jinaimachi streets, remembering our strolls during the spring vacation. At dinner neither of us mentioned my impending departure. We ate our fill of tasty Japanese specialties, and enjoyed free drinks proffered by one of my former students, who was working at the bar.

Two hours later, tipsy and red-faced, we stumbled out of the restaurant. We leant on each other as we wandered down the street. I started singing.

'Let's go to karaoke,' Akko said. 'I want to sing karaoke one last time with you.'

I laughed and kissed her. 'Okay, let's go.'

Akko was on good form. She belted out her favourite songs in a sexy, husky voice. I happily butchered every song I attempted. After a while,

I lost track of time. One hilarious song followed another, and our voices grew tired and our throats hoarse.

Laughing and talking loudly, we staggered back to my apartment. We sat out on my balcony. The full moon illuminated the ancient streets and cast a ghostly glow on the Kanan Mountain Range. I smiled at Akko. She stared out at the darkness, unaware that I was looking at her. It had been a perfect night.

Mr and Mrs Oki were on my doorstep. They were an hour ahead of schedule, and keen to get on the road. Mrs Oki stood in the kitchen talking with Akko while Mr Oki and I carried my suitcases down to his car.

My landlady and her daughters appeared in the doorway. They had brought me some fruit to eat on the plane. The girls were quiet and hid their faces when I said goodbye. 'They are very sad,' Mrs Fujita said softly. 'They will miss you.' I had prepared some parting gifts—kiwi souvenirs and toy sheep. The girls sped off to show old Mrs Okuda over the road.

Old Mrs Okuda and young Mrs Okuda clustered around Mr Oki's car. It was, as usual, parked in Mrs Fujita's parking space but this time no one cared.

'You're such a great young man,' old Mrs Okuda called out. 'He cooks for himself,' she explained to Mrs Oki. Mrs Oki was horrified. 'Heymishi! What do you cook? Why doesn't Akko cook for you?'

I laughed, and Akko punched my arm. Mrs Oki nearly fell over in shock.

Young Mrs Okuda pressed some cakes into my hand. 'Please enjoy these on your journey home,' she said warmly, and stepped back with tears in her eyes.

I was reluctant to leave. As soon as I stepped into Mr Oki's car I would no longer be a resident of Tokiwa Mansion. Akko smiled at me, sensing my sudden disquiet. 'Let's go,' she said calmly. 'You need to go to the airport.'

I nodded and waved to my neighbours for the final time. 'I will miss you all very much,' I called out and climbed into Mr Oki's car.

I stared out the car window. Jinaimachi sped past. Tondabayashi sped past. Osaka sped past. I closed my eyes and held Akko's hand. My three years in Japan were nearly at an end.

A crowd of people were waiting for me at the airport: Mr Tokunaga, Mr Higo, Mr Hioki, eight other teachers from the school, the Isoi family, Wij, Matt, Justin.

Mr Higo held a banner: 'Sayonara, Mr Hamish'. 'I made this myself,' he announced proudly.

Mr Oki was already at the check-in desk, impatiently gesturing for me to join him. 'Come on,' he said hurriedly, looking at his watch. 'You have only three hours until your flight leaves.'

I laughed. 'Thank you for driving me to the airport,' I said and patted him on the back. He relaxed and smiled. 'It was a pleasure.'

I checked into my flight. It was time to go home. My long goodbye had been going on for long enough. I was tired and emotionally spent. I shook hands. Hugged people. Hugged Akko. Kissed her goodbye.

I stepped through the metal detectors and my crowd of friends vanished from view.

# Epilogue

*Three months after I returned to New Zealand*, Akko came for a visit. We spent three happy months together before her tourist visa expired and she had to return to Japan. Several months later, we agreed not to pursue a long-distance romantic relationship. We are still in regular contact and remain firm friends.

Mr Higo has married a fellow teacher, whom he had been secretly dating for several years. He is now the proud father of a baby girl.

Mr Hioki has undergone a dramatic transformation, injecting humour into his classes and replacing his trademark pudding-bowl haircut with a spiky crew cut. He wears smart designer suits to school and is now regarded as one of the 'popular' teachers.

Mr Tokunaga is still teaching at a local primary school. He works long hours and has been unable to take a holiday, let alone go on a camping trip, in years.

No one has heard from Mr Doi since his departure from the school.

The people I knew at the Board of Education have all retired, resigned, been transferred to other roles, or passed away.

Rachel Brown returned to England at the same time as I left Japan.

My Japanese mothers still meet regularly to drink tea, chat and gossip. They are all in good health and we send each other Christmas cards every year.

After I returned to New Zealand, the Okis proved mysteriously difficult to contact. Letters to their home went unanswered, and I was at a loss as to how to reach them. Finally, early in 2007, I managed to find a phone number for Mr Oki's office. The female receptionist quietly explained that Mr Oki was no longer coming in to work, and had not been doing so for some time. She hesitated before adding that both Mr and Mrs Oki were now in an 'institution' and that only immediate family members could contact them. I have heard nothing since.

# Acknowledgements

The enthusiasm of my friends and family for my stories sowed the seed of inspiration for this book, and were a driving force through some frustrating moments in the writing process. I would particularly like to thank my parents, without whom this book would never have made it on to the page. As well as saving my emails from Japan and painstakingly compiling them, they have provided sound counsel, encouragement and support.

Considerable thanks go to Karen for her ideas, comments, suggestions, advice, support, and for putting up with the reclusive lifestyle of a part-time writer. I would also like to tip my hat to my brainstorming pals Chris, Jonathan, Campbell, Geraldine, Al and Russell. Thank you for being such willing and helpful sounding-boards.

The literary advice and guidance I received from Lydia MacKinnon, Graeme Lay and Donna Wright was crucial to my stumbling my way into the publishing industry. My publisher, Awa Press, has been a professional joy to work with, and Mary Varnham has been a brilliant editor.

Finally, I would like to thank the people of Kanan Town and my friends in Osaka for their kindness, limitless hospitality and great sense of fun, all of which made my life in Japan so rewarding and enriching.